SLEEPWALKING
WITH THE BOMB

SLEEPWALKING
WITH THE
BOMB

JOHN C. WOHLSTETTER

SEATTLE   DISCOVERY INSTITUTE PRESS   2012

Description

Sleepwalking with the Bomb shows how we can forestall nuclear catastrophe. It offers familiar faces, cases and places to illustrate how the civilized world can face the most pressing nuclear dangers. Drawing from both history and current events, John Wohlstetter assembles in one place an integrated, coherent and concise picture that explains how best to avoid the "apocalyptic trinity"—suicide, genocide and surrender—in confronting emerging nuclear threats.

Library Cataloging Data

Sleepwalking with the Bomb by John C. Wohlstetter

266 pages, 6 x 9 x 0.6 inches & 0.87 lb, 229 x 152 x 15 mm. & 0.396 kg

Library of Congress Control Number: 2012940396

ISBN-13 978-1-936599066 (paperback)

BISAC: HIS027030 History/Military/Nuclear Warfare

BISAC: POL001000 Political Science/International Relations/Arms Control

BISAC: HIS032000 History/Europe/Russia & the Former Soviet Union

Publisher Information

Discovery Institute Press, 208 Columbia Street, Seattle, WA 98104

Internet: http://www.discoveryinstitutepress.com/

Published in the United States of America on acid-free paper.

First Edition, First Printing. June 2012.

Praise for *Sleepwalking with the Bomb*

JOHN WOHLSTETTER HAS GIVEN US A TOUR DE FORCE OF OUR TROU-bled nuclear condition, its roots and its prospects. It's all here: an insightful history of the nuclear aspect of the Cold War and its crises, fictional as well as real; the chilling prospects of nuclear-armed rogue states and terrorists; the dangerous links between civilian nuclear power for the grid and nuclear weapons; the fuzzy and counterproductive dreams of the zero nukes movement.

For many years *Sleepwalking With the Bomb* will be the standard against which all other work on nuclear issues will be measured.

R. JAMES WOOLSEY, FORMER DIRECTOR OF CENTRAL INTELLIGENCE, CHAIRS THE FOUNDATION FOR DEFENSE OF DEMOCRACIES.

In these perilous times of nuclear Jihad and amputational pacifism we acutely need John Wohlstetter's Reverean ride through the night, ringing out strategic alarms and insights in the grand tradition of Herman Kahn and Albert Wohlstetter. *Sleepwalking With the Bomb* is as lucid, sophisticated, and wide awake as America's current leadership is muddled, naive, and somnambulant.

GEORGE GILDER, AUTHOR OF *THE ISRAEL TEST* (ENCOUNTER BOOKS, 2012) AND *WEALTH & POVERTY* (REGNERY, 2012).

To family, friends, and others who educated me in coping with life's challenges, including the challenge of thinking about how best to avoid man-made catastrophes—of which nuclear conflict is most fearsome and destructive of all.

CONTENTS

FOREWORD

Richard Perle

WHEN RICHARD NIXON RETURNED FROM MOSCOW IN 1972 HE brought with him the apparent triumph of a comprehensive agreement with Leonid Brezhnev that would end a nuclear weapons "arms race" and usher in a new era of constructive cooperation between the superpowers. Neither he, nor his grand strategist Henry Kissinger, understood that the ABM Treaty and separate offensive arms limitation agreements they negotiated would lead to a massive Soviet build-up that left the United States (and its allies) in a situation far worse than the one they hoped to improve.

Far from reducing the Soviets' already vast nuclear arsenal, the agreements of 1972 actually increased both the number and lethality of Moscow's nuclear forces. And they led directly to a challenge to the United States and its allies that was as grave as any in the Cold War.

The 1972 interim agreement fixed the number of launchers for nuclear armed intercontinental ballistic missiles, but it allowed for the enlargement of those launchers and the replacement of older, single warhead missiles by new missiles with multiple warheads. The Soviets promptly began to exploit both provisions of the agreement, first by replacing a class of missiles carrying a single warhead with a new class carrying three warheads. But not content with using an arms control "freeze" to triple the number of their warheads, they then proceeded to develop an entirely new missile, which was excluded from any limit because it lacked intercontinental range. The Soviets assigned this new missile (known as the SS-20) to the European targets that had been pre- viously assigned missiles limited by the agreement. This freed up hun- dreds of missiles that could now be aimed at the United States. By the time Ronald Reagan took office in 1981, the SS-20 and NATO's plan to respond had created a crisis in the NATO alliance, as our allies debated whether to approve a plan to balance the new SS-20s with American missiles of comparable range. For much of Reagan's first term the crisis dominated America's relations with Russia and its NATO allies.

The unintended consequences of the 1972 arms agreement is but one example of a lesson that the Obama administration has yet to learn: arms control is seldom a solution but is often a problem. Today, the ill-founded belief that arms control treaties with Russia are vital to American interests militates against sensible policies regarding missile defense and nuclear weapons proliferation. By their nature, international treaties treat all signatories alike. Yet the great challenge of halting the proliferation of nuclear weapons will not be met until we accept that not all states or regimes are the same: nuclear weapons in the hands of Britain or France or the United States are not the same as nuclear weapons belonging to North Korea or Iran.

It was a misplaced global/legal sentiment that helped get us into today's situation where nuclear technology has been freely distributed around the world, waiting only for "peaceful" nuclear programs to be transformed into programs for nuclear weapons. The chances are that a future nuclear conflict will involve weapons acquired by one or more states that benefited from outside technical assistance based on, and justified by, the Atoms for Peace program and its progeny, the Nuclear Proliferation Treaty (NPT).

John Wohlstetter knows all this and a great deal more. With great clarity and effortless instruction he has astutely analyzed and explained the history and current issues surrounding nuclear weapons. Anyone wishing to understand the past, present and future of nuclear weapons should read this fine book before saying or writing a word on the subject. I can't think of a single journalist or government official, especially those with strong opinions on nuclear matters, who would not benefit from reading *Sleepwalking With The Bomb*. (The more they think they know, the greater the benefit.) But the thing most devoutly to be wished is that someone, somewhere in the Obama administration (and those that follow it) will read this important book.

—RICHARD PERLE, WASHINGTON, D.C.

PREFACE

THE IDEA FOR THIS BOOK CAME FROM WATCHING ADMINISTRA-
tions make avoidable mistakes during the period after the end of
the Cold War and the implosion of the former Soviet Union. There were
things done right as well, but nuclear policy is supremely unforgiving,
leaving little margin for error and little time to correct mistakes. Applying lessons from the failure to stop North Korea's nuclear quest, for example, would have led to better decisions and perhaps avoided the peril
we confront today with Iran. This book draws lessons that I hope will
give future leaders of the civilized world a better chance to make sound
decisions.

A book of this nature necessarily involves some technical explana-
tions and use of terms not universally familiar. I have done my best to
make this material as clear as possible for nonspecialists; some clarifica-
tions and definitions are offered in the text itself, and some are in foot-
notes or in the book's appendices.

The period covered in this book encompasses the last 46 years of the
former Soviet Union (also known by the Anglicized initials USSR, or
as Soviet Russia), and the first 20 years of its current remnant, Russia
(known as the Russian Federated Soviet Socialist Republic, or RFSFR,
when part of the USSR). "Soviet Union" and "Russia" were used colloquially during the Cold War period as interchangeable, and in the text
the names are often alternated or combined, depending on context. The
text also follows colloquial usage in referring to the United Kingdom as
Britain or Great Britain or England.

Foreign names are spelled per usage familiar to the public; if I cite
a text, I generally follow the spelling in the version cited. For Chinese
names, I follow the modern, phonetic Pinyin system (thus "Jiang Ze-

min"); but I use the older Wade-Giles Roman transliteration for Taiwanese names (thus "Chiang Kai-Shek").

I mined sources primarily for factual support for matters in the text, with analysis mine unless otherwise attributed. Where named people who have written memoirs are cited, their memoirs, if listed in the bibliography, are used as primary source material for what they said, wrote, or thought. Special attribution in the text is given to certain works unusual for their coverage of one or more parts of the puzzle, or for offering an especially valuable narrative. The text includes a bibliography of some of the more important works in the field, all of which were consulted in writing this book. Complete documentation of quotations and factual data is available online at www.SleepwalkingBomb.com.

As with any book, the author owes much to many. Bruce Chapman, founder and guide of Discovery Institute, created a home for me to think and write—at his insistence, in that order. His counsel on how best to proceed was invaluable, as was his editorial advice. Discovery's Steve Burie provided me with serial events at which to float my analyses and conclusions before a public audience.

George Gilder contributed the insights of his capacious, creative intellect, plus much encouragement and sage advice for the entire project. Others who read drafts and offered guidance and encouragement include Rosann Kaplin, Nicholas Fuhrman, Jack Oslund, and Tim Wilson. Tim brought his expert knowledge of weaponry to clear up key points. Edward Weidenfeld offered the sage advice drawn from his lifetime immersion in national security policy, politics, and history.

Special mention must be made of the late David Ginsburg, whose storied Washington career spanned 72 years, and who crossed paths with countless major national security figures around the world and in 13 American administrations. Thirty-one years of periodic lunches and serious conversation on issues of the day were an education for me and inspired me to try writing books.

Special thanks also to Richard Perle, who contributed the foreword. Meeting Herb London proved a landmark in my life. He invited me to become a trustee of the Hudson Institute, and has been a constant source of encouragement. Fellow trustees Linden Blue, Jack David, and Scooter Libby, Hudson CEO and president, and Ken Weinstein, and Hudson scholars Douglas Feith, and Christopher Ford provided essential perspectives on nuclear issues, in various contexts. Linden brought in Robert Schleicher, who offered expert advice on nuclear technology basics. Michael Ledeen offered abundant historical perspective. Peter Huessy and Sven Kramer shared their wide knowledge of arms-control and strategic weapons issues. Claudia Rosett and Gordon Chang offered deeply informed perspective on North Korea and China. Laurie Mylroie, as always, educated me on Mideast matters.

If it flies, Stu Johnson and Paul Hart know all about it. Ike Nehama aided my look at missile defense. Alan Salisbury and Marc Gunnels gave me needed military perspective on key issues. Michael Brewer applied his insightful analysis to a wide range of subjects. George Brokaw pointed me to a source I had overlooked. Jeff Gibbs lent his historical scholarship and long experience to various topics; he also pointed me to Thomas Hone, whose essay on the Washington Naval Treaty was very illuminating. Yuri Mamchur tested my Russia arguments, to my benefit. Henry Sokolski's Nonproliferation Policy Center provided a gold mine of proliferation data and analysis, plus public forums with discussion of the highest quality. Bob Zarate collaborated with Henry on editing the writings of Albert and Roberta Wohlstetter, an invaluable source. Joan Hall, my first cousin, added her insights on Albert, Roberta and issues of the day.

A September 2011 visit to Israel, under the auspices of the Hudson Institute and hosted by the Friends of the Israeli Defense Forces, provided a close-up look at the strategic situation of one of America's firmest, most trustworthy allies, a world leader in critical military and commercial technologies.

Online publishers The American Spectator, Human Events, and Daily Caller published my national security articles, enabling me to air some of my arguments during the book's long gestation. Hudson DC's Grace Terzian shepherded my twin publications on Herman Kahn for Hudson Institute. Hudson NY's former online editor, Nina Rosenwald, published my comparison between the Washington naval treaties and the SALT treaties.

I give heartfelt thanks to the talk radio hosts who provided me with hundreds of radio opportunities on stations of local, citywide, statewide, and national reach. They gave me a platform to present my national security thoughts to a broad swath of Americans—including those who called in to engage me directly.

I owe a special debt to two permanent members of the strategic community, my late uncle and aunt, Albert and Roberta Wohlstetter. Their work, which spanned the half century following World War II, has been an inspiration to me.

Albert Wohlstetter focused on issues of strategy, force structure, and nuclear proliferation and associated incentives, aiming to avoid nuclear conflict without the free world surrendering. Roberta Wohlstetter addressed nuclear proliferation as well. But she is best known for her seminal work on intelligence and strategic surprise. In *Pearl Harbor: Warning and Decision* (1962) Roberta examined the intelligence failure that led to Japan's successful destruction of the fleet at Pearl Harbor. Her work showed that evidence of an attack was never clear enough, nor highlighted sufficiently, to enable decision makers to anticipate what transpired. The perceived improbability of Japan striking such an audacious blow, impermeable bureaucratic walls between agencies, organizational sloth, and the ardent—understandable—human desire to decline to believe the worst among possibilities, combined to lead to disaster. Roberta won the Bancroft Prize in history for her book. To this day, many in the intelligence community refer to the problem of anticipating strategic surprise as a "Roberta problem." The *9/11 Commission Report* dealt with similar issues after what we consider the twenty-first century's first Pearl Harbor. New disclosures upon the seventieth anniversary of the attack confirm the acuity of the analysis Roberta presented 50 years ago. It was the work of Albert and Roberta that got my attention in junior high school days, and made my study of these issues a lifetime quest.

I finally thank two editors who worked on the book. Louisa Gilder edited early versions of the manuscript, and brought to bear both her knowledge as the accomplished author of a history of physics and the perspective of a younger generation—both with highly positive results. Anne Himmelfarb applied her elegant editing skills to later drafts. She also copy-edited the final manuscript, a service she ably performed for my first book.

I am, needless to say, solely responsible for all errors of analysis, context, and fact, and any other faults in my book.

Introduction: Organization of the Work

THE AIM OF THIS BOOK IS TO EQUIP READERS WITH A BROAD UN-derstanding of fundamental nuclear weapons issues and to draw lessons from history that can help us avoid nuclear catastrophe. Two generations ago "the Bomb" was uppermost in the national consciousness. For those of us who grew up in the "duck and cover" 1950s, the national shock of Sputnik's October 1957 launch is an indelible memory. The race for the moon had suspenseful moments worthy of Hollywood. As for Tinseltown, it plied us with radioactive monster movies in the 1950s, Cold War dramas or satire in the 1960s, and peace pictures in the 1970s.

The real-life parade of nuclear crises peaked with the October 1962 Cuban Missile Crisis, which put the entire country on edge for a fearful fortnight. Assassinations, riots, and wars followed. But through it all the concrete prospect of nuclear holocaust cast a baleful shadow over the body politic.

Then came the fall of the Berlin Wall in 1989, and two years later the end of the Soviet Union's "evil empire," as Ronald Reagan famously tagged it. With the "peace dividend" of the 1990s and a "Goldilocks Economy" Americans enjoyed a storied "holiday from history." Democracy and free markets were increasingly ascendant in many parts of the globe, astonishing to those who remembered how rare they once were.

Cold War–oriented curricula began to disappear from college offerings. Students looked elsewhere for fields of study—finance, law, and ecology. National security threats as a concept came to include climate change and economic growth. Nuclear nightmares receded.

The terrorist atrocities of September 11, 2001 brought home militant Islam's crusade against the West. Once again the Bomb threatened.

This time the most feared threat was not warheads atop ballistic missiles hurtling through space at several miles per second, but Islamist terrorists chauffeuring a crude atomic device inside a truck or slipping a device inside a shipping container.

Lost to a new generation that did not live through the Cold War's "delicate balance of terror" was the real sense that nuclear catastrophe was more than a theoretical prospect. Al-Qaeda has been pushed back, with its efforts abroad increasingly feeble. Its founder perished ignominiously in his hideout, cowering before the avenging angels of SEAL Team 6.

So while national security specialists continue to worry about growing nuclear threats, our citizenry is preoccupied with global economic crises. Though generally aware of present threats, many lack the grounding offered by the more than half century of tutelage that preceded 9/11. To them the prospect of an actual nuclear detonation must seem remote. It is a comforting, but perilous, assumption. Only history's lessons can supply what living memory cannot.

Nuclear strategy was once an avocation for what often was termed—rarely as a compliment—a "priesthood" of strategists, scholars, defense and foreign policy intellectuals, government officials, and a small coterie of interested onlookers from the outside. Much relevant knowledge was of necessity highly classified (some still is, most notably the precise formula for making an efficient, and hence readily deliverable, hydrogen bomb). Most discussions of what might or might not happen—even what could and could not happen—centered upon speculation. The great nuclear strategists of a half century ago exercised their keen imaginations, with only sparse data to answer central questions, among them how governments and individual leaders could acquire and use nuclear technology, and how nuclear war could best be avoided.

There was little historical guidance. America's Founding Fathers, by contrast, drew lessons extracted by painstaking study of historical examples dating back to ancient Greece, traced through imperial Rome, medieval England, and more. Over 2,000 years of history were encompassed in such narratives.

Now, after two-thirds of a century, global nuclear history offers multiple clear examples that teach lessons on how to minimize the risk of nuclear catastrophe in the present and future. Yesterday's history gives us concrete evidence of what has worked and what has failed. Now there are enough examples to illustrate—for the public and policy makers alike—how to most effectively address the nuclear issues we face. This book applies lessons of nuclear-age history to chart a less utopian, more prudent path.

Support for nuclear disarmament—so-called nuclear zero—flies in the face of history's lessons. Proponents of nuclear zero hold that the possibility of nuclear annihilation creates among all nations a common interest in mutual survival. They also hold that a world without nuclear weapons can be achieved by means of diplomacy. According to their view, the use of a single nuclear weapon will inevitably lead to an all-out nuclear war—that is, to mutual assured destruction; disarmament is therefore necessary to save the human race.

Public policy prescription has always been, in the main, guesswork, but there are better and worse guesses. Guesses that rely on the belief that all countries and all leaders share our core civilizational values are likely to be wrong. The strategists, with their numbers and calculations, can err with catastrophic consequences—but equally so can those who slight sound strategic principles or disdain numbers and calculations, because they pursue disarmament as an end in itself in spite of what history has to teach.

The first two chapters of the book offer some background. **Chapter 1** explains why policies driving America's arsenal towards nuclear zero would, far from making America, its allies, or the world safer, bring everyone closer to nuclear catastrophe. This is especially crucial to realize as the United States elects a president in 2012; the winner likely will face decisions of greater moment than any since at least the 1962 Cuban Missile Crisis.

Chapter 2 reviews nuclear-age history, highlighting key events from the three eras of nuclear arms evolution: 1945 to 1967, which saw an all-out arms race; 1968 to 1992, which was dominated by superpower efforts to restrain arms competition; and 1993 to the present, which has featured growing nuclear proliferation by hostile states.

Each of the next eleven chapters offers a narrative of key faces, places, and cases with an eye towards the vital lessons nuclear-age history now offers—lessons that are being ignored at grave peril to world political, economic, and social stability.

Chapter 3 looks at the former Soviet Union and today's Russia to examine the relationship—in strategic parlance the question of "linkage"—between the nuclear arms policies and foreign policies of nuclear nations. It offers the FIRST LESSON: ARMS CONTROL CANNOT BE VIEWED IN ISOLATION, BUT RATHER MUST BE CONSIDERED ALONG WITH AN ADVERSARY'S CONDUCT.

Chapter 4 examines the problem of trying to negotiate arms agreements with adversaries. The experience of the United States over several decades teaches the SECOND LESSON: ARMS AGREEMENTS MUST BE BASED UPON GENUINE, NOT PRESUMED, COMMONALITY OF STRATEGIC INTEREST.

Chapter 5 examines the risk of a future global nuclear confrontation with Iran in light of new information about the 1962 Cuban Missile Crisis. That event, properly understood, teaches the THIRD LESSON: REVOLUTIONARY POWERS CANNOT BE CONTAINED; THEY MUST BE DEFEATED.

Chapter 6 looks at North Korea to consider the risk of a rogue nuclear state blackmailing adversaries with the threat of a sudden resort to nuclear weapons. It offers the FOURTH LESSON: NUCLEAR WEAPONS GIVE NATIONS A "DYING STING" CAPABILITY THAT VIRTUALLY PRE-

CLUDES PREEMPTIVE ACTION AND CONFERS NEAR-TOTAL SURVIVAL IN-
SURANCE.

Chapter 7 looks at China and Chinese history to consider the risk
of a regional power confrontation escalating to nuclear war. The Chinese
experience teaches the FIFTH LESSON: THE NUCLEAR BALANCE MAT-
TERS IF ANY PARTY TO A CONFLICT THINKS IT MATTERS, AND THUS
ALTERS ITS BEHAVIOR.

An "interlude" between chapters 7 and 8 examines how thin is the
line between development of commercial nuclear power and the development of weapons. The discussion there serves as an important background to subsequent chapters.

Chapter 8 looks at India and Pakistan to examine the risk of regional nuclear war. It also examines the risk posed by theft of nuclear
weapons or an Islamist takeover of the country. These countries' experiences teach the SIXTH LESSON: CIVILIAN NUCLEAR POWER INHER-
ENTLY CONFERS MILITARY NUCLEAR CAPABILITY.

Chapter 9 examines the problem of obtaining accurate intelligence
on a country's nuclear power program, looking specifically at Western
experiences with Iraq and Iran. It offers the SEVENTH LESSON: INTEL-
LIGENCE CANNOT RELIABLY PREDICT WHEN CLOSED SOCIETIES GO NU-
CLEAR.

Chapter 10 examines why nations go nuclear and considers Russia,
Britain, France, and Israel in turn. It offers the EIGHTH LESSON: ALLY
PROLIFERATION CAN BE PREVENTED ONLY BY SUPERPOWER CONSTANCY.

Chapter 11 looks at the implications of popular pressure to disarm,
such as arose after the bombings of Hiroshima and Nagasaki, as well as
pressure to ban atmospheric tests. It offers the NINTH LESSON: POPU-
LAR PRESSURE FOR UNILATERAL DISARMAMENT CAN PREVAIL UNLESS
WESTERN GOVERNMENTS EXPLAIN ITS HIDDEN, GRAVE DANGERS.

Chapter 12 also looks at disarmament, though from a different
angle: it explores why nations disarm (the examples are South Africa,

Libya, Argentina, Brazil, and three former Russian republics) or are disarmed by force (Iraq and Syria). These examples teach the TENTH LESSON: DISARMING HOSTILE POWERS CANNOT BE DONE BY NEGOTIATIONS ALONE.

Chapter 13 examines the special catastrophic threat posed by surprise "electromagnetic pulse" attacks, now within reach of smaller, emerging nuclear powers such as nuclear-club-aspirant Iran. It offers the ELEVENTH LESSON: NEVER ALLOW SINGLE OR LOW-NUMBER POINTS OF CATASTROPHIC VULNERABILITY.

Chapter 14, the last chapter, ties everything together: concepts, cases, and coping with future dangers. It suggests that, if learned, the vital lessons afforded by nuclear history can reduce the risk of nuclear catastrophe, and it offers a final, summative TWELFTH LESSON: NUCLEAR POLICY MUST BE FUNDAMENTALLY DEFENSIVE: ITS GOAL SHOULD BE TO AVOID THE APOCALYPTIC TRINITY OF SUICIDE, GENOCIDE, AND SURRENDER.

Four appendices offer important context. **Appendix 1** discusses how the imaginations of novelists and filmmakers swayed the public via scenarios starkly at odds with nuclear-age realities. **Appendix 2** discusses the tightening of control over nuclear weapons since 1945. **Appendix 3** discusses intelligence failures regarding strategic arms deployment. **Appendix 4** discusses nuances of the complex relationships between missile defensive and offensive weaponry.

This book assembles in one place an integrated picture of what lessons history and strategic thinking offer us to confront today's nuclear threats. They are lessons we are well advised to absorb, and to apply to evolving events and threats today and in the future.

1.

THE RUSH TO NUCLEAR ZERO: COURTING CATASTROPHE

So today, I state clearly and with conviction America's commitment to seek the peace and security of a world without nuclear weapons. I'm not naive. This goal will not be reached quickly—perhaps not in my lifetime. It will take patience and persistence. But now we, too, must ignore the voices who tell us that the world cannot change. We have to insist, "Yes, we can."
PRESIDENT BARACK OBAMA, HRADCANY SQUARE,
PRAGUE, CZECH REPUBLIC, APRIL 5, 2009

SINCE NEWS OF THE TWIN ATOMIC BOMBINGS THAT ENDED THE SEC-ond World War first hit front pages around the world, the cause of abolishing nuclear weapons has resonated with millions. A visit to the Los Alamos "Trinity" test site, where the first atomic bomb exploded, offers mute testament to the vast scale of man-made destruction unleashed two-thirds of a century ago: the three-foot-high remnant of the 100-foot tower that cradled the massive, ungainly device; the ground littered with tiny shards of "trinitite," also called "Alamogordo glass." The explosion instantly fused the sand around the tower base into a green-gray glass that sparkles in the sun—and that emits radioactive alpha and beta particles. One site visit will give visitors about half the radiation dosage they would get from a transcontinental plane flight. A brown rock obelisk, about twice the average height of an adult, marks the spot where the world was changed forever.

Beginning with President Harry S. Truman, every American president has expressed a desire to see the world rid once and for all of nuclear weapons. All have stated that it is a goal unlikely to be achieved anytime soon. But on February 15, 2012—less than three years after President Obama joined his predecessors in cautioning that nuclear abolition is a faraway goal—"perhaps not in my lifetime"—anonymous senior administration officials leaked a "trial balloon." The Obama administration was considering three levels of arms cuts beyond those already slated in the 2010 New START Accord, down to far lower nuclear force levels than 2009's total stockpile of 5,133 warheads. The three target level ranges leaked were 1,000–1,100, 700–800, and 300–400.

It is evident that President Obama desires to push America's nuclear arsenal as low as possible, to levels near those he had originally said might be decades away. He gave the reasons in his April 5, 2009, Prague address:

> The existence of thousands of nuclear weapons is the most dangerous legacy of the Cold War. No nuclear war was fought between the United States and the Soviet Union, but generations lived with the knowledge that their world could be erased in a single flash of light....
>
> [T]he threat of global nuclear war has gone down, but the risk of a nuclear attack has gone up. More nations have acquired these weapons. Testing has continued. Black market trade in nuclear secrets and nuclear materials abound. The technology to build a bomb has spread. Terrorists are determined to buy, build or steal one. Our efforts to contain these dangers are centered on a global non-proliferation regime, but as more people and nations break the rules, we could reach the point where the center cannot hold....
>
> Some argue that the spread of these weapons cannot be stopped.... Such fatalism is a deadly adversary, for if we believe that the spread of nuclear weapons is inevitable, then in some way we are admitting to ourselves that the use of nuclear weapons is inevitable.
>
> ... [W]e must stand together for the right of people everywhere to live free from fear in the 21st century. And ... as the only nuclear power to have used a nuclear weapon, the United States has a moral responsibility to act. We cannot succeed in this endeavor alone, but we can lead it, we can start it.

Obama views himself as a transformational president. And in national security what could be more transformational than ending the world's post-1945 nuclear nightmare? The New START Treaty, ratified in December 2010, and the 2010 Nuclear Security Summit are cited as examples of success in the direction of nuclear zero. But New START was a unilateral U.S. strategic arms-reduction agreement, as the Russians were already below treaty limits. Under the treaties to which they are signatories, the Russians can actually build newer, more modern missiles and add to their arsenal; they are in fact doing so, testing several models. New START's verification provisions are far more limited than those in the treaty it replaced (the Bush Moscow Treaty of 2002). As for the Nuclear Security Summit, its participants paid more attention to Israel for its arsenal than they did to North Korea for having exited the Nonproliferation Treaty and joined the nuclear club.

Abolitionism cannot surmount several immense obstacles. *First, hostile states will not only decline to follow our good example; they will be induced to increase their arsenals, which become more valuable as our arsenal shrinks*—100 nukes in Pakistan matter much more in a world in which the U.S. has the same number than in a world in which the U.S. has a few thousand. This behavior runs counter to the psychology of civilized people who see nuclear weapons as being for deterrence only, but a nuclear Iran eager to destroy the Great Satan (U.S.) and Little Satan (Israel) will think differently.

Consider what the Soviets did in the 11 months between the November 1985 Geneva Summit and the October 1986 Reykjavik Summit. In that short span they capped off their 25-year strategic buildup by adding over 5,000 warheads, topping out at some 45,000 warheads— this despite the U.S. having frozen the total number of its warheads in 1967 at 31,255, and reducing them constantly since. Gorbachev did soon come around, as Russia's economy imploded. But it is unrealistic to expect Iran's fanatical mullahs to do the same. Pakistan's increasingly Islamist leadership plans to double its arsenal as rapidly as possible.

A second obstacle to abolitionism is that *verifying clandestine stockpiles of warheads and missiles is simply impossible at present and likely will remain so for a long time.* We failed to find a dozen jet planes Saddam hid in the sands of Iraq, until after his overthrow. Concealing missiles and nuclear warheads deep underground would be, by comparison, child's play.

China has been developing—and possibly concealing—new nuclear weapons. It revealed in December 2011 that it has built 3,000 miles of deep underground tunnels—called "the Underground Great Wall"— that may conceal an arsenal far larger than the 200 to 400 weapons China is commonly thought to possess. China has never divulged anything compatible to the extensive nuclear data that we have collected from the Russians over the past 20 years, and thus we can only guess at the size of its arsenal. A former U.S. national security official, Professor Phillip Karber, had students working for three years to compile all available data on the subject. Karber offered no specific China arsenal estimate. The data, official film footage on China's bomb and missile programs, show huge missiles shuttling inside the tunnels. Prominent skeptics argue that current estimates are correct, citing CIA estimates of arsenal size and estimates of fissile material produced in China. But CIA nuclear intelligence estimates are often wrong. Given that Chinese leaders know they may someday face the United States in a western Pacific showdown, it defies strategic logic to assume that the massive across-the-board Chinese military buildup would exempt the most powerful class of weapons.

Third, *abolitionists have no basis for their confidence in the UN's ability to stop a determined nuclear aspirant.* The worst nations will simply ignore entreaties and evade inspections. What can work—the only remedy–is positive regime change. The Soviet Union evaded arms treaty obligations for years and concealed the full size of its massive strategic buildup. Only with the accession of Mikhail Gorbachev late in the Cold War did things change for the better. Until similar change comes to Pakistan, North Korea, and Iran, abolition is chimerical.

To be sure, President Obama talked in Prague about the need to punish violators:

> Rules must be binding. Violations must be punished.... The world must stand together to prevent the spread of these weapons.... North Korea must know that the path to security and respect will never come through threats and illegal weapons. All nations must come together to build a stronger, global regime.... [W]e must stand shoulder to shoulder to pressure the North Koreans to change course.

He went on to note the threats posed by Iran and by terrorists in possession of a nuclear weapon.

But President Obama had spurned a rare opportunity for positive regime change in June 2009, when the Iranian opposition formed in fury at the stolen election that returned Islamist Mahmoud Ahmadinejad to the Iranian presidency. Instead of siding with the demonstrators and uniting a coalition to put maximum pressure on the mullahs, Obama stood aside and contented himself with feeble verbal sallies. Moreover, he pursued arms talks with a leadership that had never honored an agreement made and that was clearly determined to pursue its nuclear ambitions, in part by slow-rolling diplomatic negotiations whenever possible. He also allowed Russia and China to water down several rounds of Iran sanctions. Though since late 2011 sanctions against Iranian oil and financial interests began to bite, they have not stopped Iran's nuclear program.

As this book went to press the furies were assembling in the Mideast. It appears increasingly likely that Iran's relentless progress towards nuclear weapon capability cannot be arrested by sanctions alone, and thus that Israel, perceiving a nuclear Iran as an existential threat, will take preventive military action. Israel's determination to act has been reinforced by the Obama administration's strong public opposition to launching a strike and by a notably unsympathetic international community. A nuclear-armed Iran, declared "unacceptable" by two American presidents, does suggest how ineffective, indeed dangerous, nuclear nonproliferation efforts tend to be.

Finally, there is a fourth obstacle to abolitionism: *it creates the dangerous situation in which the public's gut sentiment favoring abolition can trump practical obstacles to verification and enforcement, and thus could push Western nations to disarm first.* Were a nuke to detonate anywhere on the planet, momentum for unilateral disarmament could snowball. Many advocates fan such emotional flames. But embarking on a course of unilateral disarmament before devising the requisite diplomatic and military arrangements needed to effectively police a nuclear-zero world—a condition nowhere near to being achieved—would begin the slide down the slippery political slope. There is no definitive correct number of nuclear weapons that the United States needs at any given time; this would be true even if every other nation's number were perfectly known. Thus there is no definitive stopping point for disarmament, and advocates can keep pressing Western democracies to cut their arsenals—pressures not felt by the world's most dangerous nuclear-armed regimes.

The president has shown an alarming willingness to trade a modest missile defense program—one that would hedge against clandestine nuclear breakout in event of countries violating nuclear-zero pledges—for the instantly revocable promises of an adversary. Ronald Reagan conditioned zeroing out nuclear missiles on keeping missile defense development, in order to erect a shield as a hedge against such cheating. But President Obama is manifestly eager to bargain away missile defense leverage—shown by the notorious "open mic" verbal exchange with a top Russian leader at the 2012 Nuclear Security Summit in Seoul.[1] Leaving America defenseless even against small nuclear-armed missile attacks invites nuclear blackmail during a crisis.

The president did announce in Prague two laudable initiatives: to curb black market smuggling of nuclear material and to secure all loose nuclear material within four years (by the end of 2013). But his opti-

---

1. The text of the exchange appears in chapter 4.

mism about negotiations follows a utopian model of resolving differences between nations, premised upon a presumed commonality of interest in mutual survival:

> When nations and peoples allow themselves to be defined by their differences, the gulf between them widens. When we fail to pursue peace, then it stays forever beyond our grasp. We know the path when we choose fear over hope. To denounce or shrug off a call for cooperation is an easy but also a cowardly thing to do. That's how wars begin. That's where human progress ends.

Put simply, the president mistakenly believes that all nations share a common interest in mutual survival. He thus rejects the idea of irreconcilable conflict. But such conflicts manifestly exist. In fact, *what irreconcilably opposed governments share is a parallel desire to survive; neither has any interest in a mortal enemy's surviving. Rather, each desires—and must aim for—the enemy's destruction.*

The United States has no common interest in survival with al-Qaeda. The United States desires to survive; so does al-Qaeda. But parallel desires are not common interests. The United States has no interest in Hamas, Hezbollah, or the Muslim Brotherhood surviving. It has no interest in the Ayatollah Khomeini's militant Islamist republic surviving. It has no interest in the North Korean regime surviving. Nor would it have an interest in militant Islamists gaining control over Pakistan's government, and thus its nuclear arsenal. Conversely, nothing would more greatly benefit militant Islamists of any stripe than the destruction of the United States. The United States, along with its allies, is the main obstacle to the global triumph of militant Islam.

In the run-up to World War II, the Western democracies had mutual interests in one another's survival, but hardly any security interest in the survival of Hitler's Nazi regime or of the militarist regime in Japan. The United States formed an alliance of convenience with Soviet Russia, but U.S. interests ceased coinciding with Russia's at war's end, and only when in 1991 the former Soviet Union collapsed could the United

States win the Cold War. While the United States and the Soviets both sought to survive, the Soviet project would have benefited most of all from the U.S.'s demise.

Just as America had no common interest with past enemies in mutual survival, it would be a deadly mistake to think that it shares such an interest today, given growing nuclear threats from hostile states, some of whose leaders embrace a fanatical religious ideology that welcomes Armageddon. Such powers may not act on ideological imperatives, but we cannot assume they will decline to do so.

Regrettably, many of Barack Obama's policies make a war more likely. Rushing towards abolition of nuclear weapons will, on the fair historical evidence, not induce dangerous nuclear states to follow the U.S. lead. Instead, our adversaries will see greater benefit in increasing their own arsenals if America's is pared to a few hundred.

We make comfortable assumptions about how our adversaries will act at our potentially grave peril.

2.

THE NUCLEAR AGE: FROM "TRINITY" TO TEHRAN

*Then it may well be that we shall by a process of sublime irony
have reached a stage in this story where safety will be the sturdy
child of terror, and survival the twin brother of annihilation.*
PRIME MINISTER WINSTON CHURCHILL, HOUSE OF COMMONS, MARCH 1, 1955

ON SEPTEMBER 24, 1924, READERS OF THE BRITISH LITERARY MAGazine *Nash's Pall Mall* opened its pages to a chilling article by Winston Churchill. In "Shall We All Commit Suicide?" Churchill—a statesman then out of political office—warned what was incubating in the embers of the recent world war. Beyond the horrors of the war he had observed on the Western Front, he wrote of the immense escalation the summer of 1919 would have seen had there been no armistice. With incredible prescience, Churchill intuited the direction towards which modern war technology was heading:

> Might not a bomb no bigger than an orange be found to possess a secret power to destroy a whole block of buildings—nay, to concentrate the force of a thousand tons of cordite and blast a township at a stroke? Could not explosives even of the existing type be guided automatically in flying machines by wireless or other rays, without a human pilot, in ceaseless procession upon a hostile city, arsenal, camp or dockyard?
>
> … Such, then, is the peril with which mankind menaces itself. Means of destruction incalculable in their effects, wholesale and frightful in their character, and unrelated to any form of human merit: the march of Science unfolding ever more appalling possibilities; and the fires of hatred burning deep in the hearts of some of the greatest peoples of the world, fanned by continual provocation and unceasing fear and fed by the deepest sense of national wrong or national danger!

Modern nuclear history began with discoveries by late nineteenth-century and early twentieth-century physicists looking into certain strange elements and mapping out the internal structure of the atom. By the time the first physicist grasped the potential of unlocking the energy contained there, the world was already on the path to a second global conflict. But the statesman who saw the future came first.

Churchill's foreboding 1924 prophecy encompassed the three components of the greatest threat humankind has faced since 1945: nuclear weapons, ballistic missiles, and fanatics in possession of both. His remarks came when guided missiles were a pipe dream, rocketry consisted of sending tiny projectiles aloft for a few seconds or minutes to reach at most a few miles' altitude, and scientists had yet to even discover the neutron particle, which made splitting the nucleus of an atom feasible. The element plutonium was still unknown, let alone the process of thermonuclear fusion that would ultimately allow the miniaturization of high-yield weapons. Though visionaries like the sci-fi writers Jules Verne and H. G. Wells had imaginatively seen ahead before Churchill spoke, among statesmen of his time Churchill's prediction was uniquely far-sighted.

The First Bomb: Earliest Research through the Trinity Test

On a drizzly London day in September 1933, only months after his Hitler-induced exile from Germany, Leo Szilard had the crucial eureka moment. The great Hungarian grasped before any of his fellow physicists that a nuclear chain reaction would release enormous energy, sufficient to destroy a city. The next step came just before Christmas 1938, when German chemists Otto Hahn and Fritz Strassman stumbled upon an unexpected effect. The physicist member of their group, Lise Meitner, had just fled to Sweden. From there, she and her nephew, fellow refugee Otto Robert Frisch, interpreted what had happened—the central nucleus of a uranium atom was apparently unstable. The absorption of an extra neutron was enough to split it, resulting in two smaller atoms and an immense release of energy—a process Frisch dubbed "nuclear fission."

Tipped off by Meitner, Szilard saw that here could be the beginning of the chain reaction he had foreseen. He persuaded Albert Einstein to write his famous 1939 letter to President Franklin Roosevelt. "[T]he element uranium may be turned into a new and important source of energy in the immediate future," Einstein wrote FDR, calling for "watchfulness, and, if necessary, quick action on the part of the Administration." He explained:

> It may become possible to set up a nuclear chain reaction in a large mass of uranium, by which vast amounts of power and large quantities of new radium-like elements would be generated.... A single bomb of this type, carried by boat and exploded in a port, might very well destroy the whole port together with some of the surrounding territory.

Szilard chose Einstein to deliver the message, to lend it the weight of his unmatched prestige. He had calculated well. On October 19 FDR convened an advisory panel to look into the matter, and by 1942 the Manhattan Project (so named to conceal its true purpose) was under way. Yet according to James B. Conant, a top FDR science adviser, FDR had "only fleeting interest in the atom," and "the program never got very far past the threshold of his consciousness."

The discoveries made by Manhattan Project scientists first led to two types of atomic bombs (A-bombs), based upon uranium and plutonium, each a thousand times more powerful than bombs with conventional explosives. These atomic bombs, in turn, laid the foundation for the later development of the hydrogen bomb (H-bomb), a thousand times more powerful than the A-bombs dropped on Japan.

Forty-two months after the founding of the Manhattan Project, the atom bomb was a reality. A flood of European scientists, refugees from Hitler, made this astonishing success possible. To Los Alamos flocked geniuses: two more Hungarians, the mathematics prodigy John von Neumann and the "father of the hydrogen bomb" Edward Teller; the great Danish founder of the atomic theory, Niels Bohr; the young Polish mathematician, Stanislaw Ulam; the brilliant German Hans Bethe, who explained how fusion energy powers the stars; and the Italian Enrico Fermi, considered by his peers the most deeply knowledgeable of them all. They joined Americans like J. Robert Oppenheimer, whose technical brilliance was complemented by his organizational ability and knack for picking the right people for each complex task; young physicist Glenn Seaborg, who created the devilish artificial element plutonium in 1941; and a contingent from Britain that included James Chadwick, discoverer of the neutron particle essential for nuclear fission.

Fear that Adolf Hitler would get the atom bomb first drove the Manhattan Project's crash program. Szilard feared that by Christmas 1943 or New Year's Day 1944, the Nazis would A-bomb Chicago. These scientists knew the truth of Winston Churchill's description of Germany's Napoleonic leader: "a maniac of ferocious genius, the repository and expression of the most virulent hatreds that have ever corroded the human breast." The Allies were certain that Hitler would not hesitate to use the bomb. Indeed, Joseph Goebbels, Hitler's infamous propaganda minister, noted in his diary in spring 1942:

> I received a report about the latest development in German science. Research in the realm of atomic destruction has now proceeded to the point where... tremendous destruction, it is claimed, can be wrought with a minimum of effort... It is essential that we be ahead of everybody.

The Nazis were, in fact, not even close to developing the bomb, but the Allies understandably erred on the side of assuming the worst case, partly out of supreme respect for legendary German physicist Werner Heisenberg. Had they passed up development, and Hitler managed somehow to build the bomb, utter annihilation surely would have befallen the great democracies. That they were not close was proven by Heisenberg's reaction upon being told about the Hiroshima bombing.

He guessed that the bomb had not been a uranium weapon, but instead a superpowerful chemical explosive bomb.

After the war, Einstein regretted having helped the Allies by persuading FDR to pursue A-bomb research. He lamented to his secretary: "Had I known that the Germans would not succeed in producing an atomic bomb, I would never have lifted a finger. Not a single finger!"

The Nazis did, however, jump into a huge lead in another department during the war. The great German rocketeer Wernher von Braun led development of "vengeance weapons"—the German "V" series of rockets. V-1s—jet-powered low-flying subsonic missiles that usually can be steered in flight (what today we call cruise missiles, albeit the pioneering V-1 was not maneuverable)—began dropping on London in 1944. Later that year, the V-2, the world's first true military ballistic missile, hit London. (A ballistic missile—from "ballista," a medieval catapult of large stones—is set on its course by a few minutes of powered flight, then coasts until gravity pulls it back to earth.) Unlike the V-1, which flew at constant speed and altitude until its final plunge, and thus could be easily shot down by ground fire or by intercepting aircraft, the V-2 attained a velocity of nearly one mile per second and thus fell on its targets with no warning, arriving before the sound of its approach. Had Hitler's warheads carried atom bombs of the kind dropped on Japan in August 1945, the heart of London could have been obliterated with but a few such hits.[2]

The nuclear age formally began on the morning of July 16, 1945, when in the New Mexico desert the Trinity device was detonated. Its blinding brightness led Oppenheimer, leader of the Manhattan Project, to famously recall a verse from the Indian epic, the *Bhagavad-Gita* ("The Song of God"):

2. In an 80-day period in 1944, 2,300 V-1s hit London. In their best day, the British defenders—using ground-based anti-aircraft guns and pursuit planes like the Spitfire—shot down all but four 4 of 101 incoming V-1s. As the strategist Bernard Brodie later observed of that day's tally, "But if those four had been atomic bombs, London survivors would not have considered the record good." Of 4,300 V-2s launched at London, 1,200 landed within the 30-mile target area.

If the radiance of a thousand suns were to burst at once into the sky, that would be like the splendor of the mighty one. For I am become Death, shatterer of worlds.

Oppenheimer's awe-induced invocation of ancient sacred poetry was spot-on: the glare from the blast would have been visible from the planet Jupiter, some one-half billion miles away from Earth.

The bombs dropped on Hiroshima and Nagasaki less than a month later changed warfare and global politics forever. The age that began two-thirds of a century ago has gone through several stages—from the all-out arms race of 1945 to 1967, to the arms control of the seventies and eighties, and finally to the era of rogue nuclear weapons proliferation we entered in the early nineties.

Nuclear History, 1945–Present

WITH A combination of wartime espionage at Los Alamos and its own scientists at Sarov (the monastery town turned closed city for the Russian bomb project), the Soviet Union lagged only four years behind the U.S. in nuclear bomb building.

The end of the war found the former allies now armed with nuclear weapons, facing off in a struggle lasting nearly 50 years, with Europe divided by Soviet aggression. Though labeled "cold," the war was very hot in several major regional proxy conflicts and numerous smaller fronts around the globe. Nuclear arsenals kept the two superpowers not only from a nuclear conflict, but from a major direct conventional-force conflict as well.

The race to develop the "Super"—the H-bomb—began right after Russia exploded its first A-bomb. In 1952, the Americans vaporized an atoll in the South Pacific with a massive hydrogen device, one far too large to qualify as a true bomb. The Soviet H-bomb was tested in August 1953 on the steppes of Kazakhstan. The vast power of these hydrogen bombs made destruction not merely of cities, but of civilization itself, a plausible prospect.

In December 1953 President Eisenhower announced his Atoms for Peace program, when only three powers—the U.S., Soviet Union, and United Kingdom—had gone nuclear. His idea was to provide a compelling reason for countries not to pursue nuclear energy for military purposes. In exchange for such forbearance they were to be guaranteed help in developing peaceful atomic energy uses. Under the aegis of Atoms for Peace, dozens of nations received economic and technical aid to develop commercial nuclear technology. Coupled with America's precipitous 1946 disclosure of Manhattan Project technology, knowledge pertaining to nuclear weapons began spreading around the globe. As there is no bright line between commercial research and military use (see the "Interlude" at the end of chapter 7), out popped the proliferation genie.

The year 1957 brought new urgency to the technology arms race with two dramatic Soviet triumphs. That August, the Soviet Union tested the world's first intercontinental ballistic missile (ICBM), a ballistic missile with a range further than 5,500 kilometers—around 3,500 miles, roughly the distance from Nova Scotia to Portugal. Such a device was hardly inevitable: FDR's wartime science adviser, Dr. Vannevar Bush, told Congress in December 1945 that such a machine could never work. But Stalin wanted it; in 1947 he was telling senior deputies that an ICBM "could be an effective straitjacket for that noisy shopkeeper Harry Truman." Two months after the Soviets tested their ICBM, they had their second triumph: they launched the world's first orbiting satellite, Sputnik ("traveler").

Between 1957 and 1967 the superpowers raced to close the window of nation-ending catastrophic vulnerability the new technologies had opened. They hid their intercontinental ballistic missiles underground in storage cylinders, encasing underground launch pads, all bearing the gentle agrarian name of "missile silos." They hid intermediate-range ballistic missiles under the oceans in submarines, and they retained air bases for their strategic bombers. As technology improved, this "triad" of nuclear systems (a nuclear "system" is a weapon plus the platform on which that weapon is mounted) reduced each side's vulnerability to a surprise nuclear first strike, what nuclear strategists call the "bolt from the blue."

In the first quarter century of nuclear weaponry, five nations conducted hundreds of above ground tests. Almost half came in 1962 alone, the peak of worldwide nuclear testing. Most of these were U.S. tests in Nevada and in the Pacific Ocean on the Marshall Islands. A few were British tests in the Australian outback and on Christmas Island. France tested in Algeria. China tested its devices in its vast western interior, and the rest were Soviet tests in Kazakhstan or in the Arctic at Novaya Zemlya. Amid rising awareness of nuclear fallout, the U.S., Soviet Union, and Great Britain agreed in the Limited Test Ban Treaty of 1963 that they would confine future tests to shots fired deep in underground testing caverns.

To reduce the risk of nuclear war between the two superpowers, a quarter century of intense efforts at arms control followed the all-out race. Arms control became a dominant theme in 1967 when the United States announced it would unilaterally freeze—that is, freeze without Russia's participation—the number of offensive nuclear weapons platforms it deployed. Arms control acquired iconic status in 1972 with the U.S.-Soviet agreement known as SALT I. Superpower arms-control agreements became central strategic policy. Many politicians and analysts treated arms control as uniquely important among national security issues.

The 1973 Arab-Israeli Yom Kippur War brought the superpowers close to nuclear war again—notwithstanding their arms-control talks of the previous year. Soviet and American naval ships drifted into a tense confrontation in the Mediterranean, as the U.S. declared the highest nuclear alert since the Cuban Missile Crisis. As in 1962, cooler heads prevailed, and catastrophe was averted.

How limited was the influence of arms talks became clear as the Soviet Union began aggressively backing Third World Marxist movements, often with gifts of sophisticated conventional weapons. The Soviets induced Cuba to send soldiers to fight "wars of national liberation" in Africa. These actions revived a policy that strategists called "linkage." More and more, American politicians and diplomats called for linking strategic arms negotiations to the increasingly bellicose geopolitical conduct of the Soviet Union. Total Soviet warheads surpassed America's in 1978, with America's number declining and the Soviets' count climbing (to a peak in 1986). After the 1979 Soviet occupation of Afghanistan, ardent arms controllers found that their position—that nuclear arms control is of unique and overriding importance and can be divorced from other considerations—had become politically untenable. "Linkage" became enshrined as a bedrock principle of superpower relations.

President Reagan's 1983 Strategic Defense Initiative restored missile defense as a legitimate option to limit the destructiveness of a nuclear attack. In 1987, the U.S. and USSR signed the first true arms-reduction treaty, eliminating their intermediate- and medium-range nuclear ballistic missiles (those that can reach targets roughly 600 to 3,500 miles away). The Berlin Wall fell in 1989, symbolizing liberation of Eastern Europe from Moscow's jackboot. Just before the breakup of the Soviet Union on the last day of 1991, the superpowers negotiated the first major strategic nuclear-warhead-reduction accord—that is, one involving long-range weapons such as ICBMs. The next year, the U.S. unilaterally ended warhead modernization.

But as the U.S. was making this momentous decision—and as superpower arsenals were plunging, from a peak of 12,000 deployed nuclear warheads in 1992 to 2,200 by 2002—there was a parallel acceleration in what is known in strategic parlance as nuclear proliferation. India (which had in 1974 set off what it called a "peaceful" nuclear explosion) in May 1998 tested a series of nuclear weapons beneath the sands of the Thar Desert near Pakistan. Pakistan followed a fortnight later with its own series of tests within a mountain in the foothills of its west Afghan border, becoming the first nuclear-armed Islamic nation. Nearby, Iran continued its clandestine nuclear weapons program begun in the 1980s. So did North Korea.

In the middle of this period of nuclear proliferation came the September 11, 2001, attacks on America, whose success raised plausible fears that terrorists could someday strike America using weapons of mass destruction. Such fears were only heightened by North Korea's first nuclear test in October 2006 (at an underground location not far from its northernmost coast), while Iran continued its march towards nuclear weapons capability. Enemy states like these, recognizing no restraints on what they do, are fertile soil for nuclear proliferation. Spreading nuclear-weapon-capable technology—for example, to Libya and Syria—has been the hallmark of Pakistan and North Korea.

Proliferation, however, can sometimes be staved off. The crumbling of the former Soviet Union posed a great danger, as new and not necessarily stable states found themselves the possessors of Soviet weapons stored within their borders. But a massive and largely successful effort over the past 20 years brought all far-flung ex-Soviet weapons back to Russia. Remarkably, this time of upheaval saw no known theft of nuclear-weapons-grade material.

Thus the nonstop all-out arms race so often portrayed is sharply at odds with the more complex history of nuclear policy since 1945. What began as an all-out superpower technology race morphed into a protracted period of superpower bargaining, and finally was superseded by proliferating smaller powers, most of them hostile to the West.

The emerging era in which less stable powers obtain nuclear weapons will create an international environment more dangerous than that of the Cold War. This danger will be especially acute if the traditional calculus of deterrence fails to impress a new breed of leaders, who may prefer a fanatical calculus to more traditional approaches. By learning how events unfolded in the past and which choices made by leaders were sound versus faulty, perhaps we can minimize the risk of nuclear catastrophe in the future.

3.

RUSSIA: LINKING ARMS CONTROL
TO AN ADVERSARY'S CONDUCT

*We do not want war any more than the West does, but
we are less interested than the West in peace, and
therein lies the strength of our position.*

JOSEPH STALIN, WHO HAD JUST ANNEXED EASTERN EUROPE BY FORCE, TO
AMERICA'S AMBASSADOR TO RUSSIA, WALTER BEDELL SMITH, IN 1949

THE COLD WAR SAW SUPERPOWER COMPETITION TAKE CENTER stage. At the heart of this epic struggle were two features: Soviet "adventurism" in aggressively pushing to extend Moscow's sphere of geopolitical influence and deployment of massive strategic and tactical nuclear arsenals. Adventurism saw Moscow attempt to choke off West Berlin in 1948 then succeed in sundering Berlin in 1961. It would authorize its North Korean client state to wage a war of conquest against South Korea, and later support North Vietnam's successful conquest of the South. It would crush serial rebellions in Eastern Europe, including an especially brutal suppression of the 1956 Hungarian uprising. It would also support Marxist movements in the Third World, as well as a wave of transnational terror directed against the West. The Soviet drive for Third World dominance culminated in the 1979 invasion of Afghanistan.

The U.S. was caught flat-footed by Moscow's push. Massive demobilization had left America's armed forces denuded and under-prepared. America's military roster plummeted from 12 million under arms in June 1945 to 1.5 million two years later. Symptomatic of this sudden shift was a 1948 exercise called the Dayton Raid: the Air Force conducted a test, ordering its strategic bombers to electronically "bomb" Wright-Patterson Air Force base near Dayton, Ohio. Taking off from Omaha,

Nebraska, was every single strategic bomber in the U.S. inventory. Not a single plane successfully completed its mission.

The Soviet Union's conduct during the Cold War teaches the First Lesson of nuclear-age history: ARMS CONTROL CANNOT BE VIEWED IN ISOLATION, BUT RATHER MUST BE CONSIDERED ALONG WITH AN AD-VERSARY'S CONDUCT. Had the United States made arms control the paramount good, it would have given tacit approval to Soviet policies very much counter to America's interests.

Superpowers and "Super" Bomb: The Arms Race Begins

WHEN THE new president, Harry Truman, told Joseph Stalin about the successful first atomic test in the Jornada del Muerto desert in New Mexico, he thought he was breaking news to the Soviet dictator. But strategic arms competition was already underway between the two ostensible allies even before World War II ended. Spies—including Ted Hall, an American, and Klaus Fuchs, a German who had recently escaped to Britain—had brought Stalin the precise details of the Manhattan Project. During the chaos at the end of the war, captured German scientists also aided the Russian program. The Russians kidnapped scientists they found in their sector and kept them in Russia for six years before allowing them to return to Germany in 1952. America, too, got help from German scientists (most notably, chief German rocketeer Wernher von Braun, who led the American space program through the 1969 moon landing).

The Soviet goal was not just to have an atomic bomb. Fuchs and others had alerted the Soviets that the Americans mulled over a program to build an even mightier bomb, known around Los Alamos as the "Super." In fact, no program was begun, as all effort at Los Alamos was directed towards finishing the atomic bomb project as soon as possible, so as to hasten the end of the war.

President Truman directed at the start of 1950 that the Super be built, not knowing if Russia had an H-bomb program. Paul Nitze (who during the 45 years of the Cold War served in more senior national security capacities than anyone else) recalled that Truman's decision to build the Super was guided ultimately by fear that Stalin would go ahead if advised such a device were technically feasible. In fact, Stalin had authorized the Russian H-bomb program two months after the Soviet Union's first atomic test, and three months before Truman authorized the American one.

For decades the myth persisted that if only the U.S. had refrained from developing the hydrogen bomb, the Russians might well have reciprocated. But the memoirs of Andrei Sakharov, the so-called father of the Soviet hydrogen bomb and later a prominent antinuclear weapons advocate, demolish that theory. Sakharov makes clear that had America held back, Stalin and his legendarily sadistic secret-police chief Lavrenti Beria would have exploited such restraint:

> The Soviet Government (or, more properly, those in power: Stalin, Beria and company) already understood the potential of the new weapon, and *nothing could have dissuaded them from going forward with its development.* Any U.S. move toward abandoning or suspending work on a thermonuclear weapon would have been perceived either as a cunning, deceitful maneuver or as evidence of stupidity or weakness. In any case, the Soviet reaction would have been the same: to avoid a possible trap, and to exploit the adversary's folly at the earliest opportunity. (Emphasis added.)

American diplomat George Kennan, a senior official serving in Russia during much of Stalin's tenure, gave this grim assessment of Stalin:

> His words were few. They generally sounded reasonable and sensible; indeed, often they were. An unforewarned visitor would never have guessed what depths of calculation, ambition, love of power, jealousy, cruelty, and sly vindictiveness lurked behind this unpretentious façade.

The need to raise public awareness of the challenge posed by Stalin prompted Winston Churchill's famous words in his March 5, 1946, address at Fulton, Missouri: "From Stettin in the Baltic to Trieste in the Adriatic, an iron curtain has descended across the Continent."

Kennan, for his part, writing in 1947 under the pseudonym "X" for the influential journal *Foreign Affairs*, literally defined America's postwar "containment" strategy:

> The main element of any United States policy toward the Soviet Union must be that of a long-term, patient but firm and vigilant containment of Russian expansive tendencies....
>
> Soviet pressure against the free institutions of the Western world is something that can be contained by the adroit and vigilant application of counterforce at a series of constantly shifting geographic and political points.

The U.S. won the race to detonate a thermonuclear device. "Ivy Mike" was exploded November 1, 1952, on a Pacific atoll named Elugelab. It demolished the atoll and yielded an awesome 10.4 megatons, 700 times more powerful than the yield of the Hiroshima bomb and 500 times more powerful than the bomb that destroyed Nagasaki. But the device was, at 62 tons, not deliverable as a practical weapon.

The first Russian H-bomb test followed on August 12, 1953, 16 days after North and South Korea signed their armistice. Yet America did not test an operational H-bomb, carried by a bomber, until May 1956. The official American reaction to early nuclear bomb milestones was to treat potential nuclear war as merely souped-up conventional conflict. Eisenhower's secretary of state, John Foster Dulles, propounded his "massive retaliation" policy at the beginning of 1954: any kind of attack launched by the Soviet Union would be met—at least, in theory—with an all-out nuclear response. In October 1953 President Eisenhower authorized full-scale production of the B-52 Stratofortress strategic heavy bomber in anticipation of America deploying a deliverable H-bomb. The massive eight-jet plane, designed to reach the Soviet Union at high subsonic jet speed and deliver H-bombs without refueling, entered service in 1955 and remains in the U.S. inventory today.

The prime consequence of these thermonuclear weapons has turned out quite different from what was originally forecast. The early bombs' massive devastation gave them, as noted by the eminent strategist Herman Kahn, the plausible potential to literally destroy civilizations, not just to level small cities, as atom bombs could. Uranium or plutonium atomic bombs produce explosive yields in kilotons—the equivalent of thousands of tons of conventional explosives like TNT. (The Hiroshima device was estimated to yield 14 kilotons.) But hydrogen bomb yields are theoretically without limit. The largest devices yield megatons (millions of tons of TNT), whereas the highest yield ever achieved with an A-bomb is 500 kilotons. (The 1961 test of Russia's Tsar Bomba produced a stupefying yield of 50 megatons.) Though that huge bomb—too large to fit in a bomb bay, let alone inside a missile warhead—was not deliverable as a weapon, a 25-megaton H-bomb was—still is—very deliverable.

Yet the longer-term impact of H-bombs was to enable packing more explosive power into smaller, lighter warheads and not to destroy the largest possible area. Miniaturization was driven by the need to maximize firepower carried by bombers and missiles and, in the West, to reduce collateral casualties—especially arising from use of tactical nuclear weapons deployed in Western Europe, which might have had to be fired against targets on Allied soil.

In a 1959 article, "The Delicate Balance of Terror," nuclear strategist Albert Wohlstetter evaluated strategy in a world containing such devastating weapons. In the early 1950s, he had led a team at a new research-and-development think tank for the armed forces (the storied RAND Corporation, founded in 1948), which had stunned air force brass in its evaluation of the extreme risks posed by Soviet A-bombs to U.S. forces overseas—risks that early warning systems, hardened shelters for bombers, and more intelligent basing of bombers and ballistic missiles could drastically reduce. In his seminal article, Wohlstetter concisely laid down the theoretical foundation for strategic nuclear force structure.

He saw that a force should be designed to deter first strikes by promising effective retaliation if deterrence failed.

For that strategy to work the American force had to be able to survive a massive nuclear attack and still retain enough forces to retaliate. Nuclear submarines, because they are exceptionally hard to detect and track, provided the ideal missile bases—especially as the range of submarine-launched ballistic missiles increased, enabling the subs to cruise underneath ever-larger portions of the world's oceans. Eventually their range would reach 6,000 miles, making the job of locating them almost impossible. On land, missile silos could be "hardened"—with concrete and powerful shock-absorbing springs between the missile canister and the outside walls of the underground silo—to radically improve their ability to withstand a nuclear near miss.

A properly designed force, Wohlstetter wrote, could increase what strategists call "crisis stability": the ability of a nuclear state to ride out an attack would obviate the need to launch missiles instantly—either during a crisis, or upon (potentially fallible) warning of an attack, or during the attack itself—before damage assessment has been done. In contrast, forces vulnerable to a surprise attack would leave leaders with a "use or lose" proposition in times of extreme tension between nuclear-armed powers, encouraging them to fire when otherwise they might not do so.

Herman Kahn attempted to bring nuclear strategy to the educated lay pubic with his massive tome, *On Thermonuclear War* (1960). In it Kahn pointed out that in the early 1950s as few as one dozen well-placed Russian nuclear bombs could have wiped out America's tiny and vulnerable surface-based arsenal. In event of war America's B-29s were to fly to Fort Hood and get their A-bombs—after completing paperwork!— then fly to New England bases, and from there head to Russia. Kahn's provocative arguments stirred up considerable controversy, with people recoiling at his analytical treatment of horrific prospects. In *Thinking about the Unthinkable* (1962), Kahn tried to explain why the issue could not be avoided: dangers do not disappear just because one ignores them; on the contrary, they may increase.

But the lay public was not getting its information about nuclear weapons and strategy from Wohlstetter or Kahn. They were reading various popular nuclear-war-themed books, at least five of which were written in the six years from Sputnik to the Cuban Missile Crisis. These include Peter Bryant's 1958 novel, *Red Alert*, the source material for the acclaimed 1964 Stanley Kubrick black comedy *Dr. Strangelove, or How I Stopped Worrying and Learned to Love the Bomb*.[3] However, amid the exaggerations of popular fiction, some fictional assertions were close to the truth. The cliché that pushing one button could start a war by launching strategic weapons was true of the Soviet Union at the time of *Strangelove*. That soon changed. After the Cuban Missile Crisis, the Soviet leadership made intensive efforts to reduce the risk of accidental war, and, starting in 1967 a series of upgrades were put into place. The U.S. had strict controls on arming most nuclear weapons from the start.[4]

Strangelove features a secret Russian "doomsday device" that, upon a U.S. attack, automatically triggers an all-out Russian nuclear counter-strike. No such automatic system existed. However, two decades later, the Soviets built a semiautomatic system, known as "Dead Hand," in which a small cadre of duty officers, sheltered in a deep underground bunker, could decide to launch an all-out retaliatory strike. Dead Hand was tested late in 1984 and activated January 1, 1985.

Kennedy, Khrushchev, and Berlin: Nuclear Blackmail Succeeds

DECADES BEFORE Dead Hand (and years before *Strangelove*) the Kennedy administration thought the Dulles policy—of all-out nuclear response to any kind of Soviet attack—unrealistic, and sought a more credible deterrent. "Flexible response" became the order of the day: the options ranged from conventional forces only to battlefield nuclear use to strategic nuclear use. Instead of making a threat of all-out war that

3. Appendix 1 discusses how novels distorted public perceptions of nuclear risks.
4. Appendix 2 discusses the evolution of command and control over nuclear weapons.

might well not be believed, flexible response enabled the U.S. to decide what level of force would be needed on a case-by-case basis.

The Western powers had agreed never to launch a nuclear "first strike" but retained the option of "first use" of nuclear weapons given a conflict already under way. That was essential to prevent the Soviets from overrunning Western Europe by sheer weight of numbers. As Winston Churchill put it in 1948:

> Nothing stands between Europe today and complete subjugation to Communist tyranny but the atomic bomb in American possession.... What do you suppose would be the position this afternoon if it had been Communist Russia instead of free enterprise America which had created the atomic weapon? Instead of being a somber guarantee of peace and freedom it would have become an irresistible method of human enslavement.

Proof of this was provided in 1948, at the outset of the Berlin Airlift. President Truman let word leak that U.S. bombers capable of carrying A-bombs were deployed to Britain. Duly warned, Stalin dared not shoot down Allied planes dropping supplies to Berliners.

The first test of the Kennedy administration's resolve came right away. In April of 1961 the infamous "Bay of Pigs" invasion of Cuba was easily crushed by the forces of the charismatic revolutionary Fidel Castro. At a crucial moment during the operation, Kennedy lost his nerve and abandoned the Cuban exiles that had landed on the beach. They were slaughtered or imprisoned by Castro's forces.

Only six weeks after this embarrassing failure in Cuba came another test, a summit in Vienna with Soviet premier Nikita Khrushchev to discuss divided Berlin. U.S. intelligence described the Soviet premier as a "chronic, optimistic opportunist" with "resourcefulness, audacity, a good sense of political timing and showmanship, and a touch of the gambler's instinct." Khrushchev had survived Stalin's purges in the late 1930s and the power struggle after Stalin died; he denounced Stalin in his landmark 1956 "Secret Speech" and consolidated his grip on power. The summit was to have fateful consequences.

Author Frederick Kempe, in his magisterial *Berlin 1961*, recounts how nuclear risks played a crucial role in the Berlin Crisis, from run-up to conclusion and thereafter.

At 2 a.m. on the first day of 1960, late into a Kremlin New Year's Eve party, Khrushchev had cut loose with a drunken tirade in which he threatened to start World War III if he did not get his way on Berlin, scaring the wits out of U.S. ambassador Llewellyn Thompson. Khrushchev boasted that he had 30 nuclear weapons aimed at France, and 50 each aimed at West Germany and Britain, plus a "secret" number targeting the United States. Six hydrogen bombs could destroy Britain, Khrushchev told the British ambassador six months later, and nine could destroy France. "Berlin," said the notoriously earthy Khrushchev on an equally diplomatic visit to West Germany, "is the testicles of the West. Each time I give them a yank, they holler."

At that point, East Germans were crossing the border into West Berlin—and on into West Germany—by the thousands daily, and the Soviets wanted to seal off this access. West Berlin, 200 miles inside East Germany and connected to the rest of West Germany by only a single highway, would be easy to blockade. That the Potsdam Treaty guaranteed the four occupying powers—the U.S., Great Britain, France, and the Soviet Union—full right of access to the whole city mattered little to Khrushchev or to the East German dictator, Walter Ulbricht, who was seeing his country's population shrinking daily.

West German chancellor Konrad Adenauer and French president Charles de Gaulle wanted Kennedy to guarantee that if necessary to stop a Russian takeover of Berlin, the U.S. would escalate to nuclear war. But Kennedy told de Gaulle he understood why France sought an independent nuclear force—the French leader had earlier said that he did not believe the U.S. would sacrifice New York for Paris or Berlin. Former secretary of state Dean Acheson, a close adviser of Kennedy's, was convinced that a U.S. threat to use nuclear weapons against the Soviets over the status of Berlin might not suffice to deter Khrushchev. Famed columnist Walter Lippmann interviewed Khrushchev before the Vienna summit. "[T]here are no such stupid statesmen in the West to unleash a war in which hundreds of millions would perish" over the status of Berlin, the Soviet premier told the columnist. "Such idiots have not yet been born."

On June 1, two days before the meeting in Vienna, Kennedy had told his aides it was "silly for us to be facing an atomic war over a treaty preserving Berlin as the future capital of a reunified Germany when all of us know that Germany will probably never be reunified. But we're committed to that agreement, and so are the Russians, so we can't let them back out of it." During the summit, Kennedy raised the prospect of miscalculation leading to nuclear war, but the Soviet dictator brushed it aside contemptuously: "All I ever hear ... is that damned word 'miscalculation!'... [W]e will not start a war by mistake.... You ought to take that word 'miscalculation' and bury it in cold storage and never use it again."

Khrushchev threatened war if he did not get his way, and convincingly suggested his indifference to the devastating toll a nuclear exchange would take. Kennedy yielded, allowing Khrushchev to treat East Berlin as if it were Soviet territory. The result, beginning on the night of August 13, 1961, was the sudden, swift erection of the Berlin Wall, which virtually shut down cross-border traffic. The Soviets' plan, at least as understood by Bobby Kennedy, the president's brother and attorney general, was to "break our will in Berlin [so] that we will never be good for anything else and they will have won the battle in 1961.... Their plan is ... to terrorize the world into submission."

Kennedy's advisers put to him a graduated plan for the August 1961 Berlin showdown. If the Soviets were not stopped by allied conventional forces, the U.S. would consider three nuclear options: a demonstration shot to establish will to use such weapons, a limited use on the battlefield, and all-out general war. A top Kennedy defense official, Roswell Gilpatric, warned in a speech that the U.S. would not allow itself to be defeated over Berlin. At least one senior American official, arms negotiator Paul Nitze, believed Berlin more dangerous than Cuba.

Kennedy had designated U.S. General Lucius Clay to command the Berlin crisis with White House supervision. Clay unilaterally sent forces up the Berlin access road, daring the Soviets to prevent their entry into Berlin. Exceeding his orders, Clay also sent tanks to the Berlin Wall, where they confronted Soviet tanks a few hundred yards away across the dividing line. No shots were fired.

The confrontation at the "Checkpoint Charlie" crossing point took place with Soviet forces under a first-ever nuclear alert. In the end, Khrushchev succeeded, and the status of Berlin was changed, with access to the eastern sector cut off despite the postwar treaty. Kennedy told a senior aide, Kenny O'Donnell, that only if the freedom of all Western Europe were at stake would he risk nuclear Armageddon. The Wall stayed, undercutting stern U.S. warnings over Berlin. The day the Wall went up Kennedy stated: "It's not a very nice solution, but a wall is a hell of a lot better than a war."

Khrushchev took what proved to be the wrong lesson from Berlin. He told Soviet officials: "I know for certain, that Kennedy doesn't have ... the courage to stand up to a serious challenge." In September 1962 the earthy Soviet dictator told interior secretary Stewart Udall, "It's been a long time since you could spank us like a little boy. Now we can swat your ass." He told his son Sergei that over Cuba Kennedy "would make a fuss, make more of a fuss, then agree."

That the subsequent 1962 Cuban Missile Crisis ended with neither an all-out war nor a city-trade was dismissed as a lucky accident by many observers. Luck was indeed involved, but so were the two sober leaders Kennedy and Khrushchev, both wounded on wartime battlefields and bereft of family members killed in combat. It was Cuban dictator Fidel Castro who asked Moscow to launch an all-out nuclear strike. Moscow warned Fidel that Cuba would be made to disappear—American B-47 bombers based in Florida during the crisis carried 20-megaton H-bombs, a single one of which would have erased Havana. Castro was not moved. Seething with hatred of the United States as his main tormentor, he wanted the strike launched anyway. In 2010, wiser at age 84, Castro admitted that he had made a mistake in urging that contingent course of action in 1962.

In reality, while accidental war was chillingly possible during the Cold War, the superpower leaders were too sober to deliberately launch a nuclear strike. During the Cuban Missile crisis a Russian submarine commander almost launched a nuclear torpedo to sink a U.S. destroyer that was trying to force his diesel sub to surface, using depth charges. Had he done do, does anyone really think that Kennedy would have launched an all-out nuclear strike at the Soviet Union, in the act dooming more than 100 million Americans to incineration? However, fifty years later, as newer powers join the nuclear club, with some possibly led by hotheads like the young Castro, the risk of what Herman Kahn called "spasm war" will grow.

Cold War, Cool Heads, a "Mad" Freeze

AFTER THE close shave of the Cuban Missile Crisis, the United States turned towards arms control. But Kennedy's assassination and the escalation of the Vietnam War delayed any action until June 1967, when, in Glassboro, New Jersey, President Lyndon Johnson and Soviet premier Alexei Kosygin laid the final political groundwork for negotiating superpower arms limitation agreements. The Soviet Union's August 1968 invasion of Czechoslovakia, however, again derailed such efforts, and for the remainder of LBJ's administration. Tanks rumbling through Prague provided poor political video to accompany simultaneous arms talks.

The 1967 U.S.-Soviet summit, in the midst of the Vietnam War, coincided with a remarkable decision made by Secretary of Defense Robert McNamara: freezing the U.S. nuclear arsenal at 1967 numerical levels. In a speech in San Francisco in September of that year, McNamara presented his "assured destruction" doctrine. The McNamara view assumed that each side would deliberately hold its own civilian population hostage to the other side's offensive forces. Deterring a nuclear attack on the U.S. or its allies was "the cornerstone of our strategic policy," he explained:

> We do this by maintaining a highly reliable ability to inflict unacceptable damage upon any single aggressor or combination of aggressors at any time during the course of a strategic nuclear exchange, even after absorbing a surprise first strike. This can be defined as our assured-destruction capability.

McNamara had helped General Curtis LeMay plan his firebombing campaign of 1945 against Japanese cities and was in the midst of rethinking the course of the Vietnam War. He decided that America's 1967 arsenal—able to destroy roughly a quarter of the Russian population and half of Russian industry—was powerful enough as it stood.

Strategist Donald Brennan appended "mutual" to McNamara's phrase "assured destruction" to create an acronym indicating how mad the policy seemed to him and other critics. In its grisly logic of deterrence by mutual suicide pact, MAD meant that each side would deliberately keep its own civilian populace without protection—in effect, hostage to the other side's nuclear striking forces— while protecting commanders and retaliatory forces. (McNamara's policy prescriptions to the president, however, did not actually focus only on civilian destruction but also included options for targeting Soviet missiles and bombers.) On their side, the Soviets clearly did not believe that mutual assured destruction would be enough to deter a U.S. attack. They ran a massive civil defense program, building underground shelters that could keep millions alive after a strike, while U.S. civil defense efforts, even before MAD, were minimal.

Soon after proclaiming the MAD policy, McNamara left office. Between 1967 and 2009, the U.S. reduced its stockpile of nuclear warheads from 31,255 to 5,133, an 84 percent drop. Russia, meanwhile, continued its own arms buildup for some two decades after the U.S. froze its arsenal—the U.S. call having been made based upon intelligence estimates that were egregiously optimistic.[5]

Despite this reduction, the U.S. could not stop developing new weapons. America was faced with the plausible prospect that Russian ICBMs, if not countered, would create catastrophic U.S. vulnerability. It was a risk that the U.S. could not prudently take, and thus a bipartisan domestic consensus supported ICBM development.

Such a consensus required support for H-bomb deployment, because only the hydrogen weapon packed sufficient explosive power to enable a megaton warhead to fit on a missile. In the 1950s and early 1960s warhead delivery accuracies were measured in miles. Megaton yields were essential to destroy surface targets a few miles away. As missile accuracy improved, thermonuclear warheads could be shrunk in physical size, while ratcheting their yield down to a few hundred kilotons for U.S. warheads; for underground targets like missile silos, improvements in accuracy were vastly more important than increasing yield.

The next step in this shrinking-warhead progression was the multiwarhead-missile platform, the so-called MIRV. MIRVs—"multiple independently targetable re-entry vehicles"—carry several warheads, each capable of hitting a different target. U.S. ICBMs carry three nuclear warheads. Russia's ICBMs can carry many more—its giant SS-18 ICBM can carry up to 38.

In 1962 the first "Single Integrated Operational Plan" (SIOP)—a comprehensive war plan covering all forces and how they would be used—was presented by military chiefs to President Kennedy. He and McNamara were horrified. It envisioned a massive nuclear strike to obliterate Russia, which surely would have led to reciprocal obliteration of the United States—reflecting the attitude of the leader of the Stra-

---

5. Appendix 3 discusses intelligence failures as to arms deployments.

tegic Air Command, General Thomas Power, who quipped: "Look, at the end of the war, if there are two Americans and one Russian, we win!"

Superpower leaders who held the power of final decision were not flippant. In his study of superpower nuclear affairs, *The Dead Hand*, David Hoffman notes that Richard Nixon was similarly aghast when he saw the 1969 SIOP, with some 90 variations on the apocalypse. In 1972 Soviet dictator Leonid Brezhnev played in a nuclear war game in which it was assumed that a U.S. first strike had killed 80 million Russians and demolished 85 percent of Soviet industry, as well as leaving the military with a thousandth of its original striking power. Asked to launch three dummy Soviet ICBMs as part of the exercise, a shaky Brezhnev asked his defense minister, "Are you sure this is just an exercise?"

Ronald Reagan, whose political opponents portrayed him as a nuclear cowboy, was equally unnerved when, two months after assuming office, he received a detailed briefing on presidential nuclear command and control matters. In *Reagan's Secret War*, longtime policy advisers Martin and Annelise Anderson quote from President Reagan's diary entries:

> The decision to launch the weapons was mine alone to make.
>
> … The Russians sometimes kept submarines off our East Coast with nuclear missiles that could turn the White House into a pile of radioactive rubble within eight minutes.
>
> *Six minutes* to decide how to respond to a blip on a radar scope and decide whether to unleash Armageddon!
>
> How could anyone apply reason at a time like that?
>
> … A nuclear war couldn't be won by either side. It must never be fought. But how do we go about trying to prevent it and pulling back from this hair-trigger existence? (Emphasis in original.)

As recounted by the Andersons, on September 25, 1983, Lieutenant Stanislav Petrov, the duty officer on watch, decided to ignore an alarm showing five U.S. ICBMs headed for Russian soil. The Soviet command protocol dictated immediate launch on warning, but Petrov ignored the rule book, figuring that a real American attack would involve more than five missiles. It turned out that the Soviet satellite had misread sunlight glinting off clouds over a U.S. missile site. *This amazing near-Armageddon—turning on one mid-level officer's instant judgment—underscored the wisdom of nuclear doctrine calling for an ability to absorb a surprise first strike, with an assured second-strike response.* But Soviet forces were concentrated in land-based offensive missiles, and thus more vulnerable to a first strike: the U.S. had a greater share of its forces based at sea, better able to ride out a surprise attack. The Soviets' posture of relying primarily on the most accurate silo-killing missiles despite their own greater vulnerability suggests that the Soviets valued the ability to threaten U.S. forces more than they feared a U.S. first strike.

Reagan entered office in 1981 stating publicly that the Soviets enjoyed strategic nuclear superiority. Yet Hoffman notes that Reagan concluded by late 1983 that Soviet fears of a U.S. first strike were not made up. Reagan wrote in his memoirs:

> Three years had taught me something surprising about the Russians: Many people at the top of the Soviet hierarchy were genuinely afraid of America and Americans. Perhaps this shouldn't have surprised me, but it did. In fact, I had difficulty accepting my own conclusion at first.

Lieutenant Petrov was not the only Soviet officer to decline to fire missiles upon instrumental signals showing an attack, and U.S. officials behaved in similar fashion in refusing to launch on signal warning. Put simply, both sides desired to survive and worked hard to avoid accidental Armageddon.

Reagan had in fact declared war against the Soviets, but not a shooting, let alone nuclear one. In 1983 he issued a presidential directive for conducting what amounted to political and economic war against the "evil empire." It sought to aggravate internal political pressures against the Soviet regime, and subject it to increasingly severe economic straits as well.

Paul Nitze wrote in 1956 about the role of nuclear weapons in the Cold War beyond deterring a war or waging one, using Russian chess prowess as metaphor: "The atomic queens may never be brought into play. But the position of the atomic queens may still have a decisive bearing on which side can safely advance a limited-war bishop or even a cold-war pawn."

Nitze's assessment reinforces the lesson of this chapter: ARMS CONTROL CANNOT BE VIEWED AS SUPREME IN RELATIONS WITH ADVERSARIES. The full spectrum of an adversary's conduct must be taken into account in formulating policy.

4.

AMERICA: THE LIMITS OF WHAT ARMS PACTS CAN ACCOMPLISH

We may be likened to two scorpions in a bottle, each capable
of killing each other, but only at the risk of his own life.
J. ROBERT OPPENHEIMER, 1953

AMERICAN ARMS CONTROL AGREEMENTS DATE BACK TO THE EARLY days of the American republic. The first U.S. arms agreement, the Rush-Bagot Treaty with Great Britain, was signed after the War of 1812 and limited armaments on the Great Lakes and Lake Champlain. (Each side got one or two 100-ton vessels carrying a cannon with an 18-pound shell.) In 1871 the U.S. and Great Britain signed the Treaty of Washington, which called for complete demilitarization along the U.S.-Canadian border. The agreement has been periodically modified and is still in force.

In the two centuries since Rush-Bagot, and in particular in the last 40 or so years as nuclear arms agreements have been reached, the United States has had ample opportunity to see what types of agreements, signed in what circumstances, are effective. It is in the months and years after agreements are signed that the Second Lesson of nuclear-age history emerges: ARMS AGREEMENTS MUST BE BASED UPON GENUINE, NOT PRESUMED, COMMONALITY OF STRATEGIC INTEREST.

"Big Ships Cause Big Wars": Arms Control before World War II

IT IS instructive to begin this consideration of nuclear arms agreements with a look at agreements preceding the development of nuclear weapons, following the First World War. The ghastly carnage in the trenches of Europe spurred calls for global disarmament. Fifteen million were dead—the "Lost Generation." The Big Four victorious Allies—the U.S., Britain, France, and Italy—drew up the treaty, a spectacularly unsuccessful one. The harsh terms it imposed on Germany fueled the resentments of, among others, one Corporal Adolf Hitler. The boundary lines it laid down spawned wars in Europe, the Mideast, and Africa. The League of Nations it founded was totally ineffectual. The U.S. Senate rejected the Treaty of Versailles, keeping America out of the new organization and guaranteeing that its writ would be ignored worldwide. However, there is little reason to believe that things would have been different had the U.S. ratified the treaty—as shown by experience with the League's successor, the United Nations.

But in the short term, the deep revulsion against war among the victorious Allies spurred further arms-control efforts. The modern idea of disarmament was an invention of liberal Western societies. Either adversaries were coerced to participate after a military defeat, or they voluntarily participated while pursuing secret strategic advantage. The 1922 Washington Naval Treaty set limits on naval ship size for the United States, Great Britain, France, and Japan. Three subsequent treaties (1930, 1935, and 1936) further limited ship sizes for the signatory powers. (Japan signed only the 1930 pact. Germany only the 1935 pact.) A regnant maxim of the day succinctly captured the idealism driving disarmament: "Big ships cause big wars, little ships cause little wars, and no ships cause no wars." President Warren Harding, in presenting the treaty to the Senate for ratification, described the negotiation as "a conference of friends, proceeding in deliberation and sympathy, appraising their friendly and peaceful relations and resolved to maintain them."

Between the two world wars, the idea that fewer arms are always safer was common currency, among leaders as well as with the general public. Thus Secretary of State Charles Evans Hughes (whom President Wilson had defeated in 1916 with the slogan "He kept us out of war") said of arms limitation: "How was it possible to stop this mad race? By an international agreement for the limitation of armaments."

Staunch conservative president Herbert Hoover went even further. He endorsed the 1928 Kellogg-Briand Pact between the U.S. and

France, which expressly outlawed war as an instrument of national policy and sought reductions—not just limitations—in arms.

In June 1933, as Hitler took power, two future prime ministers squared off in Parliament. Winston Churchill presciently called for Britain and France to rearm, and Anthony Eden opposed rearmament in order "to secure for Europe that period of appeasement which is needed." The British Peace Pledge Union formed and collected 10 million "Peace Ballots" (from a British population of 46 million), with 87 percent of those casting ballots voting to totally disarm and have the League of Nations keep world peace. Yet another future prime minister, Clement Atlee, told the House of Commons on December 21, 1933: "We are unalterably opposed to anything in the nature of rearmament."

But the leaders of the world's democracies were to discover that treaties with German nationalists and Nazis, and with Japanese militarists as well, could and would be broken. Put simply, they learned that with arms accords it matters greatly whether your partners are friends, neutrals, or adversaries.

In 1934 the Japanese began breaking out of the ship size limits of the 1922 Washington Naval Treaty, which had limited, with a few grandfathered exceptions, single-ship tonnage to 35,000 and gun bore widths to 16 inches. Japan built the two largest battleships ever to ride the high seas: the 70,000-ton leviathans *Yamato* and *Musashi*. They carried nine 18.1-inch guns, the largest ever mounted on a ship; the guns' recoil was so powerful that all nine could not be fired at once, lest the ship roll over. They could hurl a 3,200-pound projectile—a half-ton heavier than an American 16-inch shell—26 miles with unmatched accuracy.

Disarmament efforts fared no better with Nazi Germany. The June 18, 1935, Anglo-German Naval Treaty limited the German Navy to 35 percent of the British Royal Navy's tonnage. But on July 1, 1936, the keel of the super battleship *Bismarck*, a 45,000-ton behemoth to be fitted with eight 15-inch guns, was laid. By September 1938—as British prime minister Neville Chamberlain returned from Munich proclaiming to his countrymen that he had achieved "peace in our time"—the *Bismarck* was complete to the upper deck level, and it was launched a few months later. The keel of her sister ship, *Tirpitz*, was laid in November 1936, and the 47,000-ton ship was launched in April 1939. Hitler denounced the treaty on April 28, 1939, having already swallowed up the Rhineland, Austria, and Czechoslovakia. In the event, neither the German nor Japanese super ships played a decisive role in maritime combat during the war.[6]

World War II rendered ship size limits moot. Yet the prewar arms-control concepts endured—limits upon platform size (ships then, submarines and bombers today), explosive payload (shells then, bombs and warheads now), and finally sites (bases then, silos now). They would return to bedevil arms-control efforts after the war, because the complexity of modern strategic systems made setting appropriate benchmarks nearly impossible.

How Much Is Enough?: Early Cold War Arms Talks

THE NEAR-NUCLEAR miss of the Cuban Missile Crisis spurred renewed efforts to secure superpower disarmament. During arms negotiations between the U.S. and the USSR, much was made about the folly of adding yet more weapons to already gigantic stockpiles. Was their sole utility to "make the rubble bounce" after Armageddon? These talks were

---

6. The Nazi ships posed a fearsome maritime threat, but they were defeated by British air power: *Bismarck*, named for Germany's unifier and "Iron Chancellor" Otto von Bismarck, sank Britain's battle cruiser *HMS Hood*, on May 24, 1941. After an epic chase the British sank it three days later. *Tirpitz*, named after the World War I admiral who built up Germany's navy, shelled the island of Spitsbergen in January 1943; she was sunk in her pen November 12, 1944, by British bombers.

As for the Japanese titans, both saw action in the landmark Battle of Leyte Gulf, from October 23 to October 26, 1944; the Japanese threw all their naval assets into the battle in a desperate attempt to prevent General MacArthur from fulfilling his wartime pledge to return to the Philippines. *Musashi* was sunk by American planes and submarines in the opening engagement. *Yamato* retreated ignominiously after surviving a torpedo charge by American destroyers on Leyte's final day, before she could shell troops landing on the beach; the reason for her retreat remains unclear to the present day. She was sunk by American carrier planes in April 1945 off Okinawa, where she had been sent as a last-ditch decoy.

based upon what Western arms controllers presumed was a common interest with the USSR in reducing massive stockpiles of nuclear weapons and potential vulnerability to surprise attack.

The "rubble" metaphor was superficially appealing but misleading. A "bolt from the blue" attack could be totally successful (and thus inviting) if a country did not have enough armaments remaining to retaliate afterwards. (Recall the previous chapter's discussion of why the ability to absorb a surprise first strike, with enough force left to retaliate, is so important.) The attacked country's entire force, then, must incorporate a multiple of the requisite destructive retaliatory power needed. If, as some strategic planners feared early on, the Soviets in a best-case attack possibly could destroy 90 percent of America's land-based ICBMs, half of America's submarines sitting in port, and 90 percent of the bombers, the small portion that survived would have to cover all targets.[7]

Pessimistic estimates presented to President Eisenhower were based in part on reconnaissance flights showing Soviet missiles being deployed; the United States estimated that the Soviets would deploy 100 ICBMs by 1960. At the time, both sides based missiles above ground, leaving them highly vulnerable.

The "nuclear strategic triad" doctrine held that each leg of the triad—land, sea, and air—must itself be able to accomplish full postattack retaliation, to guard against Russian breakthroughs that neutralized the other two legs. Such secure, survivable forces would remove any temptation the Soviets might feel to launch such an attack, thus strengthening deterrence. In other words, no one intended to "make the rubble bounce."

In November 1969, the new Nixon administration met with the Soviets in Helsinki for the first Strategic Arms Limitation Talks, known

---

7. Factors include how much of the attacking force reaches the target, how well sheltered targets are, whether there is sufficient warning, whether bombs burst in the air or on the ground, how hard and which way the winds blow, how well protected targets are. Calculations of the destructive effects of large-scale nuclear attacks are dizzyingly complex and, under the best of circumstances, highly subjective, with huge margins of error. Serious strategists understood these limitations and used calculations to help frame problems in broad brush strokes so as to better address them.

by the acronym "SALT." The talks were from the outset muddled by fundamental cultural differences in the way American and Russian negotiators approached their complex task. Henry Kissinger, who superintended the Nixon and Ford administration arms talks, explained the problem in his memoirs.

American negotiators ardently seek agreement, and thus look for ways to break deadlocks with initiatives, find some compromise. They even at times urge far-reaching concessions to reach a provisional accord, secure that other officials will oppose them and thus temper the final result. They continually seek to convince their opposite numbers of America's good intentions, in hope of getting a reciprocal conciliatory gesture. Soviet negotiators were almost the polar opposite in approach and temperament. Their diplomacy "substitute[d] persistence for imagination." They derived no reward for making proposals or concessions. They could sit rigid for years without any domestic pressure, and wait for the other side, under heavy domestic pressure, to give in. (So can Russian negotiators today. Neither their bargaining culture, nor ours, has changed.)

The SALT treaties followed the regnant doctrine of the day: mutual assured destruction—founded on the idea that holding mass populations hostage better preserved deterrence than protecting them by shelters or missile defense, given vast amounts of offensive weapons. The Nixon administration enshrined MAD in SALT I, via the Anti-Ballistic Missile Treaty. The ABM Treaty—which the Senate ratified 88 votes to 2—sharply limited the deployment of missiles designed to intercept and destroy other missiles in flight. Of the many objections to this treaty, three were most salient:

1. The vast throw-weight (payload deliverable over distance capability) of Russia's missiles, concentrated in highly accurate, land-based ICBMs.
2. The inability to verify actual numbers of Russian warheads.

3. The limits the treaty placed on missile defense.

Russia had deployed huge missiles—far larger than any in the American arsenal. The missiles possessed the requisite combination of accuracy and yield so that they could plausibly destroy large numbers of American missiles inside their silos. Russia's monster SS-18 ICBM had seven to eight times the payload capacity of America's mainstay Minuteman III ICBM. Its multiwarhead SS-19 missile, taking advantage of loose treaty language, replaced a far smaller (and less accurate) single warhead missile (SS-11); its monster SS-9 missile was topped with a 25-megaton warhead, the largest ever deployed on an ICBM. The SS-18 was the 1970s equivalent (on a vastly more destructive scale) of Japan's leviathan battleships armed with 18-inch guns. Just as those guns could hurl a heavier shell farther than a U.S. 16-inch bore, so the throw-weight of Russia's largest missiles was superior to anything in America's forces.

The Soviets refused to consent to on-site inspections, and would not even tell the United States how many warheads and missiles they had or confirm U.S. estimates. So the treaty was based upon our counting what could be verified—silos in the ground, detectable by surveillance satellite cameras.[8] As to things that could not be seen, like warheads inside a missile nose cone, the United States devised "counting rules"—based upon the observed size of nose cones—to apply limits.[9] SALT I limited *launchers*, not missiles or warheads, for precisely this reason. A complex

8. Military surveillance satellites, in contrast to the communications satellites we use every day, usually make a highly elliptical orbit of Earth—for example, 700 miles perigee (lowest point) and 12,000 miles apogee (highest point). At low altitude over their photo reconnaissance target, they can photograph objects as small as a tennis ball and clearly display license plate numbers. But weather over the target area can complicate observation, and—as its orbital path is a matter of the laws of physics—the people whose assets are under surveillance can enhance concealment every 90 minutes when the satellite passes overhead.

9. Counting rules were complex. Rules had to be devised not only for missiles based on land, but also for those carried deep underwater by missile submarines. Rules for the latter were devised by counting launching tubes, with estimates of possible extra missiles based upon the size of the submarine and the types of missiles it carried. Counting warheads on bombers also proved very hard: rules had to be devised for bomb bay sizes and the size of bombs carried externally—under wings or under the fuselage.

technical and strategic calculus underlay judgments as to the balance between offensive and defensive systems.[10]

As to missile defense, SALT I limited each side to radar to protect one major city and one ICBM base, a compromise designed so that the Russians could keep their primitive systems protecting Moscow and one missile base. (The United States briefly deployed an ABM under treaty rules, but scrapped it later in the 1970s.) The treaty decreed that ABM radars could be deployed only on the periphery of the country. This was to prevent them from being used for the "battle management" of a national missile defense system—that is, for the countrywide detection and interception of incoming hostile objects (and damage assessment after a hit). In the 1980s the Soviets deployed a massive battle-management radar installation in central Russia, in violation of the treaty, but denied it until the Cold War ended. SALT I's Standing Consultative Commission regulating treaty implementation was a two-party affair with no final outside arbiter (none existed). Thus the U.S. could not force the Soviets to comply.

Disenchantment with SALT I did not stop the arms-control process—the new Carter administration unilaterally cancelled the strategic B-1 heavy bomber in 1977.[11] The next year, Carter did away with the proposed battlefield weapon known colloquially as the "neutron bomb." Formally termed the "enhanced radiation, reduced blast" warhead, it combined intense neutron radiation with relatively limited explosive and heat energy. Covering a small area—typically, within a quarter-mile radius of the bomb's low-altitude airburst detonation, half the physically destructive radius of the Hiroshima bomb—the highly lethal neutron radiation penetrated tanks and buildings, killing personnel inside (or outside) within hours. As any tank battle in Germany would have to take place close to heavily populated cities, German chancellor Helmut

---

10. Appendix 4 discusses SALT trade-offs and judgments balancing MIRV and ABM.
11. President Reagan put the B-1 back in production in 1981. It remains part of America's bomber force.

Schmidt had staked his prestige on the deployment of this weapon, and was enraged at Carter's unilateral cancellation of it.[12]

The Carter administration signed the SALT II treaty in June 1979, essentially freezing new missile development at levels that left the Soviet heavy-missile arsenal intact. Its ratification—already an acrimonious subject in the Senate—became impossible when the Soviets invaded Afghanistan on Christmas Eve.

A Search for Common Interests: Late Cold War Arms Talks

THE ADVENT of the Reagan administration in 1981 bid fair to change the arms-control picture. Reagan had campaigned against the SALT II treaty as a symbol of the deteriorating military balance between the United States and the Soviet Union. Despite never ratifying the treaty, as president he informally adhered to its limits, for want of congressional support to build beyond them. In Paul Nitze's view, by not seeking Senate ratification of SALT II Reagan allowed future arms talks to begin from scratch, rather than be treated as a continuation of SALT II and thus bound by SALT II's foundation principles.

While a Republican Senate from 1981 to 1986 gave President Reagan support for new weapon systems, a Democratic House of Representatives and the tug of arms-control politics severely limited his options. The House shrunk the domestically unpopular MX "Peacekeeper" program—200 missiles with 10 warheads each, shuttling on railroad tracks between 4,600 launching points in vast western rural tracts—down to 50 missiles in existing silos. Russia could deploy large numbers of such land mobile missiles because its populace had no say in such matters. Strong domestic political opposition—NIMBY: Not In My Back Yard—made mobile missile ICBMs politically toxic in America.

Ronald Reagan dramatically changed arms-control direction. On March 23, 1983, he called for the development of a comprehensive missile

---

12. In order to boost support for the SALT II treaty, Carter committed to developing the Trident submarine-launched missile, and deployed it in 1979. Its intercontinental range and MIRV warhead payload greatly enhanced the sea leg of the U.S. triad.

defense system to protect the entire population—the Strategic Defense Initiative (SDI, or "Star Wars" to its critics)—in a decisive rejection of MAD. In truth, even though MAD had been public-official declaratory doctrine since 1967, no president ever fully accepted it. Richard Nixon attempted to deploy missile defense but critics crippled the system, which was finally done in by SALT I. Gerald Ford's years saw James Schlesinger's tenure as secretary of defense, during which Schlesinger pushed for "limited nuclear options" short of all-out retaliation. In effect, this was a refinement of Kennedy's flexible response doctrine, seeking options between all-out mutual suicide and total surrender.

Even dovish Jimmy Carter authorized targeting leadership cadres, who were exempt from targeting under a pure MAD doctrine.[13] Carter's defense secretary, Harold Brown, endorsed limited nuclear options, telling Congress that even if it were likely that an initial nuclear exchange would escalate to all-out nuclear war, "it would be the height of folly to put the United States in a position in which uncontrolled escalation would be the only course we could follow." But these refinements were easily swamped in sound-bite public political debate, and thus stayed in the shadows.

Reagan—unafraid to call the Soviet Union an "evil empire" and to trumpet "we win, they lose" as his Cold War philosophy—supported stringent high-technology embargoes, and even sabotage, against the Soviet Union. In 1982, with the help of "Farewell," a rare high-level mole placed by the French inside the top Soviet leader circle, the U.S. arranged for defective computer chips to be sent to Russia for use in its biggest natural gas pipeline. The malicious software in the defective chips caused system malfunctions that led to a massive conventional ex-

---

13. Presidential Directive 58 (PD-58), issued June 30, 1980, established a program to protect the president and top U.S. leaders in event of nuclear attack. PD-59, issued July 25, 1980, called for targeting Soviet leadership cadres in event of nuclear war between the superpowers. The latter directive ran flatly counter to the precepts of MAD, which called for targeting deliberately unprotected civilians, while leaving alone offensive military assets (missile defense was banned). By inescapable implication, the Soviet leadership would not be targeted under MAD, so it could survive to order retaliation after an American attack.

plosion—at three kilotons, more powerful than small nuclear devices—that destroyed key parts of the pipeline and set Moscow back years.

Reagan formed his view of the Soviets in the early years of the Cold War, which Brezhnev reinforced with a memorable speech in 1973 at a major Communist party conclave in Prague. The Soviet leader predicted:

> We are achieving with détente what our predecessors have been unable to achieve using the mailed fist.... Trust us comrades, for by 1985, as a consequence of what we are now achieving with détente, we will have achieved most of our objectives in Western Europe.... A decisive shift in the correlation of forces will be such that come 1985, we will be able to extend our will wherever we need to.

By 1985 the Soviets came to see things differently, with the accession of Mikhail Gorbachev to the position of general secretary of the Communist Party in March. Facing a resurgent America and a president reelected by a landslide, Gorbachev decided to try to reform the Soviet system, which was mired in terminal catatonia.

Even before Gorbachev rose to General Secretary, in late 1984 he gave Prime Minister Margaret Thatcher the first plausible indication that the Soviets might be willing to bargain seriously. Thatcher recalled in her memoir, *The Downing Street Years*, that before meeting Gorbachev she had heard "modestly encouraging" things, but she remained wary.

On December 16 Gorbachev visited Lady Thatcher at the prime minister's country residence, Chequers. The two discussed the risk of accidental war, with Gorbachev quoting a Russian proverb: "[O]nce a year even an unloaded gun can go off." Thatcher ascertained that the Soviets were petrified of Reagan's missile defense ideas. The Soviets knew they could not match America's technological prowess and feared a comprehensive U.S. missile defense system might succeed. (Despite their claim that Reagan's SDI would "militarize space," the Soviets, notes Paul Nitze, had put more military satellites in orbit than the U.S. had and had the world's only operational anti-satellite systems.)[14] Thatcher found Gorbachev's dream of abolishing missile defense as unrealistic as Reagan's belief that nuclear weapons could be abolished but told the press after the meeting she thought the West could "do business" with Gorbachev.

Reagan and Gorbachev first met at Geneva in November 1985. Reagan found someone he could indeed "do business" with. As for Gorbachev, he learned the truth of what his note taker had written after watching Reagan at the first meeting: "When you touch raw nerve, Reagan's flare will fill the room. He feel something close to his heart, he is like lion!" The two leaders issued a joint statement on November 21, 1985: "[A] nuclear war cannot be won and should never be fought." Russia was in the midst of a five-year spree during which it deployed 15,000 new nuclear weapons, bringing its arsenal to its 1986 peak of 45,000; it added 5,803 alone between the 1985 Geneva Summit and the Reykjavik Summit 11 months later. This was more than the total U.S. stockpile of 5,133 when President Obama took the oath of office.

In Reykjavik in October 1986, Ronald Reagan committed the biggest blunder of his presidency—only to find himself saved from its consequences by an even bigger blunder made by Gorbachev. Seized by a long-held idealistic impulse to push for abolition of nuclear weapons, Reagan accepted Gorbachev's offer to phase out all offensive nuclear weapons by 2000. (Lady Thatcher later wrote: "My own reaction when I heard how far the Americans had been prepared to go was as if there had been an earthquake beneath my feet.") The deal died when Reagan insisted that there be no restrictions on his cherished missile defense program—he wanted an exception to the 1972 ABM Treaty, allowing for a defense against a surprise attack. He offered to wait 10 years before withdrawing from that restrictive treaty and to share missile defense technology, but Gorbachev refused. Ironically, had Gorbachev accepted Reagan's offer, SDI would surely have been killed in the euphoria of the post-Cold War, "peace dividend" 1990s.

14. The Outer Space Treaty of 1967, between the U.S., UK, and USSR, barred offensive weapons and weapons of mass destruction in space.

Nuclear zero would have given the Russians a grand opportunity, one related to what Herman Kahn called "the problem of the clandestine cache": When each side has thousands of weapons, a few hundred hidden weapons count for little. But if both sides supposedly go to zero, the strategic value of a few hundred hidden weapons would be supreme—aces of trumps in geopolitics. Detection methods are sophisticated, but hardly foolproof. Hiding weapons in a country the size of Russia is, as Herman Kahn put it, child's play. It is far easier than concealing WMD facilities inside Iraq. President Reagan grasped this verification limitation, and it drove his insistence on missile defense as insurance.

Just over a year after that double blunder in Reykjavik, the two leaders met in Washington to sign the Treaty on Intermediate-Range Nuclear Forces (known as the INF Treaty), which eliminated missiles with ranges between roughly 300 and 3,500 miles). This treaty of late 1987 was the culmination of something Reagan had been proposing since 1981—if the Soviets dismantled their ballistic and cruise missiles aimed at Europe, then the U.S. would cancel the 464 cruise missiles and 108 Pershing II ballistic missiles it planned to deploy there. The Russians were petrified of the 1,000-mile range Pershing II, which could have hit Moscow with 100-foot accuracy within eight minutes of launch from West Germany. In late 1983 they walked out of arms talks to protest the initial NATO "Euromissile" deployments. Despite intense pressure to remove the missiles and suspend deployment, not only from Democrats, but also from much of the media and even some prominent Republicans, Reagan stood fast. Eight months after Gorbachev became General Secretary, the Soviets returned to the table, ending a two-year arms talk hiatus. So Reagan's arms-control legacy, the INF Treaty—under which the U.S. destroyed 846 nuclear weapons and Russia 1,846—became the first nuclear arms accord to eliminate an entire class of weapons.[15]

---

15. The INF Treaty has not worked perfectly. Reportedly Russia shipped two rocket motor models—the RD-214 and RD-216 motors, stripped from scrapped INF Treaty–covered missiles (SS-4 and SS-5) and sent them to Iran for testing.

Scaling Back Massive Arsenals: Arms Talks after the Cold War

The November after Reagan left office, the Berlin Wall fell. Before George H. W. Bush's presidential term ended, the Soviet Union exited the world stage. In 1992, President Bush Sr.'s last year, the country passed three arms-control milestones. Firstly, the United States unilaterally ended nuclear warhead modernization, a step even our allies did not follow, let alone our adversaries. (Modernized warheads can be made both safer and more reliable.) Secondly, Senators Sam Nunn (D-GA) and Richard Lugar (R-IN) created the Nunn-Lugar Cooperative Threat Reduction Program to secure from theft loose nuclear materials at hundreds of sites inside Russia and find work for thousands of Russian nuclear scientists. Nunn-Lugar is nearing the end, with the close of 2013 set for completion of its myriad monumental tasks.

Nunn came to the view early in his career that nuclear material must be stored far more securely than it typically was. As a 24-year-old congressional intern he visited NATO's massive Ramstein Air Base (in what then was West Germany) during the Cuban Missile Crisis. He was told by an air force general that in event of a Soviet attack he had one minute to get his planes aloft so they could escape destruction. Visiting NATO sites in 1974 as a freshman senator, Nunn was stunned to learn that ground commanders facing Warsaw Pact forces far larger than their own envisioned early recourse to nuclear weapons, to prevent the Soviet Union's huge army from overrunning Western Europe. On that same visit one base security officer told Nunn that a team of terrorists could conceivably storm the base and make off with a nuclear weapon; three or four terrorists might not succeed, but a team of 10 possibly could. Safety procedures were subsequently stepped up. By the end of 1976 all tactical nuclear weapons were equipped with trigger locks known as Permissive Action Links (PALs), which made unauthorized detonation of a U.S. nuclear weapon virtually impossible.

The third arms-control milestone was the adoption by the U.S. and Russia of a pact scrapping long-range nuclear missiles. Russia's nuclear arsenal had surpassed America's in 1978 (when the U.S. level fell below 23,000), and it peaked at around 45,000 weapons in 1986. The end of the Cold War made deep arms reductions possible. Bush Sr. negotiated the first Strategic Arms Reduction Treaty (START) with Gorbachev in 1991. At the time the superpowers had 12,000 deployed strategic nuclear weapons. The treaty cut the total to 6,000, but Bush also unilaterally reduced America's 6,000 *tactical* nuclear weapons to 500.

Bush Sr. and Gorbachev's successor, Boris Yeltsin, signed the START II (De-MIRVing) Treaty in 1993, to replace multiple-warhead missiles with single-warhead missiles. The Senate ratified it 87 to 4 three years later, but—in a case of the Russians practicing linkage—the Duma (parliament) delayed it, protesting the enlargement of NATO into Eastern Europe and the American interventions in Kosovo and Iraq. Though the Duma finally ratified the treaty in 2000, it attached conditions on missile defense that the George W. Bush administration could not accept, and the treaty never came into force.

In 2002, George W. Bush and Vladimir Putin negotiated the steepest weapons cut yet, slashing deployed strategic weapons to 2,200, in a treaty known as Strategic Offensive Reduction Treaty (SORT, or the Moscow Treaty). In the same year Bush exercised America's legal right to exit the 1972 ABM Treaty upon six months' notice, a step Moscow did not protest.

President Obama came into office determined to go for nuclear zero sooner rather than later, based upon his belief that all countries have a genuine common interest in abolishing nuclear weapons. But in pushing this goal he has been speeding through yellow caution signals.

In April 2010 he signed the New START Treaty, which cut American nuclear weapons while permitting the Russians to increase theirs, since they were already below the treaty levels—despite the fact that they could not maintain their existing weapons. Further, Russia's rail-mobile missiles (shuttled around Russia's vast rural interior) did not count towards treaty limits. Verification was more limited than under

START: Russia was required to decrypt telemetry information—radio signals with missile flight data, immensely valuable for understanding how a missile performs in actual flight—for only five missile tests. *Thus Russia can conceal data on its newest missiles, about which we know least, by revealing decrypted information only for obsolete models about which we already know a great deal.*

In his eagerness to "reset" relations with Russia, Obama threw away all the negotiating leverage that would have enabled him to extract concessions from an economically strapped Moscow. U.S. negotiators allowed treaty preamble language relinking missile defense to offensive deployment—in other words, Russia could assert that U.S. deployment of missile defense negates Russia's offensive missiles, and thus impairs Russian deterrence. Washington says this language does not legally bind; Moscow says it does. (Russia also objects to the limited missile defense deployments slated for Eastern Europe.) This in practical terms means an unenforceable standoff on missile defense.

Officials selected exclusively by the U.S. and Russia make up the Bilateral Consultative Commission in charge of adjudication. This legal arrangement yielded serial stalemates under SALT I a generation ago, and figures to produce more of the same this time around. The United States is in the odd position of having a legal right dependent upon Russia's acceptance of guilt. The U.S. has, in effect, the right to sue—but can win only if its adversary admits liability.

In a landmark 1961 article, "After Detection, What?," nuclear and arms-control strategist Fred C. Ikle, later to become the third-ranking defense official in the Reagan administration, presciently warned that detecting an arms agreement violation is only the beginning:

> If the violator resumes testing, the injured country will do likewise; if the violator reoccupies his part of a neutralized zone, the other will move back into his; and if the violator rearms, his opponent will rearm to the same extent.

The problem of deterring violations has often been oversimplified by assuming that a detected evasion would automatically be taken care of by the cancellation of the agreement and the application of such "restorative measures." But three conditions have to be met if "restorative measures" by themselves are to be an adequate deterrent:

(1) The potential violator must fear the risk of being detected.

(2) He must also fear that a detected violation will cause an unwanted response by the injured country.

(3) He must not expect a violation to bring him an irrevocable advantage that would outweigh whatever gain he derives from abiding by the agreement.

No one effectively sanctioned Soviet violations of Cold War arms pacts. (Circumventing on-site inspection can be easy—as Paul Nitze discussed with a Soviet negotiator in 1969, it takes only six hours to place a warhead on a Russian ICBM.) Enforcing the New START Treaty will run up against the same real-world hurdles that allowed Cold War violations to occur.

The Senate ratified New START in December 2010, but—in contrast to the SORT Treaty, devoid of missile defense language—attached strict conditions. New START as ratified separated missile defense from limits on offensive systems and committed the administration both to fully implement planned missile defense deployments and also to modernize America's aging nuclear arsenal—regardless of Russian offensive missile deployment.

Such ratification conditions have the same legal effect on the Russians, said former Reagan-era arms-control and international law expert Eugene Rostow, as "a letter from my mother."

The Political and Principled Limits of Arms Control

ARMS-CONTROL HISTORY gives us common sense political insights about what deals can be negotiated, with whom, and under what circumstances.

1. *If an arms treaty is perceived as sound, it will command huge ratification majorities.* The 1987 INF, 1991 START I, and 2002 SORT treaties all commanded over 90 ratifying votes—the 2002 vote was 95–0. The SALT I accord won 88 Senate votes. Treaties that got into trouble were those regarded as poor bargains by many senators: unratified SALT II in 1979 and New START in 2010, whose 71–26 vote garnered only 13 of 46 Republicans.

2. *The circumstances in which leaders present arms treaties affect how people perceive them.* A broad bipartisan consensus that the time had come to find common ground with America's superpower adversary greeted SALT I, whereas SALT II met a deeply divided public. The INF Treaty and the arms treaties of the Bush Sr., Clinton, and Bush Jr. administrations came when public support was broad, whereas most Republicans sharply opposed New START, and the public—focused on the economy—barely noticed it.

3. *A leader people perceive as strong can get large ratification majorities for treaties.* Just as it took staunch anticommunist president Richard Nixon to go to China, Presidents Reagan, Bush Sr., Clinton, and Bush Jr. won large majorities for arms pacts because the public trusted them. President Obama is less well trusted, and the modest margin of passage for New START reflects this reality.

These factors have to do with gaining support for and ratifying treaties; they apply before the fact. The more important lesson of arms-control agreements, stated at the beginning of the chapter as the Second Lesson of nuclear-age history and repeated here, has to do with how the treaties work in the months and years after they are signed: ARMS AGREEMENTS WORK WELL ONLY IF THE PARTIES CORRECTLY PERCEIVE COMMONALITY OF STRATEGIC INTEREST. The Soviet Union ruthlessly exploited loopholes in SALT I, while ardent arms-control supporters held America to narrow interpretations of what the treaty permitted. The INF and START I treaties worked well, because Mikhail Gorbachev indeed was a different Soviet leader: he ended the Soviet quest for global dominance, freed his country's captive nations, and turned the country inward for reform efforts. The 2002 SORT Treaty came when Russian leader Vladimir Putin was acting as an ally of the United States, and worked well. But Putin ended linkage of arms treaties to country conduct later in the decade. Most notably, he invaded Georgia—America's ally and Russia's former satellite republic—in 2008.

The years 1967–1992 were the apogee of arms control. Arms-control primacy in Western countries elevated it to an exalted place, supreme above all other competing security priorities, as the path to escape nuclear nightmares. Formalist objections to particular provisions in SALT I were put aside, in pursuit of ending "the arms race"; not until several years later did it become clear that America's freeze of its arsenal did not encourage the Soviets to freeze its arsenal. Jimmy Carter's own defense secretary, Harold Brown, conceded that the Soviets built even while we were cutting.

Ironically, New START reflected the Obama administration's Cold War mindset: a treaty between superpowers. Yet Russia is no longer a true superpower, although it is still able to cause lots of trouble around the world. It makes no sense to place current-day Russia's concerns at a level higher than those of all other nations. In terms of arms control and deterrence, Barack Obama has traveled in time back to 1967, to the days of mutual assured destruction, placing superpower arms concord above deploying full-scale missile defense as insurance against future "clandestine cache" strategic surprise. To put that in perspective, imagine that President Johnson in 1967 had based American policy on how things looked in 1922. That was the year the Washington Naval Treaty put limits on ships and their armaments. Leaders of the great democracies thought these limits would prevent a second world war. Tyrants in Germany and Japan ended that fantasy.

The Cold War turned out better, but arms accords did not bring about the collapse of the evil empire, nor can it be proven that they alone prevented a nuclear war. All that can be known are two truths: The accords, whether wise or not, did not realize the worst fears of their critics. Equally, it can be said, they did not realize the high hopes of their ardent supporters. They were politically salient, bringing a measure of political peace in Western countries, but ultimately of marginal impact on strategic affairs save for missile defense. Missile defense research lagged and was skewed by arms-control priorities. We are thus more vulnerable to small-power strikes than likely we would be had our research and development on missile defense proceeded without impediments arising out of the prevailing U.S. interpretation of Cold War arms agreements.

President Obama's "open mic" exchange with Russian President Dmitri Medvedev at the March 2012 Nuclear Summit exemplified his preoccupation with arms control over missile defense, an attitude that animated the now-defunct ABM Treaty.[16] The president noted that missile defense is a "particular" concern, thus indicating an intention to move towards Moscow's position after the U.S. 2012 election. Indeed, the White House has sought to share sensitive missile defense data with Moscow, a move strongly opposed by many members of Congress.

Arms control is an essential tool, not a talisman. Agreements with adversaries are possible, but only when interests in fact coincide, as they do with efforts to avoid accidental war, and with several later arms treaties. It is dangerous for America to assume that an enemy's strategic interests are the same as its own—as Jimmy Carter learned when the Soviets invaded Afghanistan, and George W. Bush learned when Vladimir Putin invaded Georgia. Commonality of strategic goals was, in those cases, simply absent. With Russia, President Reagan put it best by often citing a Russian proverb: "Trust, but verify."

Soviet leaders were hardly immune to mirror-imaging fallacies—that is, the assumption that one's opponent behaves like oneself. Riding

---

16. OBAMA: "On all these issues, but particularly missile defense, this can be solved but it's important for [incoming president Vladimir Putin] to give me space."
MEDVEDEV: "Yeah, I understand. I understand your message about space. Space for you."
OBAMA: "This is my last election. After my election I have more flexibility."
MEDVEDEV: "I understand. I will transmit this information to Vladimir."

in Los Angeles during his 1959 visit to America, Khrushchev spotted a sign held up by a woman protesting the Hungarian revolt, brutally suppressed by the Soviets in 1956. The sign read: "Death to Khrushchev, the Butcher of Hungary." Khrushchev angrily turned to American UN Ambassador Henry Cabot Lodge: "Well, if Eisenhower wanted to have me insulted, why did he invite me to come to the United States?" Lodge was incredulous at this question, but Khrushchev persisted: "In the Soviet Union, she wouldn't be there unless I had given the order." This was no idle boast. Dean Rusk, secretary of state during the Kennedy and Johnson administrations, recounted how during a demonstration in front of the U.S. Embassy in Moscow, a staffer asked a Russian soldier how long it would last. The Russian glanced at his watch and replied: "Sixteen minutes."

It would take the end of the Cold War to relieve much public anxiety about nuclear arms races that had in fact long since ended. What is remarkable to anyone who lived through the height of the Cold War was how little a splash the New START strategic arms treaty of 2010 made in the public imagination. There were, by then, even scarier prospects than that of superpower nuclear war.

The question pending after the ratification of New START is not one of war between Russia and America. Russia never did want a direct shooting war with America, and throughout the Cold War fought hot wars by proxy only. Dangers elsewhere—proliferation in North Korea, Iran's nuclear quest, a potential Islamist takeover in nuclear-armed Pakistan—are unaffected by New START. History simply fails to support the hope expressed by President Obama and Secretary of State Hillary Clinton that we are furthering nuclear arms control elsewhere by setting an example with our own reductions. With America's huge arsenal dramatically shrunk and its needed modernization stalled, other powers large (Russia, China) and small (Pakistan, North Korea, Iran) cheerfully ignore us.

5.

IRAN AND THE MIDEAST: SLIDING TOWARDS NUCLEAR WAR

Our dear Imam [Khomeini] ordered that the occupying regime
in Al-Qods [Jerusalem] be wiped off the face of the earth. This
was a very wise statement. The issue of Palestine is not one
on which we could make a piecemeal compromise.... This
would mean our defeat. [Anyone who recognizes Israel] has
put his signature under the defeat of the Islamic world.

IRANIAN PRESIDENT MAHMOUD AHMADINEJAD,
"WORLD WITHOUT ZIONISM" CONFERENCE, 2005

IRAN'S QUEST FOR NUCLEAR WEAPONS IS WIDELY ACKNOWLEDGED throughout the West, after disclosure in late 2011 that Iran has pursued components of advanced nuclear weapons and has gotten the help of a renegade Russian weapons designer. A February 2012 inspection report compiled by the UN's International Atomic Energy Agency found that Iran had conducted high explosive and detonator tests for a nuclear warhead, as well as computer modeling of a nuclear warhead core, in a facility whose suspect activities were detected by satellite surveillance. In February 2012 Iran installed higher-speed centrifuges at its Fordo facility in order to more rapidly enrich uranium that could fuel an atom bomb; the facility is buried more than 200 feet in solid rock, and may be impregnable to attack from the air using presently available conventional munitions—even by the United States.

This march towards nuclear weapons status—the most dangerous proliferation development in the post–Cold War era—highlights the importance of a Third Lesson of nuclear-age history: REVOLUTIONARY POWERS CANNOT BE CONTAINED; THEY MUST BE DEFEATED.

Iran's Nuclear Quest

Situated on the eastern side of the volatile Mideast, Iran menaces traffic passing through the Strait of Hormuz, 34 miles long and at its narrowest ("choke-point") 21 miles wide, yet deep enough to handle supertankers. Through its waters pass 15.5 million barrels of crude oil daily, about one-sixth of global daily oil consumption. Iran has threatened to close off the waterway, which could plunge the global economy into a deep recession. Were Iran a nuclear power, military options against it would virtually vanish.

The shah of Iran pursued a commercial nuclear power program in the 1950s, under President Eisenhower's Atoms for Peace plan. But few doubted that the shah desired a nuclear weapons capability; the program was suspended when the shah's regime fell in early 1979. Iran began a clandestine nuclear program in 1984. The Nonproliferation Treaty allows peaceful nuclear activity—commercial power and research, provided the country accepts safeguards and monitoring. *A clandestine program makes sense only if its objective is to develop nuclear weapons.*

According to investigative reporter Kenneth Timmerman, by 1991 nuclear-club member China was aiding Pakistan, North Korea, and Iran. One Iranian official publicly stated that Iran "was keeping its options open." The feckless efforts to confront Iran over its nuclear program were perhaps best summed up that year by a comment from a German foreign ministry official. He responded to the Iranian official's comment: "If you are a piano player, keeping your options open means you are practicing."

The apparently successful 2010 Stuxnet worm—a malicious self-replicating program that spreads itself, computer to computer, throughout a network—inflicted considerable mechanical damage at key Iranian nuclear facilities. It cost Iran's uranium enrichment program an estimated year. This cyber-sabotage was presumably the work of either Israel or the U.S. (or both).

But Iran is closing in on nuclear weapons capability. Specific and reliable intelligence as to when it will be ready to cross the nuclear threshold is nearly impossible to acquire. Those whose job it is to determine this have revised, even reversed, their assessments. The historical record shows that more often than not intelligence fails to predict when closed societies will acquire nuclear capability or test a nuclear device, the task being an exceedingly difficult one under the best of circumstances (see chapter 9).

Historical Parallels

IRAN'S DETERMINATION to develop nuclear weapons is the most dangerous proliferation development in the post–Cold War era (Pakistan's ascendancy to nuclear membership was all but complete by 1984). Complicating efforts to confront the threat posed by a nuclear Iran are two factors:

1. Lack of a fully effective missile defense screen for Western nations within the potential reach of an Iranian arsenal.

2. Lack of confidence that Iran's leaders will be as effectively deterred from starting a nuclear war as was the Soviet Union during the Cold War (and as are Russia and China today).

The U.S. failure to deploy an effective missile defense against a small-power attack is a product of superpower arms control. Arms-control constraints began with offensive missile systems. That approach changed in 1972, when the Antiballistic Missile Treaty severely limited missile defense design and deployment in the United States. Defensive system design since then has aimed not for the best products that technology and innovation can produce. Rather, system design has been governed by the maximum technological result deemed permissible under strategic arms-control principles as they have been narrowly interpreted since 1972. The result has been systems of perilously stunted capability.

The risks of a nuclear Iran getting into a war can be illustrated by historic examples: the two world wars and the 1962 Cuban Missile Crisis. World War I shows how great powers can be drawn into utterly un-anticipated suicidal carnage for failure to understand the real risks of a major conflict. World War II is an example of a war started in part because of efforts to appease rather than confront tyrants with Napoleon's ambition for conquest, though far more brutal than Napoleon. The Cuban episode shows how a great-power gamble can lead to the brink of total catastrophe. All these elements can be in play if Iran goes nuclear.

The Two World Wars

Asked once how a world war would start, German Chancellor Otto von Bismarck, who united Germany during his long late nineteenth-century tenure, is reputed to have quipped: "some damn fool thing in the Balkans." On June 28, 1914, the assassination of the Austrian archduke Francis Ferdinand by Bosnian Serb ultranationalist Gavrilo Princip set in motion a series of events that in five weeks triggered the Great War.

First, in Germany, France, and Russia, poisonous ultranationalist sentiments incited popular support for a war expected to last at most a few weeks. The same sentiments drove the conflict even after the calamitous carnage of the opening months alerted leaders to the monstrous destructive power at their command.

Second, individual leaders—Winston Churchill notably excepted[17]—lacked meaningful understanding of the destructive power of emerging military technologies, especially the artillery barrage and machine-gun fire. The resulting futile sanguinary conflict was prolonged by the public's desire to see revenge exacted from the enemy for inflicting mass casualties. Commanders shockingly indifferent to the fate of their subordinates sent them in endless charges across no-man's-land moonscapes, unable to imagine anything beyond premodern notions of martial spirit to counter massive firepower.

---

17. In 1900, his first year in Parliament, Churchill warned that a European war would be far more costly than colonial wars. It would involve a long, all-out effort engaging the entire population and suspending operation of peaceful industries. Said Churchill: "Democracy is more vindictive than Cabinets. The wars of people will be more terrible than the wars of kings."

Third, and perhaps most significant of all, technologies of destruction had simply outrun technologies of command, communications, and control. Once troop trains left their home depots, those authorizing departure could not reverse their passage. Between the trenches messengers sprinted on foot or rode on horseback, as had been done for thousands of years. There were limited telegraph lines suitable for fixed installation for intermittent communications with battlefield commanders, and virtually no radio communications to allow true real-time communication.

A fourth factor—the intense revulsion over war following the devastation of World War I—is also instructive for Western nations looking towards the Middle East today. The failure to control arms during battle led to attempts to control arms via diplomacy, and to an international organization, the League of Nations, charged with keeping peace. Those attempts were trampled under the jackboots of totalitarian Axis tyrants who armed for and ultimately started wars, while the memories of modern war's grisly toll paralyzed the leaders of the free world.

1962: The Cuban Missile Crisis

The most worrisome problem posed by hostile states—Islamic or otherwise—is the mental state of their leaders and the fear that deterrence may not work against millenarian zealots. During the Cold War the Soviet leaders were, in the main, rational calculators. While ruthless adversaries, they were acutely cognizant of the potential consequences of starting a nuclear war. Even Joseph Stalin, paranoid mass murderer of tens of millions, confined his strategic goal to victory without fighting a war.

Later Soviet leaders were similarly deterred. Leonid Brezhnev seriously considered a preemptive nuclear strike against China in 1969, when the two countries engaged in a series of bloody clashes along their Ussuri River border. At the time Russia's arsenal vastly exceeded that of China, whose nascent program had produced perhaps 25 to 40 bombs. But Brezhnev decided to pass. Had Brezhnev struck China first, his chance to get a strategic arms pact with America would have evaporated. America's immense arsenal troubled him more than China's relatively puny one at the time.[18]

Once indeed the world did come to the very brink of a shooting nuclear war, during the Cuban Missile Crisis. Let us return to 1962, and see what context this story can give us to apply to Iran today. That August, U.S. reconnaissance planes discovered that Russian construction teams were placing intermediate-range ballistic missiles at bases in the Cuban countryside. In response, the Kennedy administration imposed a naval "quarantine" (blockading contraband supplies only) around the island.

On October 15, Kennedy convened an executive committee of 13 "wise men" to suggest ways to resolve the crisis. Their firmly shared belief was that it was unacceptable to have Russian missiles armed with nuclear warheads sitting 90 miles south of Florida. One of them, Paul Nitze, wrote later that at the outset nearly all "ExComm" members—including the president and his brother Robert—believed that military action to remove the missiles was almost inevitable. In his Cuban Missile Crisis history, *Nine Minutes to Midnight*, Michael Dobbs superbly described what happened next.

On October 27, which the White House dubbed "Black Saturday," things nearly spun out of control. A U.S. U-2 spy plane was downed and its space-suited pilot killed, by a Soviet surface-to-air missile at Castro's

---

18. Late in the Cold War similar fears arose inside the Kremlin, though they were without foundation in fact. In 1983, Brezhnev's successor, Yuri Andropov, reportedly feared a first nuclear strike from the planned NATO deployment of 108 Pershing II missiles, which could span the 1,000 miles from their Western European bases to Moscow within eight minutes and with great accuracy. One possible set of targets was command centers in Moscow. Andropov considered but ultimately declined to launch a preemptive nuclear attack on America. At that time, Fidel Castro reportedly asked—as he had during the 1962 Cuban Missile crisis—that the Soviets launch an all-out strike at the United States. Adrian Danilevitch, a former top Soviet war planner, described how Moscow "had to actively disabuse him of this view by spelling out the ecological consequences for Cuba (in a nutshell, it would disappear) of a Soviet strike against the U.S." Castro's request went nowhere.

orders. Another U-2 pilot on an Arctic surveillance mission was tricked by an intense aurora borealis ("Northern Lights") into taking a wrong turn, penetrating 300 miles into Soviet airspace. That spy plane eluded Russian interceptors and by a major miracle made it back to friendly territory. This was not a true fail-safe scenario (inability to recall in time a hostile plane carrying bombs), as the plane was unarmed, but a shoot down would hardly have helped resolve the crisis.

Meanwhile, a U.S. destroyer was dropping depth charges to force a quarantine-breaking Russian diesel submarine to surface. Unbeknownst to the destroyer crew, the sub was armed with a 10-kiloton nuclear-tipped torpedo, some 70 percent as powerful as the Hiroshima bomb. Its commander was under strict orders not to fire a nuclear device without direct authorization from Moscow, but only by surfacing could the sub exchange messages with the authorities. But after being tracked by U.S. ships continuously—and being forced to stay below despite tropical conditions inside the sub—the Soviet commander was ready to fire his nuclear torpedo. His crew prevailed upon him to surface instead, noting the lack of authorization from Moscow. The sub surfaced to find itself in the midst of four U.S. destroyers. Moscow ordered the sub to depart the area, and the U.S. did not try to stop its departure. Had the submarine commander used his nuclear torpedo in 1962, it is inconceivable that Kennedy would have responded with an all-out attack over the loss of one of four small ships. It is hard to credit assertions that the USSR would have chosen mutual annihilation either.

Unknown to Kennedy and his advisers then was how many nuclear warheads and types of nuclear-capable delivery systems were on the island, or what command and control arrangements were in place between the Soviet and Cuban strategic forces. Dobbs writes (surely accurately) that Cuba's nuclear arsenal "far exceeded the worst nightmares of anyone in Washington." Specifically, deployed or en route to Cuba by ship were no less than 158 warheads. Ninety were already on the island, including 36 one-megaton warheads that could be hurled almost 1,300 miles and 36 14-kiloton warheads (Hiroshima-size) mounted on small tactical nuclear missiles. An estimated 150,000 American troops were to be sent to take the island, and 1,397 separate targets had been marked for destruction as part of the invasion. The Russians were prepared to send tactical bombers carrying Hiroshima-size A-bombs to annihilate any major invasion force.

Even without nuclear missile strikes on American soil, the instant carnage that would have been inflicted by the invasion force alone—by some 45,000 Soviets armed with atomic weapons, plus a much larger volunteer Cuban contingent—would have been the worst in American military history. The invasion force had the potential to suffer in a single day the death toll of Americans killed by enemy fire in the Korean and Vietnam wars combined.

En route on ships were 68 warheads, including two dozen for ballistic missiles, which could deliver one megaton 2,800 miles away (roughly the distance from Havana to Seattle). Khrushchev recalled these to Russia—weapon security on Cuba was dicey. The island heat made storage hotter than was safe for the warheads; accidental megaton-level ground detonation was a serious possibility. Without trigger locks, most nuclear weapons on Cuba could be released by the local commander—in some cases, a lieutenant—ignoring orders to the contrary from Moscow. Had an invasion come, as one Russian former soldier stationed in Cuba then put it, "You have to understand the psychology of the military person. If you are being attacked, why shouldn't you reciprocate?" Ironically, the minimal level of perimeter and site security at the Bejucal nuclear storage bunker led CIA analysts to conclude that the facility did not house nuclear weapons.

Things were better, but far from secure, on the U.S. side. Pilots had unilateral release discretion for nuclear-armed air-to-air missiles, designed to vaporize strategic bomber squadrons. During the course of the 1950s and 1960s, several nuclear-armed strategic bombers crashed. One was carrying a pair of hydrogen bombs, each able to wipe out a major city. A crash cannot detonate a modern nuclear bomb, but such events are extremely dangerous nonetheless, in that any explosion can scatter highly radioactive nuclear material.

America's fighter jets also could carry nuclear bombs. A nuclear-armed F-106 interceptor, armed with the MB-1 Genie air-to-air missile (a one-kiloton device that could be armed and fired at the pilot's sole discretion), had a near mishap taking off. Designed to destroy all enemy planes within a quarter-mile radius, it was called by one pilot "the dumbest weapons system ever purchased." F-102 interceptors had similar armament, and F-100 Super Sabres based in Europe carried hydrogen bombs to drop inside Russia. A young Navy pilot named John McCain sat in his A-4D Skyhawk jet on the aircraft carrier *Enterprise*, awaiting orders to drop A-bombs on selected Cuban targets.

Slow communications made matters worse. Both sides sent signals over broadcast television, sacrificing privacy for celerity. The Russian ambassador in Washington sent telegrams via Western Union, complete with pick-up via bicycle messenger. Informed by this potentially catastrophic infirmity, the superpowers established the Washington-Moscow Hot Line in 1963.

The Cuban Missile Crisis ended without millions perishing because at crucial moments Kennedy and Khrushchev chose caution. On October 24, three days before the crisis ended, Russian ships sailed away from the American "quarantine" line, avoiding what could have been a catastrophic confrontation at sea. As Secretary of State Dean Rusk said upon hearing the news, "We were eyeball to eyeball and the other fellow just blinked." In reality, Khrushchev had ordered the missile-carrying ships to turn back a day earlier, and only a few minor ships had proceeded to the quarantine line. But newspapers printed and broadcasters printed the legend.

The Twenty-first Century Mideast: Cuban Crisis Revisited?

THE DANGER in the twenty-first century Mideast with a nuclear-armed Iran would be vastly greater than that posed by Cuba and the USSR in 1962 for four reasons:

1. Greater vulnerability of geographically small states to nuclear strikes.

2. Inability to absorb a blow and retaliate due to short warning times.

3. A near-complete lack of rapid communication channels.

4. Leaders who have no experience in managing nuclear crises, and thus may either overestimate their chances of success with a surprise attack, or in extreme cases may succumb to an apocalyptic impulse to bring about the end of days.

Vulnerability. In the 1950s and early 1960s, the two superpowers faced each other with strategic forces that were primarily above ground and small in number. But missiles were not nearly accurate enough then to threaten them, and bombers alone could not ensure success. Furthermore, their vast size and widely dispersed populations made only a large-area attack capable of ending national life.

Today, missiles are frighteningly accurate, but the Gulf states cannot yet build such weapons. If one of them had a nuclear bomb, it would have to use military aircraft as a delivery system. (The advanced jets that the Gulf states purchase from the United States can carry nuclear bombs.) Such planes are vulnerable to a first strike. Given far fewer military installations and few cities with populations above 100,000 in the tiny kingdoms of the Gulf, countries could face devastation beyond recovery if caught in a surprise salvo of Hiroshima-sized bombs.

Short Warning Times. A Russian ICBM, launched from the Ural Mountains and hurtling through space at four miles per second, will travel the roughly 6,000 miles to America's Atlantic coast in about 30 minutes. With flight distances between potential targets in the Mideast often less than 1,000 miles, a high-speed jet can cover the distance in little more time than an ICBM can traverse oceans. Factor in missiles that fly at "merely" several times the speed of sound; in some cases, times from launch to impact within the Mideast would be less than 10 minutes. Iran has solid-fuel rockets, which use a gel fuel that (unlike liquid rocket fuel) is highly stable. Once loaded it can sit indefinitely and launch quickly.

Nor are jets the only Gulf state assets. In 1986 China sold 36 CSS-2 intermediate-range ballistic missiles to the Saudis. With a one metric-ton conventional warhead and 1,750-mile range they can easily reach Iran. But the Saudis may elect to purchase nuclear warheads for the CSS-2, or try to buy newer, more accurate models complete with nuclear warheads.

Communications Confusion. Between Washington and Moscow in 1962 there was only one functioning private communications channel, commercial telegraphy. Imagine a Mideast with a nuclear Iran, Saudi Arabia, Kuwait, Turkey, Egypt, and Israel. With six nations there are 64 possible two-way interactions, with all the attendant prospects for misunderstandings during a crisis. Israel has used hot-line telephonic communications with adversaries, including the Palestinians, with mixed results. *If with a single channel results are mixed, how will the result be with many diplomatic channels, and only hours—perhaps minutes—to Mideast Armageddon?* Add in that these countries do not trust each other, making communication problematic at best. Assurance that a single unintended missile launch was in fact accidental may easily fail to convince a nervous target's leaders.

Less Stable Leaders. Perhaps the most important personality of the 1962 crisis, one whose impulse control was, to put it charitably, weak, was Fidel Castro. He was flush with his improbable revolutionary triumph and seething with rage at the United States—rage that stemmed partly from ideological Marxist fervor and partly from the efforts of the Kennedy administration to get rid of him. Fidel wanted the Russians to incinerate the United States and was willing to sacrifice his 6 million subjects in a nuclear holocaust.

It is today's Islamic version of Castro who should worry us the most. Religious messianism and secular militarism can be as lethal as romantic revolutionary fervor. Both partake of the "monstrous self-confidence" that Henry Kissinger saw as characterizing the "true revolutionary."[19] The region's combination of religious zealotry and nuclear capability offers a clear recipe for accidental nuclear war. Fidel's reckless abandon may well be the augury of nuclear wars to come.

One Iranian Castro candidate is, of course, Iranian President Mahmoud Ahmadinejad. He has infamously said that Israel should be wiped off the map. And consider a 2001 statement by former Iranian president Ali Akbar Hashemi Rafsanjani, still in 2012 a major Iranian power broker, as to nuclear war against Israel:

> If a day comes when the world of Islam is duly equipped with the arms Israel has in possession, the strategy of colonialism would face a stalemate because application of an atomic bomb would not leave any thing in Israel but the same thing would just produce damages in the Muslim world.

This comes from an Iranian leader often called by Western analysts a moderate. Rafsanjani has also been quoted as saying in 2001 that if Iran lost 15 million people in a nuclear exchange with Israel but killed 5 million Israelis, Iran would survive but Israel would be extinguished.

As for Israel, though it has been a nuclear power (albeit undeclared) for over 40 years, its status has not ignited a Mideast arms race. When Israel took out the North Korea–supplied nuclear plant in Iran-backed

---

19. "To be a true revolutionary one requires a monstrous self-confidence. Who else would presume of his followers the inevitable deprivations of revolutionary struggle, except one monomaniacally dedicated to the victory of his convictions and free of doubt about whether they justified the inevitable suffering? It is the pursuit of this charismatic truth— sometimes transcendental, as often diabolical—that has produced the gross misery as well as the profound upheavals that mark modern history. For 'truth' knows no restraint and 'virtue' can accept no limits; they are their own justification. Opponents are either ignorant or wicked, and must be either reeducated or eliminated."

Syria in September 2007, the silence that followed in the Mideast was deafening. American diplomatic cable traffic published online by WikiLeaks showed repeated expression of intense anxiety by America's Arab allies, who fear a nuclear Iran, not a nuclear Israel.

These problems of a century ago menace the Middle East today. Many statesmen and much of the public seem to think nuclear conflict is unlikely because they assume traditional Cold War deterrence will again prevail. But dangers are growing as time passes, especially as regional instability worsens.

The Resurgence of Militant Islam

LET US be clear about in whose hands a Mideast bomb would be. When the Ayatollah Khomeini took power in Iran in 1979, Western analysts were unaware that Khomenei had published a collection of speeches, under the title *Islamic Government*, because the volume was then available only in Persian and Arabic editions. According to the great historian Bernard Lewis, the book "made it very clear who he was and what his aims were; and the popular idea that this was going to mean the establishment of a liberal, open, modern society in place of the reactionary Shah was utter nonsense."

Hailed as Imam ("priest"), Khomeini openly declared an intention to go back 1,400 years to the days of the Prophet—first in Iran and, ultimately all over the world. He imposed a political version of Twelver Shi'ism (the apocalyptic mainstream of the Shia faith; Twelvers await a child imam, who disappeared circa 873 and who will return and bring Judgment Day to the world).

In the 1980s and 1990s Iran was the world's leading sponsor of global terrorism. Indeed, Iran's Islamist regime had a role in the planning and logistical support behind the September 11, 2001 attacks, according to findings of fact made by a federal district judge in New York in a lawsuit filed against al-Qaeda. Iran also midwifed Hezbollah (Party of God), which took root in Lebanon, aided by the secular fascist Syrian regime. Hezbollah carried out the October 1983 truck-bomb attack that killed 241 Marine peacekeepers, the worst single-day loss for the Marines since the closing battles of World War II. It also launched a six-week war against Israel in 2006, firing thousands of rockets into northern Israel and virtually paralyzing one-third of the Jewish state's population.

Followers of Khomeini's creed include the current leader of Iran, Supreme Guide Ali Khamenei, and Iran's President, Mahmoud Ahmadinejad—who speaks of an apocalyptic Judgment Day. Of course Iran is just part of a broader global resurgence in Islamism. Among Islamist countries, Pakistan has achieved nuclear weapons status. Now Iran stands at the front of the Islamist queue, with potentially fateful consequences for global stability.

Compounding the problem of Iran's radical Shi'ism is a parallel resurgence of militant Sunni Islam. Eighty-five percent of the world's 1.4 billion Muslims are Sunnis—including most of the Muslims the West considers allies. Yet the Sunni turning point in 1979 was little noticed in the West. Fundamentalists that year seized Saudi Arabia's Great Mosque of Mecca and demanded that the Saudi regime return to a more fundamentalist creed. The Saudi rulers had to summon French commandos in order to retake the symbolic heart of Islam. Paradoxically, the agenda of those vanquished became the agenda of Saudi Arabia in the Muslim world. The back story to this episode was to prove of fateful significance after 1979.

By 1979 Saudi Arabia's rulers—members of the al-Saud family—were living lavish lives and cavorting with other jet setters. Resentments among fundamentalists grew, and led in time to the seizure of the Great Mosque. The fundamentalists—members of the Wahhabi movement who were mostly Bedouin students and ex-National Guard, following a charismatic Wahhabi zealot—could be dislodged only if the most senior Wahhabi clerics gave consent to the al-Saud to storm the immense Great Mosque, something the Prophet had specifically prohibited. The clerics gave their consent, but for a fateful price: the al-Saud would fund with petrodollars the global spread of militant Sunni Islam. Then they would be permitted to live with one foot, so to speak, in the modern world and the other in the world of Islamic piety. Thereafter Saudi money spread the militant Wahhabist creed to mosques and *madrassas* (religious schools) around the world.

The radical Sunni creed in Saudi Arabia and the militant Shia theocracy in Iran are ingredients for a Mideast arms race. If Iran crosses the nuclear weapons threshold, the Gulf states will not start a 25-year development program. Saudi Arabia, Kuwait, and Qatar will simply call Pakistan and ask how many atomic bombs the Pakistanis will part with for how many petrodollars. Saudi Arabia reportedly has already done this. Cash-strapped Pakistan can easily afford to sell part of its arsenal or make A-bombs to order.

With their Pakistani bombs and their American bombers, the parties would be armed fully, without the extended learning curve that taught the United States and the former Soviet Union how to safeguard their weapons from unauthorized use or surprise attack. The oft-decried immense size of these countries' arsenals also helped wean them from a dangerous "use it or lose it" attitude. Countries who might lose their whole arsenal in a single attack are much more likely to use that arsenal upon warning of an attack—a "launch on warning" posture. (If the "warning" was really a flock of geese on the radar screen, the bomb thus launched would be an unintended first strike.) Countries that strike back before the full extent of an attack is known (in strategic parlance, a "launch under attack" posture), could vastly overreact and thus precipitate a full-blown conflict after an initial accidental launch.

In his history of the Strategic Air Command, *15 Minutes*, L. Douglas Keeney recounts the November 24, 1961 "Black Forest" incident. Upon an alarm signaling that a Soviet first strike was underway, a full-blown Strategic Air Command alert was triggered, with well over 500 bombers and almost 400 tankers sitting on the runway. The alert was cancelled when the alarm signal was traced to a faulty component in a microwave radio tower in Black Forest, Colorado.

The U.S. and USSR had one luxury denied small states: the ability to absorb a small or medium strike and survive, albeit greatly and permanently diminished. Even a small-scale attack can extinguish tiny statelets like those in the Persian Gulf. Unlike the United States, Russia, and other large states, whose huge territories and vast, dispersed populations make only a large-area attack capable of ending national life, a few well-placed nuclear bombs could virtually extinguish the national life of a small country.

Nuclear crises arise suddenly, take novel forms, and impose immense stress on leaders, with little margin for error. With survival at stake, the temptation to strike first could well prove irresistible. Revolutionary powers are more likely than others to take gambles that generate crises. In 1962 the Soviet Union was avowedly revolutionary, seeking world domination. Its deployment of nuclear missiles in Cuba brought the world to the brink of nuclear war. Its demise was essential to end the revolutionary threat posed by Communism. The demise of the revolutionary Islamist regime in Iran, and its replacement by a moderate government, is the only way to defuse the growing confrontation in the Mideast. REVOLUTIONARY POWERS CANNOT BE CONTAINED; THEY MUST BE DEFEATED. If this Third Lesson of nuclear of nuclear-age history is ignored, the consequences could be devastating.

6.

North Korea: Nuclear Hostage Taking

It was already one in the morning; the rain pattered
dismally against the panes, and my candle was nearly
burnt out, when, by the glimmer of the half-extinguished
light, I saw the dull yellow eye of the creature open.
Mary Shelley, Frankenstein, or the Modern Prometheus, chapter 5 (1818)

The contrasting fates of Iraq, Libya, and North Korea illustrate how nuclear weapons can determine whether a dictatorship survives despite adverse international pressure. Saddam's nuclear program was not complete in 1991, when the Gulf War coalition moved to eject his forces from Kuwait. Had Saddam been able to threaten Turkey and Saudi Arabia with nuclear attack, neither country would likely have permitted coalition forces to launch military action from its soil.

On the eve of the coalition's March 2003 invasion of Iraq, Libyan dictator Muammar Qaddafi agreed to surrender his WMD arsenal, including nuclear materials. He feared that after Saddam Hussein's regime was toppled for failure to comply with UN WMD resolutions, Libya would be next in line. In 2011, with Qaddafi bereft of nuclear materials, NATO and the Arab League were willing to support Libyan rebels, and Qaddafi found himself on history's ash heap.

This was in stark contrast to the reaction of outside powers when, in 2006, North Korea detonated its first nuclear device. The reaction has been mostly the serial offering of bribes, in what has been the vain hope that Pyongyang would in return surrender its nuclear arsenal. Preventive military options are now off the table.

These cases collectively offer the Fourth Lesson of nuclear-age history: NUCLEAR WEAPONS GIVE NATIONS A "DYING STING" CAPABIL-

ITY THAT VIRTUALLY PRECLUDES PREEMPTIVE ACTION AND CONFERS NEAR-TOTAL SURVIVAL INSURANCE.

This lesson applies in particular to dictatorships, which rule by force rather than by consent of the governed. Their nuclear status gives them greater freedom to forcibly suppress dissent, because outsiders are less likely to intervene militarily. Rogue states like North Korea are a little less dangerous than revolutionary states like Iran, because they have more limited strategic objectives. North Korea does not aspire to overthrow the existing world order, as does the Islamic state established by the Ayatollah Khomeini. But rogues still can be very dangerous. Not only does the North foment trouble on the Korean Peninsula and in the northwest Pacific, it has distributed nuclear technology to Iran and Syria. For these reasons the ultimate goal regarding rogue states, as with revolutionary states, is positive regime change that brings in a moderate government capable of peaceful coexistence with other nations.

As this book went to press North Korea had violated its international commitments once again by conducting a satellite launch test using its newest ballistic missile, a three-stage vehicle with intercontinental range and the ability to carry a 2,200-pound warhead. This test failed. But an operational missile would put north Alaska at risk. Pyongyang's claim that it was launching a civilian satellite launch was dismissed the world over as risible, given that the North's commercial economy is virtually nonexistent. As for the missile itself, all missiles today are universally regarded as exclusively military in purpose; only one nation, the U.S., has ever attempted to create a commercial missile.[20] Thus North Korea's launch is universally considered a test of its staging capability for an ICBM.

---

20. On June 8, 1959, the submarine *USS Barbero* fired a cruise missile carrying 3,000 letters in the direction of Mayport, Florida. The missile landed safely and the mail was delivered. The postmaster general, Arthur Summerfield, offered this prediction: "Before man reaches the moon, mail will be delivered within hours from New York to California, to England, to India or to Australia by guided missiles." Summerfield's prediction came partly true: mail is hauled overnight worldwide, but by cargo plane.

In the Shadow of Stalin's Nuclear-Armed Monster

THE TRANSFER of power in North Korea in December 2011 was only the second such transfer in the 63 years since the country's inception in 1948. The new regime combines the totalitarian tyranny of the two prior absolute rulers with a new instability. How power will be shared in 2012 and beyond is unclear. Because North Korea has nuclear weapons (albeit a small stock), the risk of war on the Korean Peninsula may be fairly judged as the highest since the end of the Korean War in 1953. It was not for nothing that in January 2012 the Nuclear Threat Initiative, a high-level, bipartisan private group whose membership includes many former top national security figures, ranked North Korea dead last in nuclear security among 32 nations having enough nuclear material to make a nuclear weapon.

The prime target for the North's military power will be Seoul, capital of South Korea, in significant measure due to an accidental intersection of geography and diplomacy in 1945, when two junior American diplomats set the 38th parallel as the boundary between North and South. One, Dean Rusk (later secretary of state for Kennedy and Johnson), recounted the astonishing tale in his memoir: "We were forced by events to act as statesmen beyond our years."

On the night of August 14 Rusk studied a map of Korea, to find where the Allies would accept Japan's surrender. He and his fellow diplomat, neither of them having specialized knowledge of Korea, were informed that the navy wanted the dividing line drawn as far north as possible, while the army did not want a foothold on the Korean Peninsula at all, lacking as it did enough troops to put in. Deciding that Seoul, which had been capital of prewar Korea, should be in the southern sector, the two diplomats looked for a convenient natural geographic dividing line. Finding none they settled on the 38th parallel. Neither they nor the superiors who reviewed their selection knew a crucial historical fact: When Russia and Japan had discussed dividing up Korea into spheres of influence half a century earlier they had chosen the 38th parallel as the dividing line. Thus the Soviets interpreted the U.S. selection of the same line as an implied concession of legitimate Russian influence in the North and concluded the United States did not genuinely desire reunification of the two Koreas.

With a population of over 10 million people, Seoul is one of the largest cities in the world, and at 17,000 people per square mile, it is also one of the densest. It has double the population density of Mexico City, more than triple that of Tokyo-Yokohama or London, and more than eight times that of New York. The city and its outskirts hold over half the population of the Republic of Korea, better known as South Korea.

All these people and brightly lit skyscrapers are clustered together a mere 25 miles south of the 38th parallel dividing the two Koreas. Across the demilitarized zone, one of the largest armies in the world faces Seoul. A hundred miles further north lies Pyongyang, a capital city of gigantic monuments (including an extra-large version of Paris's Arc de Triomphe) and massive, low-slung buildings. The North's capital is a thousand square miles bigger than Seoul, but has less than one-third its population. Former Secretary of Defense Donald Rumsfeld liked to display a satellite photo taken at night of the Korean Peninsula that showed a brilliantly lit South Korea versus a nearly totally dark North. In the nineteenth century, Westerners called Korea the "Hermit Kingdom"; now the name fits only its northern half.

Were Seoul even 50 more miles from the 38th parallel, the strategic situation would be quite different. But at half that distance, it lies well inside the range of Pyongyang's artillery. The North, effectively insulated from attack since it became a nuclear power in 2006, is, metaphorically, the cornered criminal holding a gun to the head of a hostage and shouting "One false move."

Russia created, and then China protected, a monster rump state that has held peninsular peace hostage since 1948. Joseph Stalin's Asian satellite state gave the United States its first stalemate in a major conflict, and established practical limits to nuclear use by a superpower with Western values.

Stalin had a definite strategic plan when, with one week to go in the Pacific War, his troops invaded Manchuria. Put simply, he wanted to seize territory from a collapsing empire before borders were set at war's end. Stalin knew about the power of the atom bomb even before President Truman told him of it in late July at the Potsdam Conference. He prepared his troops to invade Manchuria, the area northeast of China from whence came the last dynastic rulers of China, the Manchu. On August 8, 1945, two days after the Hiroshima bomb exploded and one day before the Nagasaki bomb, Soviet troops poured into Manchuria.

Stalin's army overwhelmed the Japanese garrisons in Manchuria and continued fighting southwards despite Japan's informal surrender on August 14. By September 2, when the Japanese foreign minister signed his country's unconditional surrender on the deck of the battleship *USS Missouri*, ending World War II, Stalin had taken the northern half of the Korean Peninsula.

He created in North Korea a tyranny in his own image, risibly named the Democratic People's Republic of Korea, though neither governed by leaders elected by its people nor in any sense of the term a republic. His last-minute land grab gave Stalin a seat at the Asian part of the diplomatic table, one utterly undeserved.

North Korea persisted in its nuclear program for more than a quarter century, even as 1 or 2 million of its people literally starved to death within a society virtually devoid of normal commercial activity. With its ongoing nuclear program—and even while adding uranium enrichment to plutonium extraction as a method of nuclear weapon fuel production—Pyongyang has serially blackmailed the West for assistance. It has been able to do this for two reasons. First, there is the "dying sting" threat. Once a rogue state goes nuclear, any attempt to disarm it risks failing to find and destroy (or otherwise gain control over) all its weapons. A nuclear state like North Korea, if facing imminent extinction, might decide to fire its nuclear weapons and inflict maximum damage before it falls. Second, 11,000 North Korean artillery pieces are pointed at Seoul, the South's capital. Those pieces can lay an estimated minimum of 300,000 shells per hour on the Seoul metropolitan area. In 1994 the Pentagon assessed the risks of a military strike on the North's plutonium reactor, but stood down because artillery could well inflict 100,000 casualties on Seoul's populace.

Thus the options for America and its Asia-Pacific allies in the confrontation with Pyongyang are severely limited. The United States, in particular, has to take care not to undercut its alliance partners by dealing directly with the North—or with the North and China. Given North Korea's consistent violation of every commitment it has ever made, there is no credible reason to believe that any further negotiations will bear fruit. The true significance of diplomatic talks is symbolic. Western countries that break off talks risk alienating portions of their publics. Rogue states cheerfully will use international media outlets to blame the West for rising tensions and gain traction with the idealistic and credulous.

The failure to stop North Korea risks encouraging nuclear proliferation by America's increasingly nervous allies. South Korea, Taiwan, Japan, and Australia each could go nuclear in less than a year, having stocks of nuclear fuel and all the technical expertise needed to rapidly weaponize.

Yesterday's Korea: The Hermit Gets a Bomb

At the beginning of 1950, the normally astute and far-sighted Dean Acheson, the U.S. secretary of state, made a speech in which he excluded South Korea from the reach of America's vital geostrategic interests—issuing, albeit unintentionally, an invitation for conquest. Stalin, the wrong person to whom to send such an invitation, accepted the offer. He gave his puppet, Kim Il-Sung—a former Red Army sniper who would fill his starving country with 34,000 monuments to himself—his express consent to start a war. Another interpretation of events is offered by Henry Kissinger. Because he found no Russian reference to Acheson's speech as the reason Stalin consented to the war option, Kissinger concludes that the culprit was National Security Council memorandum 48/2,[21] adopted December 30, 1949. It excluded Taiwan and South Korea from the sphere of vital American security interests in Asia—those over which America would go to war. Soviet-era files showed references to this document in assessing whether to invade the South.

Less than six months after America's all-but-engraved invitation, on June 25, 1950, Kim Il-Sung's Soviet-equipped troops crossed the 38th parallel and invaded South Korea. The attack caught the United States flat-footed.

Acheson alerted President Truman, at home in Missouri, and the UN Secretary-General, Trygvye Lie, who immediately convened the Security Council. Charged at the end of World War II with the ambitious goal of maintaining international peace, the Security Council faced a major test. Of its five permanent members with the power of veto—the United States, the United Kingdom, France, Nationalist China, and the USSR—one had encouraged North Korea's aggression and would likely veto any effort to help South Korea. Meanwhile, Chiang Kai-Shek's Nationalist China, the loser of China's quarter century of intermittent civil war, had retreated to the island of Taiwan the year before. This left the mainland—and the Korean border—to Mao Zedong's Chinese Communist Party.

Less than 24 hours after the North Korean attack, the Security Council met in New York City to discuss the crisis. In a diplomatic blunder they did not repeat until 2011 (as to intervention in Libya), the Russians boycotted the meeting and lost their chance to veto. President Truman assembled a 16-nation coalition under the auspices of the Unit-

---

21. Established in 1947, the National Security Council is an advisory body that is part of the White House staff. The NSC advises the president and coordinates foreign and defense policy matters within the White House.

ed Nations, and American soldiers soon were fighting what became officially known as a "police action" under the UN aegis.

General Douglas MacArthur—who himself had publicly excluded South Korea from the sphere of vital American interests on March 14, 1949—took back the southern half of the peninsula and decided to press onward, crossing the 38th parallel and eventually reaching the North Korea–China border. MacArthur, who viewed nuclear weapons as a legitimate military option, calculated that a nuclear-armed United States need not fear Chinese intervention. Paul Nitze, then President Truman's national security adviser, saw cable traffic indicating that MacArthur's goal was to invade China, overthrow Mao Zedong, and restore Chiang Kai-Shek to power. Nitze noted that MacArthur had no idea how small the U.S. nuclear arsenal was in 1950.[22]

On October 7 the UN authorized combat operations inside North Korea, as the Truman administration adopted reunification of North and South as a war aim. But catching MacArthur by surprise, the People's Republic of China (like North Korea, neither a true people's government nor a republic) entered the war on October 23. Its confrontation with the UN-led army was the first direct military engagement between American and Communist troops, an initially disastrous one for the Americans. China had 4 million men under arms, dwarfing the UN forces.

It is a common misperception that MacArthur's decision to go to the Yalu River was the reason that China entered the war. In fact, Henry

22. The Natural Resources Council Database (accessed August 21, 2011) estimates that the U.S. stockpile of nuclear weapons was 369 in 1950 and 640 in 1951. These are year-end totals. Only a small fraction of stockpiled weapons was actually deployed and thus ready for use.

In his centennial history of AT&T, *Telephone*, historian John Brooks writes that production of nuclear weapons went into high gear in 1951, after the desperate government had turned to the Bell System for its managerial expertise. Bell Laboratories took over management of the Sandia facility on November 1, 1949, at which time atomic bomb production was minimal. Russia's first A-test supplied urgency. From one new design in 1948, two in 1949, and three in 1951, production increased to many designs starting in 1952. A key factor in speeding up bomb design production was the new availability of computing power.

Kissinger writes, the triggers were American forces becoming engaged in combat on July 5, plus the Seventh Fleet's "neutralizing" the Taiwan Strait, a move designed to preclude a Chinese invasion of Taiwan. For Mao, any American presence in the Korean Peninsula was an intolerable provocation, engendering Chinese historical fears of encirclement.

In Chinese dictator Mao Zedong, MacArthur faced a ruthless adversary utterly indifferent to massive loss of life. In discussing the prospect of a nuclear war, Mao remarked: "We may lose more than 300 million people. So what? War is war." Although America's nuclear weapons status did not deter Chinese aggression, the existence of nuclear weapons was not without strategic weight during the conflict. On August 5, after only six weeks of war, Truman had approved sending 10 B-29s armed with A-bombs to Guam for possible use in Korea. (Only nine planes made it, one having crashed.)

Chinese leaders knew of the American cache of atomic weapons stored on Okinawa. On November 30, 1950—a month after American forces were attacked by Chinese "volunteers" and shortly before the American retreat began—President Truman refused to rule out use of the atomic bomb in Korea. Yet Truman announced just eight days later that he would not use atomic weapons without first consulting with Great Britain, a key partner in the Korean War coalition. Then on April 6, 1951, Truman authorized General Hoyt Vandenberg to be his deputy, and at his discretion to order release of the A-bombs for use in Korea.

In 1951 MacArthur, invited to address Congress after President Truman had fired him, explained: "But once war is forced upon us, there is no other alternative than to apply every available means to bring it to a swift end. War's very object is victory, not prolonged indecision. In war there is no substitute for victory." The Korean War ended two years later, on July 27, 1953, with an armistice but no formal peace treaty. Thus, a technical legal state of war persists to this day.

Kissinger argues that in 1950 the U.S. missed a potentially great strategic opportunity. Had MacArthur not advanced all the way to the

Chinese border, but only 100 miles into North Korea, he would have taken the North's capital, Pyongyang, and also its prime port, Wonsan; and the South would have had a 100-mile wide front to defend against Mao's troops, instead of 400 miles along the Yalu River; the current front along the 38th parallel is 151 miles. Had that line been held it would have placed Seoul out of range of the North's artillery, and thus made South Korea far more secure than it is today. Had the boundary been drawn there in 1945, war would have been less likely.

For his part President Eisenhower, sworn in on January 20, 1953, never intended to use the atomic bomb in the last months of the Korean War, or on any other occasion thereafter. Proof of that came on May 1, 1954, when he rejected a request from France for help in the last days of France's war with the North Vietnamese, telling his National Security Adviser, Robert Cutler:

> I certainly do not think that the atom bomb can be used by the United States unilaterally. You boys must be crazy. We cannot use those awful things against Asians for the second time in less than ten years. My God.

Thus did Eisenhower simultaneously affirm Western values and separate them from Mao's. Later, in 1956, Eisenhower read a report estimating that in a superpower all-out nuclear exchange America would suffer at least 65 percent casualties—some 110 million out of America's then-170 million population—and wrote in his diary: "Even if the United States were 'victorious,' it would literally be a business of digging ourselves out of ashes, starting again."

North Korea's place on the geostrategic chessboard, long underwritten by the former Soviet Union, survived the end of the Cold War and dissolution of the Soviet evil empire, because China stepped in as big-power sponsor of the North. For the first 40 years after the 1953 armistice North Korea was rarely a prime focus of concern. Periodically it would threaten its southern neighbor, and from time to time precipitate border incidents by acts of low-grade aggression.

The U.S., UK, and USSR signed the Treaty on the Non-Proliferation of Nuclear Weapons (known as the Non-Proliferation Treaty or
NPT) in 1970. Grandfathering in the five self-proclaimed nuclear powers (Israel was silent)—the U.S., United Kingdom, France, USSR, and
China—the treaty requires that other countries surrender the right to
build nuclear weapons in return for the right to gain access to and to use
nuclear materials solely for peaceful purposes. The five declared powers are eventually to totally disarm, fulfilling the treaty's final goal of a
nuclear-free world. North Korea signed this treaty in 1985.

But sometime in the early 1980s the North began a nuclear program, and in 1994 this came to the outside world's attention. First, an
International Atomic Energy Agency (IAEA) inspection of Pyongyang's
nuclear power facilities discovered illegally diverted plutonium from the
Yongbyon plant, in violation of the Nonproliferation Treaty. Former
President Jimmy Carter went to Pyongyang on his own to maneuver the
Clinton administration into a negotiation, emerging with a preliminary
bargain that froze alternate diplomatic options. That July, Kim Il-Sung
died and his despot son, Kim Jong-Il, succeeded him as head of state.

In the resultant Agreed Framework accord of October 21, 1994, the
United States agreed to replace the North's graphite-moderated reactors with light-water reactor power plants, intended solely for commercial use. The U.S. hoped to move the North Korean regime towards
peaceful reconciliation with South Korea and finally towards officially
settling the Korean War. The spent fuel from the graphite plants was to
be turned over to the IAEA and not reprocessed to extract plutonium
from the nuclear waste. The U.S. agreed to ship crude oil in sufficient
quantity to replace energy loss from closing the graphite plants, and to
formally assure the North against U.S. nuclear threats or actual use.

The North, for its part, committed to (1) remain within the regulatory regime of the treaty, (2) allow inspections of its nuclear plants
pursuant to the treaty's rules, (3) implement jointly with South Ko-

rea denuclearization of the Korean Peninsula, and (4) participate in a North-South dialogue.

The North, needless to say, did not do any of these things. In October 2002 it told U.S. negotiators that it had a nuclear weapon (the North denies having said this). In December, it expelled inspectors, and two weeks later announced it was withdrawing from the Non-Proliferation Treaty. In August 2003, after the North's withdrawal became effective, the UN Security Council tried to calm the situation by convening six-party talks with the United States, Russia, China, and Japan, in addition to the two Koreas. In October 2006 North Korea exploded its first nuclear weapon in an underground test. The only known route to produce a North Korean bomb was to reprocess spent fuel from a commercial uranium reactor and extract the plutonium by-product. But in May 2010 Pyongyang revealed a previously undisclosed uranium enrichment plant. This plant gave the country a direct route to uranium nuclear bombs, easier to make than plutonium ones.

As former vice president Dick Cheney notes in his memoir, *In My Time*, U.S. intelligence concluded that North Korea likely had begun cooperating with Syria in nuclear matters as early as 1997. This is further evidence that the North had violated its 1994 Agreed Framework deal with the United States. Cheney notes that Pyongyang followed a pattern of making, then breaking deals; of threatening dire consequences if not offered more concessions, then winning more concessions—all without moderating its behavior. At a January 16, 2007, meeting, Cheney reports, American diplomats treated their North Korean counterparts to a lavish dinner and offered concessions. One delegation member summed it up perfectly: "We pulled out all the stops because we wanted to demonstrate that we were serious and sincere." That the United States proceeded this way without asking similar proof of North Korea's sincerity speaks volumes about the effectiveness of the "negotiations."

Attempts to coerce the North into ending its nuclear program—the Security Council's resolutions, the United States' targeting of North

Korean trade and finances (including restrictions on trade in embargoed goods and freezing of key officials' assets)—have all failed. Meanwhile, the North seriously escalated the Korean Peninsula crisis in 2010, sinking a South Korean ship without provocation and shelling a small island controlled by the South, equally without provocation. However, when South Korea responded with military moves and threatened to use force, the North retreated.

The North did not simply pursue its own nuclear program. It entered into the shadowy network set up by renegade Pakistani nuclear scientist Abdul Qadeer Khan, which distributed nuclear technology until Khan's cover was blown and it was shut down. It has closely cooperated with Iran, helped the now defunct Libyan program, and built the partially completed nuclear plant in the Syrian Desert that Israel destroyed on September 6, 2007. Its latest effort, according to some Western intelligence sources, is a venture with Burma to build a nuclear plant to make fuel for either North Korean or Burmese bombs. Burma also reportedly plans to ship yellowcake uranium—a powdered, partially processed uranium ore—to Iran, which has the facilities to further enrich the yellowcake.

Not stopping there, the North is working on its ballistic missiles. In 2009, it fired a test shot in the direction of Hawaii, passing over Japan en route. One North Korean model, the TD-2, reportedly has a planned design range of 9,300 miles when operational. At that distance it could hit anywhere in the 50 states. Recent large-rocket test failures suggest, however, that it could be several years before the U.S. will be in range of the North's operational rocketry.

Today's Korea: The Perils of Regime Change

THE DECEMBER 2011 death of Kim Jong-Il creates new uncertainty about the North's future. The North Korean people surely want change, but they face a heavily armed police state. Western sanctions are riddled with loopholes. Can positive regime change happen?

Third son Kim Jong-Eun, designated "Great Successor," is apparently but a figurehead, with one or more relatives ruling as regents, so to speak. He is young (about 28) and has lived much of his life in Japan—not a plus to Koreans, whose national memory includes a brutal Japanese occupation of the Peninsula from 1910 to 1945 and especially brutal treatment during World War II. Lacking the careful grooming the regime's founding ruler gave his son, Kim Jong-Eun depends upon the loyalty of his Praetorian Guard. The *praetors*—elite guards of the Roman Emperor—were known at times to turn on their ruler. Modern editions can play much the same role; should inner-circle loyalties shift, regime change could come from within. While Kim Jong-Il took steps to purge possibly disloyal elements, there is no assurance that such steps will succeed in protecting his son. With neither his grandfather's charismatic authority nor the training his grandfather gave his father, Kim Jong-Eun is vulnerable. That Kim Jong-Il designated his successor only in September 2010, two years after he had suffered a major debilitating stroke, made his pick less likely to be accepted. Successors in dictatorial regimes must be chosen when the leader in place has full power to command allegiance from potential rivals. Callow youth is moreover hardly likely to be trusted as sole custodian of the nuclear car keys.

For the foreseeable future the successor regime will remain a dictatorship, likely a brutal and dangerous one. The possibility that such a change instead could prove beneficial hinges on whether the new regime eventually surrenders its nuclear program in exchange for better political and economic relations with the West. There is no present indication that such a shift is in the cards.

There is one long-shot possibility from outside: the Chinese can easily topple the regime. China supplies about 90 percent of the North's energy needs. An energy cutoff would sink the state within months. But China has at least two reasons not to proceed this way.

First, China only lightly polices its 843-mile border with North Korea. The fall of Stalin's Frankenstein's monster would leave starving millions fleeing northward across the porous border, entering provinces where the ethnic makeup differs from that in the rest of China, and thus where the risk of increased unrest after a refugee influx is real. The country that built the world's longest and most famous wall (the Great Wall is 4,200 miles, five times longer than its Korean border) could build a security fence, but so far China has not done so.

Second, China benefits from the North being a major thorn in the Western-Asian alliance. North Korea ties up South Korea's military forces, along with some 28,500 American troops. The threat of a war between the two Koreas gives Western planners nightmares, especially with American military strength stretched thin around the globe. A major insurgency in Afghanistan is still winding down, and the United States has only just departed Iraq. Troops brought home will need extensive recuperation and rebuilding before being deployable again.

But these problems are only minor in comparison with the problems a preemptive strike would face. North Korea's conventional military arsenal is in itself a major threat to the South, but its nuclear component confers substantial immunity from preemptive attack. Nor is a nuclear preemptive option against the North feasible. Targeting artillery along the 38th parallel would require ground-burst strikes, throwing up countless tons of intensely radioactive debris—simply unthinkable in light of the close proximity of Seoul's 10 million people, who would be hostage to wind direction at zero hour. In addition, as Eisenhower noted, the political impact of a second nuclear use by a predominantly Caucasian country upon an Asian people would be seismic.

Also at issue would be the huge political impact of breaking a "nuclear taboo" that has existed since the end of World War II. Allied powers in the West have long stressed the "firebreak" between conventional and nuclear use, a concept that makes the decision to use nuclear weapons one far more than a mere continuance of gradual war escalation. The Soviet Union showed no signs of recognizing this firebreak; nor should we assume that emerging powers would. But the United States should not be the nation to disregard it.

According to Herman Kahn, the RAND corporation genius who could both joke and think clearly about "the unthinkable," to break the taboo against using nuclear weapons would be to court unpredictable, potentially horrific dangers. The value of the taboo, Kahn explained in his 1965 book, *On Escalation,* is that, "once war has started no other line of demarcation is at once so clear, so sanctified by convention, so ratified by emotion, so low on the scale of violence, and—perhaps most important of all—so easily defined and understood as the line between not using and using nuclear weapons."

He held that breaching the taboo, especially more than once, would be to weaken it forever:

[T]wo or three uses of nuclear weapons would certainly weaken the nuclear threshold, at least to a degree where it would no longer be a strong barrier to additional uses of nuclear weapons in intense or vital disputes. There would ensue a gradual or precipitate erosion of the current belief ... that the use of nuclear weapons is exceptional or immoral. The feared uncontrolled escalation would be rather more likely to occur at the second, third or later use of nuclear weapons than as a consequence of first use.

He reminded his readers of the situation in which the world has always found itself. He feared that once broken the nuclear taboo might never be restorable:

[I]n a world in which there is no legislature to set new rules, and the only method of changing rules is through a complex and unreliable systems-bargaining process, each side should—other things being equal—be anxious to preserve whatever thresholds there are. This is a counsel of prudence, but a serious one: it is not often possible to restore traditions, customs or conventions that have been shattered. Once they are gone, or weakened, the world may be "permanently" worse off.

Thus, because of the danger to Seoul, two atom bombs dropped on Japan, and the nuclear taboo, the Western powers arrayed against North Korea cannot contemplate nuclear first use—absent absolutely certain intelligence that a nuclear strike from North Korea is imminent. After the WMD intelligence fiasco in Iraq—CIA director George Tenet famously told Congress in 2002 that the continued presence of weapons of mass destruction in Iraq was a "slam dunk"—the standard of proof to convince skeptics has become absolute certitude.

Tomorrow's Korea: The Double-Edged Sword of Reunification

WHAT CHINA fears above all is a reunified Korea allied with the West, sitting on its border. Reunification, the stated goal of South Korean policy, envisions a democratic state living in peace alongside its neighbors. But a prosperous, democratic, unified Korea clearly would incite more unrest in China among those chafing under the rule of aging autocrats.

Even if the most beneficial kind of regime change—reunification—were to come to pass, the problems would be monumental. Combining an advanced industrial society with a stupefyingly backward, desperately poor garrison state run like a concentration camp for more than six decades is a far more difficult task than reunifying West and East Germany—which was still a difficult task, although the latter was not nearly as backward or poor as North Korea.

Thus South Korea itself, as well as China, should fear reunification. The 1990 reuniting of West and East Germany added to West Germany's 61.4 million nearly 17 million people—all of them a generation behind the West Germans in economic development. The 1990 per capita GDP of West Germany was $24,485; the 1990 East German figure was $10,430, making the Western population two and one-third times more productive per year. By 2008, after nearly 2 trillion dollars spent in reunification costs, the combined figure for Germany stood at $35,400, but East Germans continued to lag far behind their Western countrymen. Reuniting the North's 24 million with the South's 49 million people is a

50 percent population add-on for the South (versus 29 percent for West Germany). South Korea's 2010 per capita GDP was $30,200, nearly *17 times* North Korea's 2009 figure of $1,800. The difference is *seven times* bigger than the gap West Germany faced in absorbing the East.

Moreover, while East Germans were not schooled in entrepreneurial ways, they knew some semblance of economic life. North Korea has virtually no civilian sector at all. Its people have no real idea how to function in a modern economy like that of South Korea. Sadly, the Cold War jest about Russian factory workers wondering why, if they work in a baby carriage factory, all they can assemble are machine guns likely describes much of the North Korean economy.

Finally there is massive malnutrition in the North. The estimates of people dying of starvation during Kim Jong-Il's 17-year rule run over 2 million. The surviving population's physical growth is stunted. The public health and economic implications are simply staggering. For the South, the ancient Chinese admonition about being careful what you wish for may prove all too applicable if the South absorbs the primitive Hermit Kingdom.

Only reunification can end the North Korean nuclear threat. Such would prove a security boon to South Korea and the U.S. as principal nuclear guarantor of the South. But reunification might bankrupt the South. At minimum, the economic strain would be severe, with ultimate success by no means guaranteed.

That the Hermit Kingdom has endured for more than sixty years, despite serial aggressive behavior, mass starvation of its people, and development of a rogue nuclear weapon capability, attests anew to the validity of the Fourth Lesson of nuclear-age history: NUCLEAR WEAPONS GIVE NATIONS A "DYING STING" CAPABILITY THAT VIRTUALLY PRECLUDES PREEMPTIVE ACTION AND CONFERS NEAR-TOTAL SURVIVAL INSURANCE.

7.

CHINA: IMPERIAL ASPIRATION AMIDST A SHIFTING NUCLEAR BALANCE

Political power grows out of the barrel of a gun.
—QUOTATIONS FROM CHAIRMAN MAO ZEDONG,
A.K.A. THE LITTLE RED BOOK (1966)

CHINA'S DRIVE TO REGAIN ITS ERSTWHILE POSITION AS A PREEMInent world power is but a generation old. Its effort to regain what it regards as its rightful place begins with supremacy in the western Pacific region. It is this intensely felt national ambition that makes ultimate confrontation between China and the United States, currently the world's preeminent Pacific power, increasingly likely, though strategic accommodation remains a distinct possibility.

Such a confrontation could come as early as the end of this decade. And if it occurs, it could lead—even without either the U.S. or China desiring it—to a regional conflict, possibly involving the use of nuclear weapons. China is not a revolutionary power like Iran, with ambitions to remake the world order. Nor is it a rogue power like North Korea, utterly indifferent to world concerns. It is, as is Russia, a rival: it desires to supplant the U.S. as the most influential world power, starting in Asia, then projecting influence globally. It does not, like Iran, wish to destroy America; China's fortunes are inextricably linked with ours in many ways.

But because China's drive for ascendancy carries risk of a confrontation with the U.S., miscalculation during a crisis could lead to a war neither side desires. What emerges clearly in considering the U.S.-China relationship is the Fifth Lesson of nuclear-age history: THE NUCLEAR BALANCE MATTERS IF ANY PARTY TO A CONFLICT THINKS IT MATTERS, AND THUS ALTERS ITS BEHAVIOR.

China's Half Millennium of Self-Isolation

To SEE the roots of such a regional conflict one must begin with Chinese history, and the Chinese interpretation of it, which emphasized the harmful impact of its intercourse with the U.S. and other Western powers over the choices made by its own dictatorial rulers.

From the early nineteenth century to the beginning of the twentieth, the European powers heaped serial humiliations upon China. The Opium Wars of the mid-nineteenth century led to Britain's thuggish imposition of the degrading, enervating opium trade on the Chinese. The colonial powers pushed around the decaying Manchu Dynasty rulers at will. The crowning episode of this dolorous history was the Boxer Rebellion. Starting in 1898, the "Society of Fists of Righteous Harmony"— "Boxers" armed with guns, martial arts, and ecstatic spirit-possession— aimed to eject foreign powers and secure China's release from imperial domination and exploitation. Allied with the Manchu empress Cixi, they laid siege to the foreign embassies in Beijing for 55 days in 1900. The Eight-Nation Alliance of Japan, Russia, Britain, France, America, Germany, Austria, and Italy crushed the uprising, offering the Manchu Dynasty a settlement in 1901 in which the Chinese paid heavy indemnities to the foreign powers, particularly Russia and Germany.

All this came as the United States was beginning to flex its muscles in the Pacific. U.S. Commodore Matthew Perry's 1853 visit to Tokyo Bay ended Japan's 250-year isolation and opened trade between the U.S. and the Far East. After the U.S. Navy defeated the Spanish Navy at Manila Bay (looking out at the South China Sea), Secretary of State John Hay's 1899 Open Door Policy pressed for wider trade with China, thus increasing pressure on the decaying Manchu Dynasty to open up to all sources of Western trade.

Without in any way down playing the harm caused China by foreign powers, however, internal decisions and events were of immense consequence in retarding the global fortunes of China, arguably of greater impact than external pressures. In 1434 the Ming emperor (why remains unclear) suddenly halted the series of seven massive seagoing explorations begun in 1401, which had taken the great Admiral Zheng He as far as Africa, and dismantled the Chinese fleet. China's fleet featured ships far larger than the tiny vessels in which Christopher Columbus sailed at the end of the century, and superior in many aspects of design and construction. The "treasure ships" of the fleet were purportedly 450 feet long and 180 feet wide—half the length of a World War II aircraft carrier. Unlike the voyages of European explorers, mounted in search of trade and treasure, China's voyages, historian Daniel Boorstin explains, were simply to show the rest of the world how advanced and refined China's civilization was.

Just 26 years after China destroyed its awesome fleet, Prince Henry the Navigator launched the first of Europe's great explorations that eventually would take Christopher Columbus to the New World (in 1492) and Vasco de Gama to India (in 1498). As China began to retreat into its shell—sporadically banning private shipping and coastal settlement—the West began its 500-year rise to global supremacy.

The "Middle Kingdom" disdained "barbarians" from its perch at the center of the earth—China had a gross domestic product in 1820 that was, at 30 percent of world GDP, larger than that of the U.S. and Europe combined. (Chinese GDP was to be the world's largest for 18 of the last 20 centuries.) But its feeble military position gave it few levers in the face of foreign aggression. A China that had stayed among the leaders in military power and influence would have been in a far stronger position to resist the incursions that began a full four centuries after the dismantling of its world's-best fleet.

The next huge event impoverishing China came in the mid-nineteenth century: the 1850–1864 Tai Ping Rebellion, in which ethnic Chinese revolted against the Manchus who had ruled China since 1644. With the aid of the French and British imperial powers, the Manchu overlords prevailed over the Tai Ping rebels, but at a tremendous cost. The crushing of the rebellion, combined with other mid-nineteenth-century turmoil, resulted in a staggering 15 percent decline in China's population between 1850 and 1873, from 410 to 350 million. (Ironically, Tai Ping means "Great Peace.") By comparison, the American Civil War—which ran four years—killed 2 percent of America's population of 30 million, a slightly lower annual percentage loss, but for one-quarter the time span. To recall the impact of the Civil War on American politics to this day suggests the long-term devastation the ethnic enmities of the Tai Ping Rebellion have caused.

In the twentieth century, China suffered several other signal catastrophes—two internal, and one from its neighbor—each of which, alone, would have derailed any normal nation's progress. First was Japan's 1937 attack against a China riven by civil strife. The subsequent eight years' war was marked by extreme Japanese brutality, including the infamous Rape of Nanking that killed some 300,000 people in six weeks, and the use of outlawed chemical and bacteriological weapons. Estimates place China's casualties at 35 million, with 20 million dead and 15 million wounded. Even in a country with over 500 million people, the toll astonishes.

The second and third mega-events both came to China courtesy of one man: the self-styled "Great Helmsman," Mao Zedong, who marched into Beijing on October 1, 1949, bringing doctrinaire Marxist economics with him. In 1958 he began the grand agricultural collectivization experiment called the "Great Leap Forward." It lasted just shy of three years and claimed—through famine, oppression, and suicide—as many as 40 million lives. In a country with about 650 million in 1960, *the Great Leap thus killed one of every 16 Chinese.* For America today the equivalent figure would be over 20 million deaths. Compared to this stupefying mass murder due to ideological fervor, the 2 to 2.5 million toll from two Chinese civil wars (1928–1937 and 1946–1950) is almost lost in the shuffle.

Add the four percent death toll of the Sino-Japanese War to the six percent death toll of the Great Leap Forward, and China lost roughly ten percent of its population in the two catastrophes. Now throw in the third mega-catastrophe, Mao's 1966–1969 Cultural Revolution. In an effort to impose socialist norms, Mao purged academics, sent urban populations en masse to remote rural areas, and interred dissidents in "reeducation" camps. The result was an estimated 1 to 20 million dead.

Over 120 years, the loss of some 150 million lives through the serial carnages of the nineteenth-century conflicts, Sino-Japanese War, Great Leap Forward, and Cultural Revolution—coupled with China's half millennium retreat from world trade—surely had a vastly greater impact on China's geopolitical fortunes than the much-trumpeted Western imperial humiliations of the self-weakened country.

Today China has about 1.3 billion people. Its GDP in purchasing power parity (GDP adjusted for relative currency value) is roughly two-thirds that for the U.S., but spread over more than four times as many people. This means that once China's GDP is adjusted both for purchasing power parity and per capita, it is perhaps one-sixth of America's. One question lingers: Where would China rank today had it not suffered the series of catastrophes that began in 1434?

China's Resurgence

CHINA'S FALL began with a retreat from the world, and its resurgence began when it opened to the United States in 1971, ending the American government's refusal to recognize Mao's regime. Later that year, the Communist mainland replaced Nationalist China as permanent member of the UN Security Council—and as sole internationally recognized representative of the Chinese people. President Nixon went to China early in 1972.

Mao's China appallingly underperformed economically and wreaked havoc socially and politically. But Deng Xiaoping succeeded him after his death in 1976, and in 1979 opened China's trade to the world. Thus ended 545 years of first isolation and then reluctant limited participation in global commerce.

China's economic power can be overstated—it is well shy of the power of the U.S. economy, despite the latter's recent severe trials. Yet its sheer size makes it a force to be contended with. China is America's second-largest trading partner, holding a one-sixth share of American international trade. It holds trillions in U.S. securities and dollar-denominated reserves. It is not for nothing that in 2011 Chinese president Hu Jintao questioned the dollar's status as global reserve currency.

China is in the midst of a huge push to upgrade its military. It is building modern nuclear submarines and even an aircraft carrier—a warship only the U.S., Russia, Great Britain, and France have ever constructed. Its anti-ship missiles include models that can carry nuclear warheads a thousand miles. American air power based on carriers (or on Taiwan, often called by strategists America's largest aircraft carrier) is a major part of America's ability to project power across the Pacific. Neutralize these assets, and China's ability to dominate the western Pacific becomes a strategic reality. (Neither South Korea nor Japan would be likely to allow its territory or equipment to be used in a U.S.-China conflict, lest China target it directly.)

Most impressive of all is China's 2010 rollout of a stealth combat aircraft prototype, the J-20. Its configuration and size suggest a medium-range fighter-bomber that can target Taiwan or American naval ships (rather than an interceptor, which would shoot down bombers, or a pure air superiority fighter, designed to shoot down other fighters). The J-20 will be markedly inferior to the American F-22, the world's only operational fifth-generation combat aircraft. But that is cold comfort to allied strategic planners, since America ended its F-22 production run at one-quarter the number originally planned. The Pentagon's assessment was that China would not have a stealth fighter before the 2020s. The 2011 test flight of the J-20 suggests China is on a faster track. This comes as America's F-35, the future stealth fighter of choice for the U.S., continues to encounter technical problems that have pushed back its likely operational status into the mid-teens. Were China to deploy a sufficient number of J-20s, it could prevail over superior American quality in a major regional conflict.

Underpinning China's growing military machine is its nuclear arsenal. After American nuclear threats during the Korean War, the August 1954 first crisis over offshore islands Quemoy and Matsu, and then the American mutual defense treaty with Taiwan in December of 1954, Mao gave the go-ahead on January 15, 1955, to start China's nuclear program. Although secrets stolen from the Manhattan Project may have played a role in China's program, China early on developed a formidable in-country team of nuclear scientists. Russia also transferred technology and know-how, from 1954 through 1958 (the year of the second crisis over Quemoy and Matsu, when the United States threatened to use tactical nuclear weapons in a fight with China over its shelling of the islands). Henry Kissinger writes that a key motive behind Khrushchev's decision to transfer nuclear technology to China was so that Moscow would not feel obligated to back China in event of another major confrontation with the United States.

But in 1959 Khrushchev decided to halt Russian assistance, unnerved, Kissinger writes, by Mao Zedong's nuclear brinkmanship over Quemoy and Matsu. Weapons designers Thomas C. Reed and Danny Stillman write in *The Nuclear Express* that the Russians, upon deciding to slow China's march to nuclear weapon status, even supplied the Chinese with deliberately false data in order to sabotage their progress. But many of China's top scientists studied in other countries, including the United States, and then brought their knowledge back to China.

In 1961, Mao declared he would build nuclear weapons "even if the Chinese had to pawn their trousers." He was expressing a sentiment the West would hear often, from various leaders, in the years that followed. In starting Pakistan's quest for the bomb, Prime Minster Zulfikar Ali Bhutto famously said that his people would "eat grass," if need be, to go nuclear. Starving millions did not deflect North Korea from its program.

Put simply, no police state has qualms about pursuing weapons amidst its population's destitution, even literal starvation.

Mao rejected Russia as patron and ally in 1962, sundering China's alliance with Russia after Khrushchev stopped supporting his nuclear program. The next year, President Kennedy approached the Russians about seeking to stop China's program, possibly by nuclear means. Despite their split with China, the Russians refused to join the U.S. effort, as the superpower rivalry then was at its height.

Like Russia's 1949 test of a clone of the Nagasaki bomb, China's first atomic bomb test, in October 1964, caught international observers completely by surprise. Stillman and Reed note that from the outset, China's instrumentation was "sophisticated in the extreme." This test weapon— a uranium bomb—was four times more efficient in its explosive yield-to-weight ratio than was the Hiroshima uranium device. Danny Stillman visited China's Lop Nor test facility in 1998, and the astonished weapons designer found it to be seven times larger than the U.S. test site in Nevada. In 1966 China tested its first H-bomb.

This test strained relations between the Russians and Chinese, and in 1969, the USSR apparently considered launching a nuclear first strike over border clashes with China. Chinese documents shown Henry Kissinger verify that Russia and China were so close to nuclear war that Chinese ruler Mao Zedong ordered government officials to disperse from Beijing in the summer of 1969. The Soviets deployed over a million troops along the Russo-Chinese border. Mid-level officials asked counterparts in various chancelleries around the globe how their governments would react to a Soviet nuclear first strike aimed at China's nuclear installations.

Aware of these signals, senior American officials publicly voiced grave concern that war might break out, in an effort to signal that the U.S. would not support such a move. Fear of a potential full-scale Sino-Soviet war was a key trigger that induced the newly nuclear-armed Mao to seek formal diplomatic relations with the U.S., and led to the famous 1972 handshake with Nixon.

In his penetrating diplomatic history *On China*, Kissinger assesses Mao's overall posture on nuclear weapons. Mao grasped that in the 1950s America's nuclear arsenal was far too small to destroy China, with its vast geographic area and 600 million people. Kissinger is not convinced that Mao was serious about being willing to sacrifice 300 million people in a nuclear war, but clearly Mao had a far greater willingness to tolerate mass casualties than did America and its Western allies. Mao told Kissinger in October 1975 that American public opinion would prevent the U.S. from using nuclear weapons to help overmatched NATO conventional forces ward off a Soviet attack. In the same conversation Mao rejected Kissinger's statement that the U.S. would use nuclear weapons to defend its Mideast ally Egypt.

China's current leaders seem to share Mao's view of the western Pacific as an area within China's sphere of influence, and thus can be expected to vigorously pursue a diplomatic and military strategy of seeking to supplant America as the predominant western Pacific power. It has embarked on an impressive military program, in apparent pursuit of just that objective.

Avoiding a Collision in the Pacific

CHINA'S BOMB total is not known—estimates range from the low 200s to the high 400s. Recent scholarship, however, suggests that China may have several times that many nuclear weapons. It has built an "Underground Great Wall," an incredible 3,000 miles of huge tunnels through which mobile missiles are transported. And its huge military buildup in pursuit of dominance in the western Pacific would be far more formidable if joined with a large, modern nuclear arsenal.

The International Panel on Fissile Materials, a 16-country group comprising states with and without nuclear weapons, estimated in its 2011 report that China has 16 tons of weapons-grade uranium. According to nuclear proliferation expert Henry Sokolski, that is enough to make 1,000 first-generation uranium bombs and 3,000 advanced-design uranium bombs. China also is believed to possess an estimated 1.8 tons of plutonium—enough to make 450 crude plutonium bombs and 900 advanced plutonium bombs.[23] Sokolski points out that U.S. intelligence estimates of 240 Chinese nuclear warheads make four questionable assumptions: 1. no missile reloads, 2. no tactical nuclear weapons, 3. no nuclear-armed cruise missiles, and 4. all warheads are high-yield thermonuclear weapons. These assumptions run contrary to Russian and U.S. force deployments. Both Russia and the U.S. have deployed tactical nuclear weapons, nuclear-armed cruise missiles, and warheads across a range of low to high yields. Russia has long deployed silo reload capabilities for its land-based missiles.

These factors, and their implications, seem to have escaped the Obama administration, which aims to "set an example" for other nations by reducing the number of U.S. weapons. Lost in the fog of this thinking is that *the fewer weapons the U.S. retains, the greater incentive China has to increase its arsenal.* Far from setting an example, a shrinking stockpile of American weapons increases the payoff of each bomb deployed by a rival power seeking to displace American influence, or by an enemy power seeking to destroy America outright. In a strategic environment where America has 10,000 nuclear weapons, whether China has 100, or 500—or even 1,000—probably counts for little. A China armed with far fewer nuclear weapons than America is less likely to risk a major confrontation over Taiwanese independence, or intervene in a second full-scale Korean war.

But suppose—as "minimum deterrence" proponents advocate—the U.S. was to go down to, say, 300 weapons—the number floated as an option by the Obama administration. China's weapons would instantly become more valuable on the strategic chessboard. A China armed with 1,000 nuclear weapons facing an America with only 300 would likely act

---

23. As explained below, a "bomb" is either a military "weapon" or a terrorist "device."

far more boldly—and much more boldly if the U.S. were to go all the way to nuclear zero. Even a China having nuclear parity with the United States would be tempted to act more boldly in a crisis than it is prepared to do today.

History supports this view. During the Cuban Missile Crisis the U.S. had 2,962 deliverable nuclear bombs and warheads on 15-minute alert status, dwarfing Russia's arsenal. Khrushchev was bluffing, and the Americans knew it. During the diplomatic negotiations after the crisis, Soviet special envoy Vasily V. Kuznetsov told his American counterpart, John J. McCloy: "You will never do this to us again." He meant that Washington would never again have the overwhelming nuclear superiority to force Moscow to back down. But that nuclear balance was to change by the time of the next big crisis.

The 1973 U.S.-Soviet confrontation during the Yom Kippur War offers an even closer historical parallel than the Cuban Missile Crisis to a possible future collision between the U.S. and China in the western Pacific.

Egyptian leader Anwar Sadat ordered his troops to invade the Israeli-occupied Sinai Desert on October 6, 1973, the Jewish Day of Atonement. Israeli leaders declined to mobilize despite signs of preparation for war, never imagining that Egypt would choose the holiest day of the Jewish calendar to launch its attack. As Egyptian troops breached Israel's southwestern defensive lines at the Suez Canal and sped across the Sinai Peninsula on Yom Kippur, Syria struck Israel's northeast, the rocky farmland of the Golan Heights. Israel hastily rushed troops to both fronts, but a country with little geographic strategic depth had to initially yield ground it could hardly afford to cede. The war turned around when Israeli general Ariel Sharon—in a move reminiscent of maneuvers by General George S. Patton—crossed the Suez Canal and encircled Egyptian troops.

At this point the Soviet Union began playing aggressive diplomatic and military cards. It had only been in 1972 that Sadat, in a surprise move, had expelled the Soviets from Egypt, and the Soviets saw the war as an opportunity to retrieve their geopolitical position in the Mideast as superpower sponsor of all radical Arab powers. They therefore sought to airlift Soviet commandos into the region.[24]

Oil-supply leverage became a major factor in responses to the conflict. To punish the U.S. and divide it from its pro-Arab allies, the Saudis declared an oil embargo. Only Portugal permitted American planes to land (on the Azores) and only Greece and Italy offered port facilities to the U.S. Navy. The remaining European allies even refused overflights of U.S. military planes. Worse, NATO member Turkey allowed *Russian* planes to overfly supplies en route to the Mideast.

The Russians had narrowed most of the yawning numerical gap between their nuclear forces and America's, and perhaps their senior commanders were thinking of Kuznetsov's promise during the post–Missile Crisis diplomatic negotiations. In the Mediterranean, Soviet ships confronted American ships—including, in an historical irony, the nuclear-powered aircraft carrier *John F. Kennedy*—while the war approached its climax on land.

The U.S. Sixth Fleet and the Soviet Mediterranean Fleet were in close proximity, the Soviets shadowing the U.S. Sixth Fleet with more ships than usual for several days. Admiral Daniel Murphy sent a message to headquarters at the end of one tense day: "Both fleets were obviously in a high readiness posture for whatever might come next, although it appeared that neither fleet knew exactly what that meant."

The American goal was, in significant part, to keep Soviet troops out of the Mideast, thus limiting Soviet influence in the region. Soviet leader Leonid Brezhnev proposed a joint U.S.-Soviet deployment to share the

---

24. In their 2007 book *Foxbats Over Dimona: The Soviets' Nuclear Gamble in the Six-Day War,* authors Isabella Ginor and Gideon Remez offer evidence that during the June 1967 conflict the Soviets planned to invade Israel and bomb Israel's nuclear reactor at Dimona, where Israel makes nuclear fuel for its weapons. But Israel's rapid destruction of Egyptian, Syrian, and Jordanian forces preempted Soviet plans. The Soviets moved faster in 1973, so it took a U.S. threat to stop them.

policing of cease fire lines, and in an urgent letter warned President Nixon: "In the event that the U.S. rejects this proposal, we should have to consider unilateral actions."

The situation was serious enough for President Nixon to put U.S. forces on DEFCON 3 alert status shortly after he received Brezhnev's harsh note. (DEFCON—defense condition—3 is a midrange alert status, with DEFCON 1 meaning imminent war; DEFCON 2 was declared for the Strategic Air Command during the Cuban Missile Crisis, the highest alert level since the system was inaugurated in 1959.) "You know we were close to a nuclear confrontation this morning," President Nixon told Henry Kissinger (then serving as both National Security Adviser and Secretary of State), late on October 25, 1973, the day that the cease fire went into effect.

In the end, the Russians decided not to challenge America directly by trying to land troops in the Mideast, but that month of October had been full of dangerous moments. Nuclear use, though unlikely, was not impossible in the crucible of an intense crisis engaging the fundamental foreign policy interests of both superpowers. Fortunately, in the 11 years since the Cuban Missile Crisis, the two superpowers had established instant communications and worked out protocols for managing crises. Though nothing is foolproof, such safeguards lessened the chances of a crisis escalating to a shooting war.

In the Yom Kippur War's Mediterranean crisis phase, a Soviet decision to abort a Mideast airlift avoided possible shoot down of one or more Soviet transports. A shoot down would have triggered the first direct conflict between the superpowers since Berlin in 1961—and this time a shooting war instead of a tense standoff.

Militarily, China eventually may become strong enough to believe that in a shooting war close to home it would prevail. Such a calculation would partly be based upon a perception that America would, under the circumstances, pull its forces back. Were Chinese nuclear forces at numerical parity—or even, as was the case with Russia in 1973, nearing strategic nuclear parity—China might decide to take the chance. The Yom Kippur War model suggests that aggressive moves by covetous powers become bolder as military power grows. Nuclear weapons are regarded by such powers as trump cards. We may not see it that way, but they do. Resolute action may stave off catastrophe, as with Cuba in 1962. But of course there is no cosmic law that our luck will always hold.

Military confrontation is a traditional tool by which dictators distract domestic opposition. China's autocratic leaders, though often temperamentally risk averse, might choose military confrontation if China faces one or more acute internal crises. Gaming the future always entails speculation. "Black swans"—low-probability but especially grave contingencies—have a habit of suddenly materializing. Call it Murphy's Law of High-Stakes Geopolitics.

On top of growing military leverage, how much economic leverage does China wield, given its huge trade with America and massive U.S. securities and dollar currency holdings? China expert Gordon Chang points out that because China runs a trade deficit with the rest of its partners, its huge surplus with America makes it vulnerable to the consequences of a sharp drop in trade between the countries. In 2011 China ran a record $295.5 billion trade surplus with the U.S., up 90 percent from 2008. Its 2011 surplus was 190.5 percent of its overall net trade surplus, as it ran a deficit with the rest of the world. This factor limits U.S. vulnerability to blackmail by Beijing. Further, huge debtors enjoy a perverse leverage over creditors that small debtors lack. Thus the old adage: "Owe the bank a million, you have a problem. Owe the bank a billion, the bank has a problem." Add three zeroes for country debtors and the same principle can apply: Owe a country a billion, the debtor has a problem. Owe a trillion, the creditor has a problem. Put simply, huge creditors simply cannot afford to have a mega-debtor go under. If Uncle Sam goes belly up, China's export-driven economy sells far fewer goods.

China does, however, derive considerable leverage from producing more than 90 percent of the world's rare-earth elements. This odd series of metallic elements lies just above uranium and plutonium on the periodic table. Half bear names that relate to their discovery in the Swedish island village of Ytterby. They are essential for numerous high-technology applications in computers and specialized equipment. China's near-monopoly gives it strategic leverage in a future crisis. Though deposits of such elements exist outside China, their extraction elsewhere is more costly. China accepts a level of extractive pollution that Western countries will not tolerate. Were China to put an embargo on rare-earth elements, economies dependent on them—every modern one—would be harmed as rare-earth element prices rose. Their production elsewhere, pollution notwithstanding, would become essential to the West.

America and Australia are now investing in alternate, though higher-cost, supply sources. And because Beijing inflated prices and thus encouraged alternative investment, rare-earth commodity prices are sharply down from their 2010 peaks. Yet because Beijing is potentially in a monopoly position, importing states have strong incentives to continue building alternate facilities, and firms have a strong incentive to seek substitute products where technically feasible.

China and the U.S. are rivals, not mortal enemies. China has too many interests that intersect with American ones to permit real enmity. But China's yearning to restore the position of power it enjoyed six centuries ago is real. Failure to recognize this and deter Chinese pressure in the western Pacific could lead to a war no one wants. And any shooting war between nuclear powers inherently carries risks of unintended escalation to a nuclear exchange.

Chinese leaders are rational actors, most of whom would not encourage escalation where risk of nuclear conflict exists. But it would take only one bold leader willing to run greater risks than his predecessors—who believed, as Soviet boss Leonid Brezhnev did, that the "correlation of forces" is shifting decisively in his country's favor—to focus China's immense energies on triumph in the western Pacific. The Soviet leadership had often been cautious, wary of the immense power of the

United States. Yet Leonid Brezhnev was opportunistically tempted in 1973 to take a chance in the Mideast, even with the memory of Nikita Khrushchev's failed 1962 gamble over Cuba—which Khrushchev, unlike Brezhnev, had planned in advance. Conceivably a Chinese leader might be similarly tempted.

Consider the warning that Lieutenant General Xiong Guang issued to the Clinton administration during the 1996 crisis in the Taiwan Strait, after the U.S. sent the Seventh Fleet into the strait to warn against Chinese military action. The Chinese were trying to intimidate Taiwan during its presidential election campaign, during which the question of seeking permanent independence from the mainland took center stage. The general expressed doubt that America would trade Los Angeles to avenge a Chinese nuclear strike against Taipei.

Herman Kahn warned that strategic gambles by national leaders have been frequent in history: "We tend to forget that throughout history many decision-makers were delighted to accept 'double or nothing' tactics if the odds looked sufficiently favorable." Shifts in the nuclear balance can matter, if—as proved the case in 1973—they change how leaders behave during a crisis. Perceived vulnerability, whether in force structure, force deployment, or will to prevail, can tempt an adversary to take a reckless, potentially catastrophic gamble. U.S. policy, particularly regarding its nuclear arsenal, must focus on making sure China *always* considers the odds of such a gamble hugely unfavorable.

At the root of miscalculation in a Yom Kippur type of confrontation is the seductive trap of mirror imaging: believing an adversary assesses the nuclear balance the same way, and regards nuclear arsenals as only for last-ditch deterrence purposes. We can avoid such mistakes if we keep in mind that assessments of the nuclear balance are not intellectual exercises in philosophical pure reason. They turn rather on prosaic everyday factors—specifically, what adversaries think, which can be quite different from what America thinks.

This is especially true as to revolutionary and rogue powers, but also can apply to rivals. It forms the basis for the Fifth Lesson of nuclear-age history: The nuclear balance matters if any party to a conflict thinks it matters, and thus alters its behavior.

Interlude: A Thin Line between Peaceful and Military Nuclear Capability

The September 11 attacks brought to global public consciousness the fear that rogue nations might use or transfer nuclear weapons to terrorist groups, and that terrorist groups could themselves make a nuclear bomb. The first fear has far more foundation than does the second.

The good news is that it is very hard to make bombs; the bad news is that it is not impossible. Let's look at uranium and plutonium and see why this is so.

Uranium and Fission

All uranium atoms have 92 positively charged protons at their nucleus (with 92 almost weightless negatively charged electrons orbiting that nucleus). But all uranium atoms are not the same. Though there is no way to tell one from another chemically, different isotopes of uranium have different numbers of neutrons, the proton's neutrally-charged companion. Most atoms in a vein of natural uranium ore have 146 neutrons (for a total mass, protons plus neutrons, of 238). But a very few of them—less than 1 percent—have three fewer neutrons, and this "U-235" is extremely important for our story.

U-238 is fissionable, but not readily so. U-235, on the other hand, is fissile—its nucleus is easily split, creating two smaller nuclei, but more importantly, releasing energy plus two or three free neutrons. In a small enough space, those neutrons can each enter other uranium nuclei, splitting them to release more energy and neutrons, and so on, in a chain reaction. A critical mass of uranium-235—roughly 100–115 pounds in metal form and smaller than a soccer ball—will start a self-sustaining chain reaction on its own. If the same object is sufficiently compressed, it can become supercritical, dangerously increasing the rate of the chain reaction.

But the vast majority of uranium ore is U-238 and cannot emit neutrons rapidly enough to support a chain reaction. The solution for anyone seeking that reaction is for high-speed centrifuges to spin uranium that has been processed from ore to a powdered form called yellowcake, so that the marginally heavier U-238 molecules move to the bottom of the spinning cylinder, separating out from the precious, infinitesimally lighter U-235 that stays on top of the centrifuge. This process—of removing U-238 from U-235—is called uranium enrichment.

In order to generate an uncontrolled, supercritical chain reaction in uranium (a nuclear explosion), a would-be bomb maker must: 1. sufficiently enrich the uranium, 2. compress it ultra-rapidly into a supercritical mass, and 3. set it in an explosion-friendly physical shape.

For example, the Hiroshima bomb used uranium enriched to 80 percent U-235. Within the bomb, half the uranium was fired—by a miniature version of a World War II warship's naval gun—into the other half, causing a supercritical mass to form and detonate in microseconds (millionths of a second).

Supercritical chain reactions in uranium typically at least double with each fission. Think of the parable about the king who offers a peasant serial doublings of wheat stalks on a chessboard—one stalk of wheat on square one, two on square two, etc. Before reaching 64 doublings the kingdom goes broke; the final squares are never covered, as there is no wheat left with which to do so. The difference in the nuclear case is that doublings go past the 64th square—to the 84th. Exponential progressions look like the famed "hockey stick" curve, one that accelerates at an ever-increasing rate with each doubling.

In the 84-doubling sequence not uncommon in a fission weapon, after 70 doublings only 1 percent of the energy will have been released. After 80 doublings only 5 percent will have been released, and after 83 doublings only 50 percent. North Korea's early tests fell far short of the Hiroshima bomb in yield. A primitive weapon releases far less energy than a well-engineered one.

Commercial fuel is not sufficiently enriched to attain supercriticality, but failure to control the reaction or a failure in the cooling system can lead to an uncontrolled chain reaction and a "meltdown" in which the reactor fuel in the core overheats and melts into the floor. This is a highly radioactive event, and highly dangerous to those exposed to the intense doses of radiation (few in number, if the containment vessel protecting the reactor remains intact). A runaway chain reaction cannot generate a nuclear explosion but in water-cooled designs can cause a hydrogen explosion from the reaction of steam with core-surrounding cladding, as happened in the 1986 Chernobyl nuclear accident in Ukraine and at several reactors in the March 2011 nuclear meltdowns in Japan.

The Simple Arithmetic of Nuclear Proliferation

At first glance it seems a huge leap for a nuclear proliferator state to get from 3.5 percent, low-enriched, commercial uranium fuel for a power reactor all the way up to 93 percent, highly enriched, weapons-grade uranium fuel for a bomb. But simple arithmetic gives a counterintuitive result: *commercial-grade fuel is perilously close to weapons-grade fuel.*

Recall that significantly less than 1 percent of mined uranium is fissile—the less-desirable isotope makes up 139 out of every 140 uranium atoms. Commercial-grade fuel requires a minimum of 3.5 percent U-235, which means that 1 out of every 28 atoms must be U-235. Thus, for every 139 U-238 atoms, 112 of them must be removed. Now you can run a commercial nuclear reactor. To appreciate how close you already are to having nuclear weapons fuel, at this stage *you have done 80 percent of the isotopic separation needed to build a full weapons-grade bomb of the kind in the U.S. arsenal.*

The next important step is 20 percent enriched fuel—four atoms of U-238 for every U-235 atom—that can run a medical research reactor.

Reaching this step requires taking away a total of 135 out of the 139 U-238 atoms that originally accompanied each atom of U-235. At this stage, *you have done 97 percent of the isotopic separation work needed to make a full weapons-grade nuclear bomb.*

Put another way:

+ **Natural Uranium Ore.** In nature, there are 139 atoms of non-fissile U-238 for every one atom of fissile U-235.

+ **Commercial Nuclear Reactor Fuel.** Remove 112 U-238 atoms, leaving 27 U-238 atoms and 1 U-235 atom. This makes 3.5 percent enriched uranium.

+ **Medical Research Reactor Fuel.** Remove 23 U-238 atoms, leaving 4 U-238 atoms and 1 U-235 atom. This makes 20 percent enriched uranium.

+ **Weapons Grade Uranium.** Remove 4 U-238 atoms, leaving 1 U-235 atom. This leaves 1 U-235 atom, 100 percent enriched uranium. U.S. weapons grade uranium fuel is 93.5 percent enriched uranium.

Such separation work is by far the hardest part of the total work needed to assemble a nuclear device. One conservative estimate for Iran in early 2012 showed how enrichment times accelerate with higher levels of enrichment:

+ Start with 14,000 kilograms (15 tons) of natural unenriched uranium ore.

+ It takes 331 days to enrich to 1,400 kilograms of 3.5 percent commercial-grade fuel.

+ It takes 37 days to enrich the 1,400 kilograms of commercial fuel to make 116 kilograms of 19.75 percent medical research–grade fuel.

+ It takes only 8 days to enrich 116 kilograms of 19.75 percent enriched fuel to make 15 kilograms (33 pounds) of 90 percent enriched uranium for weapons-grade fuel, enough to make a single Hiroshima-size bomb.

Other expert calculations assume a six-fold progression through the three stages, but let us assume ten-fold, to be conservative. In round figures apply two rules of thumb:

+ **10-10-10** for the three tenfold stages of material shrinkage listed above, from uranium ore to medical-grade to weapons-grade.

+ **11-1-1** for the three time periods: 11 months for commercial reactor fuel, then 1 month more for medical reactor fuel for research, then 1 week for weapons-grade fuel for a bomb.

Thankfully, putting together the vast, industrial-scale infrastructure needed to enrich uranium via these methods is extremely difficult; no terrorist is going to do this in a garage or on a back lawn with presently available methods.

To these 11-1-1 and 10-10-10 rounding rules noted above we can add one more number each, to complete the sequences. Adding another 1 to the first sequence tells us that once all components needed for a bomb are in place it takes about one day to assemble them into an operational bomb. Adding a final 10 to the 10-10-10 sequence captures the difference between the minimum amount needed for *a crude uranium bomb* a terrorist can use (roughly 60 kilograms—the amount used in the Hiroshima bomb), and the minimum amount needed for *a highly sophisticated plutonium bomb* that a first-rank nuclear state can use to optimize its nuclear arsenal (roughly 6 kilograms).

Some specialized reactors run on fuel enriched beyond commercial grade. Nuclear-powered submarines and surface ships actually run on weapons-grade fuel, because they must provide very high power in a very small space. Such fuel, if diverted, could make fuel for a nuclear weapon. (A submarine or surface-ship reactor, though running on weapons-grade fuel, cannot generate a nuclear explosion, for want of the necessary physical configuration and compression.)

Now the bad—*very* bad—news: You do not need a full U.S. weapons-grade enriched bomb to get a nuclear explosion. *Less than 20 percent enriched uranium suffices.* In 1962 the United States tested a uranium bomb at its Nevada underground test site, and obtained a nuclear explosion with fuel enriched somewhat short of 20 percent (the exact figure remains classified). It was, in the parlance, suboptimal. If detonated in a city, such a bomb would cause less devastation and kill fewer people than a full U.S.-grade enriched bomb. But its destructive power could still be immense. The 1,336-pound (two-thirds of a ton) conventional truck bomb that exploded in a garage of the World Trade Center in 1993, had it been more carefully placed a few of yards away, would have toppled one tower into the other, killing many tens of thousands. The much bigger 1995 Oklahoma City bomb, which destroyed a large federal building and killed 168 people, used two and a half tons of conventional explosive. A "puny" A-bomb (like that detonated in North Korea's 2006 plutonium test, for example) could easily be equivalent to a few hundred tons of high explosive.

Plutonium, Fission, and Fusion

So much for uranium, the fuel of choice for proliferators. But what about plutonium? Plutonium barely exists naturally—the young American nuclear chemist, Glenn Seaborg, found it by making it from U-238,[25] and every day more accumulates in the spent fuel collected from nuclear reactors. The U-238 in nuclear reactors will catch a neutron, and instead of fissioning, become an extremely unstable atom with 239 neutrons and protons. In a series of transmutations (changes in chemical composition), this U-239 naturally becomes fissile plutonium-239, the most common modern fuel for nuclear weapons.

---

25. This was in 1941, 11 years after the discovery of Pluto, and over a century and a half after a German apothecary and chemist, Martin Klaproth, discovered uranium in 1786 and named it after the planet Uranus, newly discovered that same year. U-238 decays—transmutes itself by releasing energy—in 23 minutes to neptunium-239, named after the planet Neptune; Np-239 then decays in 2.3 days to plutonium, P-239, named after Pluto.

How a reactor is designed and run determines how readily and conveniently it creates that plutonium-239. The reactor the Iraqis built in the late 1970s was to run on weapons-grade fuel and was made to maximize plutonium production. Israel understood this perfectly well, and hence destroyed it in 1981, before it was fueled, to avoid scattering radioactive material for miles upon bombing it. Proliferation expert Henry Sokolski writes that a light-water reactor rated at a tenth the size of a commercial plant can be run so as to produce dozens of pounds of plutonium in a year. This is more than enough to fuel several nuclear bombs.

Because a reactor can produce plutonium, a terrorist might think of stealing nuclear waste to obtain it. But plutonium is just one component of some forms of nuclear waste, and most plutonium in nuclear waste is not fissile. The longer the newly made Pu-239 sits in a reactor, the longer the neutron-capture process goes on, producing heavier, less controllable, forms of plutonium.[26] These soon outnumber fissile Pu-239, and are hard to separate from it. This problem can be avoided by replacing fuel rods before they absorb too many neutrons.

Weapons-grade plutonium is a more efficient bomb fuel than weapons-grade uranium, and thus offers more explosive power per pound. The actual amount of plutonium converted into energy released by plutonium-239 nuclei that fissioned inside the core of the Nagasaki bomb was about one gram—one-third the weight of a penny. Einstein's $E = mc^2$ equation explains this. The released mass (m) is infinitesimally small—less than a thousandth of the mass that fissioned, as most of what fissioned careened around in search of other nuclei to split; the remainder was converted into and released as kinetic, thermal, and radiation energy. But the "c^2" represents the square of the free-space speed of light in kilometers per second, a huge multiplier that explains the vast energy liberated from an infinitesimally tiny nucleus. Applying this to every atom whose nucleus is split in a nuclear detonation yields a vast release of energy in various forms.

26. These include plutonium isotopes Pu-240, Pu-241, and Pu-242. The complex physics and chemistry of how they interact with Pu-239 are beyond this book's scope.

But Pu-239 is much harder to make into a nuclear bomb. It must be placed in a special configuration, far more complex than that for a uranium bomb. The Manhattan Project scientists were so certain a gun-trigger design would work with uranium that they did not even test it—uranium was in short supply and they needed it to create plutonium for the Trinity test and then the Nagasaki bomb.

A plutonium detonation occurs in about a nanosecond (a billionth of a second), a thousand times faster than a uranium detonation. To make sure as much of the plutonium as possible fissioned, the Trinity and Nagasaki bombs were "implosion" devices. A complicated arrangement of 32 symmetrically spaced conventional explosives surrounded those bombs' plutonium cores. Thirty-two lenses converted the shock waves from convex to concave, to compress the plutonium core extremely rapidly and symmetrically. A timing discrepancy among the implosion lenses of one-millionth of a second reduces symmetry and can create a dud; a timing discrepancy of 10 microseconds—10 millionths of a second—is enough to create a partial dud. In essence, plutonium bombs require super-speed, super-symmetry, and super-small compression.

For a nuclear weapons state seeking to use missiles to carry nuclear warheads, plutonium is the fuel of choice, because it provides more yield per pound, and thus is more suitable for small warheads. It is very unlikely that terrorists would be able to build a plutonium fission device on their own, due to the extreme sophistication involved.

And it is even harder to master the deep subtleties of a hydrogen bomb. This requires a conventional explosive to trigger an atomic bomb, whose radiated thermal energy then compresses the plutonium core so rapidly and compactly as to fuse hydrogen atoms and generate a thermonuclear explosion.

Terrorist Bombs and Military Bombs

In the parlance of nuclear proliferation there are three significant nouns commonly added after the adjective nuclear: "capability," "device," and "weapon." A *nuclear capability* means the ability to make a nuclear device or weapon. A *nuclear device* is the kind of weapon we have been worrying about since 9/11, a bomb too large to be delivered by traditional military means, but which can be put into a van, truck, or shipping container. A *nuclear weapon* denotes a bomb compact and light enough to fit into a missile warhead, or the business end of a bomb or artillery shell.

A nuclear device is the kind of crude weapon a terrorist would use. Once the necessary amount of enriched uranium is in hand, a crude terror device can be easily assembled. How much is needed is design dependent: for the simplest device more is needed than for a sophisticated bomb. A nuclear weapon is the kind of bomb we worried about during the Cold War and is what proliferators like North Korea and Iran are working on. What remains for them is to achieve the requisite miniaturization required to place a nuclear bomb inside a missile nose cone.

But a nuclear state need not have a weapon to aid terrorists. A device will suffice. For terrorists, a uranium-fueled atom bomb with a gun trigger is the preferred route. But even this is not duck soup for an individual, and not just any design suffices.[27] The damage a crude nuclear device—in proliferation parlance, an "Improvised Nuclear Device" or IND—can inflict if detonated in the nation's capital was recently assessed by the Federal Emergency Management Agency. A 10-kiloton blast—about 70 percent of the explosive yield of the Hiroshima bomb—would extinguish nearly all human life and obliterate most structures within a half-mile. Glass would be shattered out to 10 miles, radioactive dust would spread at least 20 miles. Severe structural damage would reach 1.5 miles from ground zero, with many casualties due to blast shockwave and thermal effects. Out to nearly 5 miles there would be light structural damage, plus numerous casualties from radioactive particulate fallout.

27. In 1976 an American high school student named John Aristotle Phillips sketched a design that Manhattan Project physicist Freeman Dyson judged *might possibly* work. Of course design alone does not a weapon make. As a kid I liked to sketch F-104 Starfighters, which I thought the coolest looking supersonic aircraft (dubbed the "Flying Coffin," it was not always thought so cool by pilots who had to fly it). But sketching it did not mean I could build one.

In all, the study estimated 45,000 fatalities and 323,000 injured. This would overwhelm local medical facilities. (The 9/11 jetliner explosions yielded about 1/10 of a kiloton.)

To go nuclear using currently available methods, a terrorist organization needs the help of a state.[28] This is especially true of the so-called "suitcase nuke" attack scenario. A truly man-portable nuclear weapon requires highly advanced miniaturization of components, to make it compact and light enough to be carried. Russia developed an atomic demolition munition (ADM) the size of a footlocker, not designed to be carried by one person. Tales of Russian "loose nukes" floating around are dubious; and they likely wouldn't work now anyway, as their core elements decay over time and eventually are no longer fissile.

With this understanding of what is required to build a nuclear weapon, and a sense of the thin line between development of commercial nuclear power and the development of weapons, we turn to the Indian subcontinent.

---

28. A technique called laser enrichment may someday enable creation of bomb fuel with far smaller-scale infrastructure.

8.

PAKISTAN AND INDIA: WHO GUARDS THE GUARDIANS?

The second myth is that nuclear weapons are OK in the hands of
'the good guys' and not OK in the hands of 'the bad guys.' We need
to have a system that is not based on subjective considerations.
MUHAMMAD EL-BARADEI, UNITED NATIONS CHIEF NUCLEAR INSPECTOR, 2006

FORTY YEARS AGO THERE WERE FIVE ACKNOWLEDGED NUCLEAR powers, all formally committed to evolving international nonproliferation legal norms: the U.S., the Soviet Union, Great Britain, France, and China. A sixth, Israel, was already an undeclared nuclear club member. The 1970s were to begin extending nuclear weapons proliferation into the Third World, with two countries—India and Pakistan—eager to take President Eisenhower's Atoms for Peace program and produce Atoms for War (at minimum, to deter each other) as well. This chapter traces the acquisition of nuclear technology by India and Pakistan, and in so doing offers the Sixth Lesson of nuclear-age history: CIVILIAN NUCLEAR POWER INHERENTLY CONFERS MILITARY CAPABILITY.

What is historically significant are two facts. First, India and Pakistan crossed the nuclear weapon threshold by equivalent routes, via proximity of civilian nuclear power generation to military nuclear deployment. India had a program for 10 years for commercial use only, until it perceived that China had come to imperil India's national security. Pakistan saw in India's bomb a mortal threat to its security. Both began their nuclear power programs in 1955, the year that the U.S. declassified atomic data under Atoms for Peace. Coincidentally, it was also the year the historic conference of underdeveloped nations was held in Bandung, Indonesia, where India assumed a leading diplomatic role.

But then their paths sharply diverged. India has never aided nuclear proliferation anywhere. In contrast, Pakistan's top nuclear scientist established a clandestine network aiding nuclear proliferation efforts in several rogue states.

"The Buddha Smiles"

IN 1947, while his nephew Phillip was marrying the future Queen of England, Lord Louis Mountbatten presided over the fateful Partition of India into two states—with the new Sunni Muslim state of Pakistan flanking Hindu India on both sides. Millions died in the subsequent mass murder and mayhem. The Kashmir and Jammu states were divided, with most of Muslim-majority Kashmir taken into India by a Hindu prince. This partition enraged parties on both sides of the border, triggering wars in 1947, 1965, and 1999. Kashmir today remains a white-hot flashpoint.[29]

The two nations also fought in 1971—a war that politically sundered East Pakistan from West, and left hundreds of thousands dead in the newly created state of Bangladesh. Two and a half years later, on May 18, 1974, Indian nuclear scientists sent India's leaders a message: "The Buddha smiles." The occasion was the detonation of what India called a "peaceful nuclear explosion."

With no bright line dividing commercial nuclear power and weapons-grade bombs, some didn't find India's blast so peaceful. Foremost among those concerned with the blast was Pakistan, India's mortal adversary. Abdul Qadeer Khan was a Pakistani metallurgist working at the Amsterdam facilities of the UN's International Atomic Energy Agency at the time of the Smiling Buddha test. In collusion with the Pakistani government he copied thousands of pages of highly confidential material on how to build enrichment facilities to extract nuclear fuel for a bomb, and spirited them back to Pakistan. Following in India's footsteps, Khan

---

29. It took delicate diplomacy conducted in 2001 and 2002 by the George W. Bush administration to defuse tensions a decade ago, but the world's first nuclear war between two countries may well be ignited by Kashmir.

took full advantage of Eisenhower's ill-starred generosity, pursuant to which the United Nations had created the agency—the International Atomic Energy Agency—for which he worked.

The idea of bringing the bounty of atomic power to the world's poor reflected the idealism of postwar decolonization. U.S. ambassador to the United Nations Arthur Goldberg—a former Supreme Court Justice and a renowned expert on international law—said in 1968 that it would be "unthinkable" and "unacceptable" to decide that nonnuclear countries, "must do without the benefits of this extremely promising energy source, nuclear power—simply because we lack an agreed means to safeguard that power for peace."[30]

The astonishing fact that he made this statement during a debate on the Nonproliferation Treaty gives a sense of how deeply rooted was the idealism behind Atoms for Peace. In the idealist view, nuclear countries were *morally obligated to place their civilizations at risk* so as to provide poor countries with access to a source of electric power that then was thought to be cheaper than likely alternatives.

This may explain why Atoms for Peace ignored a strong caveat concerning civilian nuclear fuel articulated in America's first, landmark report on atomic energy:

> We have concluded unanimously that there is no prospect of security against atomic warfare in a system of international agreements to outlaw such weapons controlled only by a system which relies on inspection and similar police-like methods.[31]

The proliferation genie released by Atoms for Peace reached the Third World only gradually. India began a plutonium production program in 1956 and succeeded in separating plutonium in a reprocessing plant by 1965—even before it had an operational commercial reactor.

---

30. Incredibly, Goldberg's statement was made to urge UN adoption of the Nonproliferation Treaty.
31. The report—the Acheson-Lilienthal Report on the International Control of Atomic Energy, issued March 14, 1946—recommended international enforcement, by armed force if necessary, to prevent diversion of materials to noncivilian use.

The adoption of the Nonproliferation Treaty in 1968—an attempt to restrict nuclear weapons to the U.S., UK, USSR, France, and China—formalized growing Western concern about nuclear proliferation. India and Pakistan have never ratified the treaty (neither has Israel) for the same reason: preserving a nuclear military option.

Only four years after the treaty came into force, India would conduct its surprise nuclear explosion. As Roberta Wohlstetter explains in her landmark 1976 study, *The Buddha Smiles*:

> The Indian case... illustrates... that a government can, without overtly proclaiming that it is going to make bombs (and while it says and possibly even means the opposite), undertake a succession of programs that progressively reduce the amount of time needed to make nuclear explosives, when and if it decides on that course.

A high-altitude 1962 border conflict between India and China, China's 1964 A-test, its 1966 H-test, and its nuclear-capable ballistic missile test later that year (a 750-mile range missile, indicating sophisticated small-warhead design), along with the wars with Pakistan, drove India's decision to seek nuclear weapon status. According to Wohlstetter, American officials could have seen India's program—which generated bomb fuel by means of a reactor built by Canada—as a risk ever since 1966. Instead, the Americans consistently accepted India's representations of lack of intent to weaponize, and simply discounted contrary evidence, even though India was not then an ally of the U.S. Officially a member of the "nonaligned" bloc at the UN, India in fact sided with the Soviet Union far more often than with America.

Then came the 1971 Indo-Pakistan war, during which prominent muckraking columnist Jack Anderson revealed confidential memos showing that the Nixon administration had decided to "tilt" its foreign policy towards Pakistan. Unlike India, Pakistan was a member of two now-defunct U.S.-sponsored alliances: the Southeast Asia Treaty Organization and the Central—i.e., Middle East—Treaty Organization). This "tilt" gave India another push in the nuclear direction.

Wohlstetter notes that the Indian case shows how even a purely civilian program can enable a country to come within *days* of fueling a bomb, and an explosion is hardly the end of the resulting problems:

> We oversimplify when we say that "the damage is done" as soon as a country explodes a nuclear device. Much more damage will be done if we do nothing to make the country regret its action. This is especially true if there has been a violation of the sense of an agreement.

She adds that India conveniently interpreted its nuclear technology agreements with the U.S. and Canada as enabling it to detonate a "peaceful" nuclear explosive. India's leaders knew full well that neither the U.S. nor Canada drew any distinction between military and "peaceful" nuclear bombs. Further, a sovereign country cannot forever renounce a military nuclear capability, because inherent in the lawful power of a sovereign is the right of a leader to change course. Thus, *as with strategic arms agreements, civilian nuclear technology agreements are nearly impossible to enforce against deliberate violators.* In 2012 India successfully tested its first nuclear-capable ballistic missile. Its ICBM range enables India to target Beijing and Shanghai.

Compounding the problem in the Indian case is that diplomats argue, as the State Department did even after India's 1974 explosion, that to crack down would rupture the diplomatic relationship and thus deprive the U.S. of leverage. Yet every time a nation defies international pressure and goes nuclear, the case for stopping nuclear proliferation by treaty suffers. Had prior efforts to stop India, Pakistan, and South Africa proven successful, they would collectively have served as powerful evidence that the treaty is fully effective. (Israel crossed the threshold before the Nonproliferation Treaty became law.)

The Islamic Bomb

PAKISTAN'S CIVILIAN nuclear program under the aegis of Atoms for Peace began in 1955. It turned military after traumatic losses in two wars with India. Once India severed East from West Pakistan in 1971 and exploded its bomb in 1974, attaining nuclear status was deemed by Pakistani leaders a matter of existential survival. In 1975 Abdul Qadeer Khan stole voluminous technical information from a UN facility in the Netherlands, where he worked in a field office of the International Atomic Energy Agency. His clandestine coup greatly accelerated Pakistan's drive towards nuclear-club membership. At one point Dutch authorities asked the CIA if they should arrest Khan for suspicious activities. The CIA declined, preferring to continue surveillance, and Khan thus evaded capture.

But American foreign policy also played a role in Pakistan's nuclear quest. The United States was well aware that Pakistan was pursuing nuclear weapon status. In 1979 the U.S. halted military and economic aid to Pakistan, citing its nuclear program. It ended the embargo in 1982, due to growing reliance on Pakistan to support the Afghan resistance. In late 1984 the CIA learned that Khan had written Pakistan's president informing him that Pakistan now had enough enriched uranium to make a bomb. The Chinese, meanwhile, provided Pakistan with a 1966 design of an atomic warhead. Anxious about proliferation, in 1985 Congress passed the Pressler Amendment (named after a Republican senator), which called for suspending aid to proliferators unless the president certified it was in the national interest for aid to continue. In Pakistan's case, the president did so certify, and aid continued in the 1980s. The U.S. sent vital equipment to the Afghan *mujaheddin* (holy warriors) that proved essential to the defeat of the Soviet invaders and their puppet rulers.[32] The strategic imperative of helping the Afghans bleed the Soviets trumped proliferation concerns. Beyond doubt, the nine-year Afghan War's brutal toll on Soviet troops hastened the end of the Cold War.

The calculation of the Reagan administration and allied conservative Democrats—ignoring proliferation was acceptable if it helped to

---

32. The film *Charlie Wilson's War* (2007) is better by far than most Hollywood films purporting to recount history accurately. It does, however, understate the strong support given Texas Democratic congressman Charles Wilson by senior Reagan administration officials, perhaps most notably by CIA director William Casey.

bring down the USSR—was defensible, provided Pakistan could be induced not to proliferate. But Pakistan's nuclear ascension itself was by then a practical reality, and it had every intention of proliferating. In 1987 Khan publicly admitted that Pakistan already had developed a nuclear weapon capability.

What was not defensible, by contrast, was what happened after the end of the Afghan War in February 1989. The nuclear horses thus had already left the nonproliferation barn. Pakistan had done everything short of exploding an actual nuclear device. However, in 1990 the George H. W. Bush administration teamed up with liberals in both parties in Congress to try to close the proverbial barn door and punish Pakistan for its pursuit of nuclear weapons. President Bush declined to certify that Pakistan was complying with nuclear proliferation safeguards, making the country ineligible to receive military aid from the U.S. And despite harboring several million Afghan War refugees, Pakistan also received no economic aid.

On May 13, 1998, India openly tested a weaponized nuclear warhead. Its Hindu nationalist government made no attempt to call this explosion "peaceful." Two weeks later, Pakistan showed how close it had been to full nuclear-weapons-club membership, responding with its own tests, one of which employed five separate devices.

The fecklessness of belatedly attempting to stop the unstoppable became abundantly clear after September 11, 2001. The terrorist attacks galvanized America into action against al-Qaeda, and Pakistan's cooperation was vital in this latest Afghan campaign. But blowback in the form of intense anti-U.S. feeling, most notably in the Pakistani intelligence agency (the Directorate for Inter-Services Intelligence, often just called "ISI"), meant Pakistani cooperation was not forthcoming.

It took Deputy Secretary of State Richard Armitage's famed dire threat ("We will bomb you back into the Stone Age!") to get Pakistan to even partially side with America again, after the 9/11 attacks. But Pakistan's support has never been wholehearted, with elements in the ISI playing on the other side, and the government either unable or unwilling to purge them. When Khan revealed his nuclear proliferation distribution network in 2004, his countrymen treated him as a national hero.

In 2005 President George W. Bush lifted military aid restrictions on Pakistan (and on India, but those restrictions had been imposed by President Clinton after India's 1998 nuclear tests), but the damage had been done, and more was to follow. The 2011 plan to kill Osama bin Laden in a U.S. raid deep inside Pakistan had to be kept secret from Pakistani officials for fear that Islamists within the Pakistan government would tip off bin Laden. (An August 1998 U.S. cruise missile strike aimed at bin Laden's Afghan base camp was compromised when Pakistani officials alerted him; bin Laden fled before the missiles completed their two-hour flight to reach their target.) Al-Qaeda sought to acquire Pakistani nuclear bombs from 1998 to 2001. American pressure after the 9/11 attacks short-circuited bin Laden's plans. The inevitable price of the 2011 raid—though clearly worth paying to get bin Laden— was a further erosion of U.S.-Pakistani relations.

The prospect that an Islamist regime could overthrow Pakistan's current government—and thus gain control over Pakistan's burgeoning nuclear arsenal—has reportedly induced the U.S. to develop contingency plans for taking out or seizing Pakistan's arsenal. But unless the U.S. knows exactly where all Pakistan's bombs are, such a mission would have no realistic prospect of complete success. Uncertainty is a huge deterrent to U.S. preemptive action.

Danger in Safety, Safety in Danger

October 27, 1970 was not a happy day for authorities in Orlando, Florida. Disney World's opening was a year away, and they found themselves facing a nuclear bomb threat: pay $1 million and guarantee an escort out of the country, or else a hydrogen bomb would be detonated. Looking at a drawing of the device neither the FBI nor the Atomic Energy Commission would give assurance that it could not work. With the city on the verge of paying up, local police found out that the threat was a hoax perpetrated by a 14-year-old high school student.

Nuclear knowledge is now widely enough distributed so as to answer publicly most of the questions scientists had to answer during the Manhattan Project. According to a top U.S. bomb designer, seven of the eight problems scientists then had to solve are now answered in the public record. The eighth element, the right people, the scientists themselves supplied. Even by the time of India's first bomb (1974), all the complex scientific questions were answered. A nation that could assemble the right personnel and gain access to the right resources would see the rest follow in due course.

As nuclear bomb knowledge spreads in states that might harbor terrorists, we find two fundamental truths about private parties and nuclear proliferation. First: *Private parties cannot now create nuclear fuel, nor will they be able to for some time to come.* The process of becoming nuclear capable has taken most states more than a decade. Private parties have vastly inferior resources and thus will not manage the huge set of complex tasks needed to produce nuclear fuel from scratch anytime soon. Neither the uranium nor the plutonium route can be taken without industrial-scale processes—thousands of supersonic-speed centrifuges for uranium isotopic separation, or a nuclear reactor and chemical nuclear-waste-separation system for plutonium—to create the fuel.

But there is ongoing research into laser enrichment technology. If its boosters prove correct as to its potential, it may make it possible to enrich uranium without full-size industrial facilities. Proponents claim that facilities one-quarter the size of current plants could be used, making their activities harder to monitor by satellite surveillance. However, even a quarter-size facility is well beyond realistic scale achievable in home garages and backyards.

But any smaller-scale enrichment innovation would be a boon to aspiring nuclear terrorists and their state suppliers. Pending before the Nuclear Regulatory Commission is an application to build a Global Laser Enrichment plant, filed by a consortium of GTE, Japan's Hitachi, and Cameco, a Canadian uranium mining company. The NRC is expected to rule on the application in 2013.[33]

The second truth follows from the first: *There are only three common ways private parties can obtain nuclear fuel: sale, gift, or theft.*[34] The first two ways involve a nuclear state as voluntary sponsor; the third way involves a state's gross negligence. No matter how sophisticated, all terror groups seeking to obtain and use nuclear weapons need state help. An effective counter-proliferation policy must target nuclear states as top priority.

But what of the "dirty bomb" or "radiological device"—a conventional explosive laced with radioactive material? Couldn't a private party throw that together without help from a state? Because a nuclear explosion is not involved, a potential dirty-bomb maker can select elements that are both easier to obtain and have more rapid rates of decay than uranium or plutonium.

Every radioactive element has an average half-life, the time span in which half its atoms will decay. An atom decays when its nucleus spontaneously emits radiation (often transmuting the atom into a new element). Early researchers named this nuclear radiation using the first three letters of the Greek alphabet: 1. *alpha particles*, composed of two protons and two neutrons, are the most dangerous form of radiation, but can be stopped by a sheet of paper or clothing; 2. *beta particles*, electrons, which can be stopped by a sheet of aluminum; and 3. *gamma rays*, which cause radiation sickness and are only attenuated by a much thicker shield, like a centimeter of lead.[35]

---

33. The plant would use an Australian laser enrichment technology called SILEX (separation of isotopes by laser excitation).

34. More esoteric transactions—lease, sale/leaseback—can be executed. But for practical purposes of policy analysis the three basic types of transactions suffice.

35. Note that two of the most dangerous forms of radiation do not come from radioactive decay: free neutrons, the most harmful and hard-to-stop form of nuclear radiation, come from fission or fusion, and X-rays come from high-energy electrons—including those of beta rays "braking" as they pass near a heavy nucleus.

The more gradually a radioactive substance decays, the less lethal the instant exposure. Fissile Pu-239 has a half-life of 24 *thousand* years, and this is one of the reasons that it is more dangerous than U-235, with a 700-*million*-year half-life, or U-238, with a half-life of 4.5 *billion* years— roughly the age of the Earth and one-third the age of the universe.

The bad news is that fashioning a dirty bomb is a relatively simple exercise. Simply lace a conventional explosive with radioactive material. A terrorist would want to use something that releases its radiation more rapidly than fissile plutonium, and is thus more quickly harmful. The half-life of cesium-137 and strontium-90 is a couple of decades, while cobalt-60's is just over five years, and Iodine-131's is eight days. Unfortunate for terrorists, but good news for their intended victims, is that one can't turn radioactivity on and off. Dirty bombs are thus more hazardous to the bomb maker than to their targets (except those killed by the explosion itself). As physicist Richard Muller writes in *Physics for Future Presidents* (2008):

> [A]ll dirty bombs have the same problem: intense radioactivity from the unexploded bomb that can kill the terrorists, and diluted radioactivity after it is exploded that drops below the threshold for radiation illness, unless the area attacked is very small.

Evidence of the hazards of working in close proximity to nuclear material was provided by the deaths of two Manhattan Project scientists who accidentally generated a supercritical mass by momentarily merging two spheres of beryllium around a plutonium core, unleashing a lethal dosage of radioactive neutrons.

That no radiological device has been detonated despite the many radioactive materials available (cesium-137, for example, is found all over the world in unsecured or poorly secured medical facilities) suggests that it remains too dangerous for too little payoff.

So much for a stateless entity making a radioactive bomb. What about just stealing a real nuclear bomb? Top nuclear security experts believe that Pakistan has fairly sophisticated devices to prevent unauthorized use of its arsenal (as does India). Even without terrorists, a situation with two hostile, nuclear-armed, countries facing each other is extremely dangerous. Is the solution for America, a veteran of such situations since 1949 and a pioneer of nuclear safety devices since the late 1950s, to share command safeguards with nuclear weapons states, as it did with the Soviet Union after the Cuban Missile Crisis?

At first blush it may seem like a good idea. But sharing with the former Soviet Union was a safer proposition than sharing with a highly unstable country like Pakistan, an Islamic rogue state. It was safer still than sharing with a pure rogue state like North Korea or a revolutionary Islamic regime like Iran. At issue is what may occur if a nuclear device is stolen, sold, or given away.

Consider if Pakistan, after an Islamist takeover, transfers a weakly secured device to al-Qaeda (or if Iran transfers a weapon to Hezbollah). Perhaps, as a demonstration of terrorist power, the transferring state decides to target Germany. But instead—because of some action the French government takes at the time, like banning headscarves—the terror group manages to compromise the inadequately secured device and detonates it in France.

From the viewpoint of the terrorist group, which has no physical return address of consequence (caves in Yemen, let us say), either country works fine. But the state sponsor has a return address—and thus detonation in nuclear-armed France versus in nonnuclear Germany can prove a fatal difference.

Better safety devices enable a sponsor state to transfer a weapon with greater assurance that it will be used at a time and place of its choosing, rather than used at the discretion of the terrorist group. Hostile powers that sponsor terrorism would thus highly value command and control safeguards not only for safer handling, but also for offensive strategic reasons.

For the United States, the Indo-Pakistani case illustrates the extreme difficulty of pursuing a purist anti-proliferation policy given other compelling foreign policy goals. For countries we assist, it shows that determined states can conceal clandestine nuclear programs. What it shows above all is that *whether a recipient of nuclear material initially intends to fashion a nuclear bomb is irrelevant, because the decision to pursue a bomb can be made at any time.* Once on the cusp of nuclear-club membership—i.e., in possession of a sufficient quantity of highly enriched nuclear material to make a bomb—a nuclear-capable state can cross the weaponization threshold rapidly enough to preclude preventive action.

India and Pakistan each have perhaps a hundred nuclear warheads pointed at each other. These provide, besides potential for nuclear catastrophe on the Asian subcontinent, stark evidence of the futility of the United States trying to induce others to reduce their arsenals or end their nuclear programs by "setting an example." Both countries deploy a varied arsenal of nuclear-capable missiles and aircraft.

America's 1967 decision to freeze its nuclear warhead numbers and then begin reducing them—and its 1992 unilateral decision to end qualitative improvements—has not in any way encouraged India or Pakistan to do the same. To the contrary, Pakistan aims to double its already sizeable nuclear arsenal within a few years.

There is one more major proliferation frontier for Pakistan, which it may soon enter: the Gulf Arab states. Pakistan would reap a huge petrodollar bonanza if Arab states, fearing a nuclear Iran, decide to purchase bombs from the world's only Islamic nuclear power. This prospect is far from theoretical.

Saudi Arabia's former intelligence chief, Prince Turki al-Feisal, warned several times in late 2011 that if Iran acquires a nuclear weapon capability his country would have no choice but to go nuclear. Saudi petrodollars funded Pakistan's renegade nuclear program. As it takes most countries that pursue nuclear weapons a decade or more to achieve them—Iran's post-Shah program began in 1984—the Saudis will not wait. They will purchase bombs over a barrel (of oil, literally). They need not, initially, rely on Pakistani missiles, as setting up a ballistic missile infrastructure requires years. Instead, they can take bombs and put them on the F-15 and F-16 fighter-bombers that they have purchased from the U.S.

It is important to keep in mind what America calls "nuclear capable" for America's inventory. It denotes making necessary hardware modifications to physically carry specific nuclear hardware, plus putting in a set of intricate command and control protocols with sophisticated control hardware and software. From a safety standpoint this is valuable. But a nation at grave national risk may pass on these. Put bombs in a jet aircraft, then authorize the pilot to release them and—presto. A Rolls-Royce nuclear capability standard is preferable, but hardly an absolute necessity. When facing imminent obliteration a nuclear Chevy will do.

Saudi Arabia is not the only Gulf Arab state that can afford to pay for bombs and has F-15s and F-16s to carry them: add Kuwait and Qatar. That a nuclear Iran will create a Mideast arms race is a matter of indifference to Pakistan. Its growing ties with Iran are a contrary foreign policy consideration, but enough petrodollars can swing the balance of national interest for Pakistan in favor of aiding the Arab Gulf states over closer ties with Iran. For Pakistan, an obsessive focus on India remains the top priority. As the two sides carry out ballistic missile tests of growing sophistication, the need for funds will dictate Pakistan's choice.

Thus the Sixth Lesson of nuclear-age history—CIVILIAN NUCLEAR POWER INHERENTLY CONFERS MILITARY CAPABILITY—expresses the tragedy of postwar Western technology-transfer idealism. And in the ultimate irony, the Nonproliferation Treaty was adopted when already there was conclusive evidence that the distance between civilian use established as a legal right under the NPT was perilously close to nuclear weapons production prohibited by the same treaty.

9.

IRAQ: THE INFORMATION
LIMITS OF INTELLIGENCE

*The danger is not that we shall read the signals and indicators with
too little skill; the danger is in a poverty of expectations—a routine
obsession with a few dangers that may be familiar rather than likely.*

THOMAS C. SCHELLING, FOREWORD TO PEARL HARBOR:
WARNING AND DECISION BY ROBERTA WOHLSTETTER (1962)

THE FAILURE OF THE 2003 IRAQI FREEDOM COALITION TO FIND
stockpiles of weapons of mass destruction in Iraq and earlier strategic intelligence failures of similarly grand proportion, offer the Seventh
Lesson of nuclear-age history: INTELLIGENCE CANNOT RELIABLY PREDICT WHEN CLOSED SOCIETIES GO NUCLEAR.

The difficulty of predicting when a given country will cross the
threshold of nuclear weapons capability is one of two big challenges for
intelligence collection and analysis. The other is how to head off a surprise attack—especially devastating if a nuclear strike. We begin by considering the latter challenge.

Strategic Surprise

THE NOW infamous U.S. Iraq intelligence disaster was actually not
America's first. That occurred in 1991, and played a key role in shaping
attitudes that led to the second. But to put both of these events in context, we begin in 1932.

Strategist Andrew Krepinevich tells the story of a little-known but
chilling incident—an air raid on U.S. Navy ships in Pearl Harbor exactly two months short of a decade before the famous Japanese attack.
After a week of sailing north of shipping lanes, using rain squalls for visual shelter in the stormy Pacific, a fleet of carriers launched 150 planes
to strike Pearl Harbor's Battleship Row and nearby Hickam Field on

Sunday, February 7, 1932. Appearing over the target areas at dawn, the planes caught soldiers and sailors by complete surprise.

That day the carriers were American, under the command of Rear Admiral Harry Yarnell, and the bombs dropped into Hawaiian waters were flour bags. An army-navy war game called Grand Joint Exercise 4 was being conducted, and the air mission was Raid Plan No. 1.

Were the army and navy so alarmed at the results of the war game and Admiral Yarnell's brilliant masterstroke that they began serious preparations to guard Pearl Harbor against possible Japanese surprise attack? Not quite.

The defenders claimed that there had been minimal damage to Hickam Field, and that they had found and sunk the carriers. Further, they complained that the attack was illegal under rules of the war game, because it had taken place on a Sunday. The postgame assessment shows how little they learned about the ability of sea-based air power to attack Pearl:

> It is doubtful if air attacks can be launched against Oahu in the face of strong defensive aviation without subjecting the attacking carriers to the danger of material damage and consequent great loss in the attack[ing] air force.

The Japanese thought otherwise, and December 7, 1941, was not their day of rest, as Americans found out to their chagrin. Not only did the Japanese launch their unsporting attack on a Sunday, they did so while their diplomats were ostensibly negotiating in Washington, D.C. As Admiral Yarnell had pretended to bomb in 1932, Japan's diplomats pretended to negotiate—while Vice Admiral Nagumo's real fleet launched real dive bombers and torpedo bombers. A total of 2,403 Americans lost their lives that day, with 1,103 killed when a bomb struck the powder magazine of the battleship *Arizona*. The Japanese lost 55 airmen.

At the time, some had foresight. Admiral Chester Nimitz, who commanded the Pacific Fleet during World War II, said: "Nothing that happened in the Pacific was strange or unexpected." But men of his vision were few. More typical was the attitude of the Secretary of War, Henry Stimson. He had closed down the State Department's "Black Chamber" (code-breaker) section in 1929, saying: "Gentlemen do not read each other's mail." America's adversaries were unfortunately not gentlemen.

Krepinevich, from whose superb book *Seven Deadly Scenarios* the above account was taken, discusses two other real-life war games in which there was comparably foolish disregard for lessons logically derivable from the outcomes—another from the period between the world wars and one in the twenty-first century Persian Gulf.

Krepinevich's interwar example is from 1937, when the German army played a massive land war game on an open plain just outside of Paris near Versailles, featuring two mock German Panzer (armored) divisions attacking conventional troops. The tank corps overwhelmed the far less mobile defenders, ending a planned seven-day exercise in four days. The results of the war game inspired Hitler's *blitzkrieg* through the Ardennes forests of Belgium, which pierced a gap in France's then-vaunted Maginot Line. The defensive fortifications did not cover the Ardennes approaches because the French thought the forest impassable by armored divisions.

Not only had the tanks already demonstrated their superiority on French soil, the plan of attack had, too. In attacking France via Belgium, Germany repeated its 1914 foot-marching offensive, although in different tactical form. The Allies obtained Prussian strategist Count Alfred von Schlieffen's war plan shortly after its December 1905 creation. Yet the Germans surprised France in 1914 and again in 1940.

The twenty-first-century example is from the summer of 2002, when the U.S. military conducted its Millennium Challenge 02 war game in the Persian Gulf. Set five years in the future, the war game pitted the Red Team, playing Iran, against the Blue Team, playing the U.S. Thinking creatively, Red Team captain Lieutenant General Paul van Riper used motorcycle messengers to communicate between land forces and coordinated his small boats for a "swarm" attack on the U.S. fleet via morning prayer broadcasts from (fictional) minaret towers. His ships used commercially available Swedish camouflage and signaled each other via light rather than radio. Van Riper's Red ships sank or damaged 16 warships, including an aircraft carrier.

What did the war game umpires do? They instantly refloated the Blue fleet and forced the Red Team to relocate its anti-aircraft assets out of range for taking out the attacking Blue aircraft. This time Team Blue prevailed. What had begun as an unscripted exercise became heavily scripted after the bad guys declined to play by the rules anticipated by the good guys.

In war games as well as in the real world, creative enemies can identify and exploit defensive weakness to launch a successful surprise attack.[36] Let us return to the case of Pearl Harbor, an attack brilliantly analyzed by Roberta Wohlstetter in her Bancroft Prize–winning study, *Pearl Harbor: Warning and Decision* (1962). The catastrophic intelligence failure leading to what FDR called "a date that will live in infamy," she writes, was the result of failings deeply rooted in human nature and organizational structure. First, intelligence officers were unable to separate the wheat from the chaff—in communications parlance, signals from background noise. Second, given ambiguous information susceptible of multiple good faith interpretations, the natural human impulse is to choose an interpretation consonant with one's own instinctive preferences and values.

---

36. History is full of examples of strategic surprises, in which enemies launch successful attacks by acting contrary to expectation: noteworthy instances in the twentieth century, besides Pearl Harbor, include Japan's destruction of Russia's fleet in the 1904 Russo-Japanese War, Israel's preemptive strike on Egyptian airfields at the start of the 1967 Six-Day War, and Egypt's attack to start the 1973 Yom Kippur War. In the run-up to the June 22, 1941, massive Nazi invasion of Russia, Stalin ignored warnings from Winston Churchill, choosing instead to trust Hitler, with whom he had made a nonaggression pact one week before Hitler started World War II. Hitler's pivot to the Eastern Front caught Russia completely by surprise.

Further compounding such failures was the inability of recipients of strategically decisive information to place that information in the hands of President Roosevelt and senior military leaders due to "stovepiping"— failing to share critical data among disparate agencies. Collectively the problem of extracting and then acting on the correct signals from the flood of intelligence data has been nicknamed by intelligence officials the "Roberta problem."

The Roberta problem was operative in the days before December 7, 1941: U.S. decision makers who made the fatal strategic call placed higher value on the fact that Japan's diplomats were still talking in Washington than on the interception of the message "east wind rain" extracted from Japan's top-secret diplomatic code, a signal that a possible attack operation was underway. A Japanese attack on American bases in the Philippines was thought a real prospect (and in fact happened on December 8), but the U.S. commanders did not seriously consider the far more daring strike at Pearl Harbor a possibility. Weren't its waters too shallow to allow torpedo planes to attack? The only alert that military officials ordered for the Pearl Harbor area was to watch out for local saboteurs.

Even when troops are massed at a border it is possible to be caught flat-footed. For months in the summer of 2008, Russian troops and equipment were building up along Russia's border with U.S. ally Georgia. Despite this ominous sign, as noted in chapter 3, the administration did not expect a Russian invasion while President Bush—and Russian president Vladimir Putin—were attending the Beijing Olympic Games.

Roberta problems can exist even after the fact, when analysts persist in blindness to salient features of an event. In November 2009, an American Muslim—whose private business card described him as a "soldier of Allah"—shouted "Allahu Akbar!" as he gunned down his fellow soldiers at Fort Hood in Texas. President Obama accepted a Pentagon report on the incident that contained nary a reference to militant Islam nor to the shooter's Islamist beliefs. The Defense Department treated the shooter as if he were simply a lone, mentally disturbed gunman.

Iraq I, Iraq II

THE YEAR 1932 was a fateful augury for America not only because of the Pearl Harbor war game and the U.S. military's failure to learn the right lessons. It was coincidentally the year that a new nation was born in the Mideast: Iraq under British sponsorship. America's history with Iraq and intelligence was an embarrassment long before facts disproved CIA director George Tenet's "slam dunk" conclusion regarding Iraq's weapons of mass destruction. The roots of Tenet's mistake were partly generic—the difficulty of amassing and analyzing intelligence information on a closed society run by a mercurial tyrant—but also deeply set in the prior intelligence failure in the run-up to the Gulf War.

In their 1995 book *The Generals' War*, Michael Gordon and retired general Bernard Trainor detail the intelligence debacle of 1990 that led to the 1991 conflict. In March 1990 American intelligence verified that Iraq had deployed short-range Scud missiles inside western Iraq and in Syria; soon after came Iraqi threats to "burn half of Israel." American and British agents intercepted components for Saddam's "supergun" project—a monster artillery piece that was to hurl projectiles several hundred miles. (The project was ultimately stopped by—who else?—Israel, whose agents killed the designer in a Paris hotel.) In May 1990, the Bush administration suspended $500 million in commodity credits (to ratchet up pressure on Saddam for his aggressive posture). But neither defense nor intelligence officials discussed the Iraqi threat. A Pentagon study from Saddam's first year as president of Iraq (1979) counseled moving forces into the Mideast early to head off Saddam's possible aggression.

As Iraq escalated its intimidation of Kuwait—complaining that Kuwait's oil-pricing policy hurt Iraq's economy—members of the Bush administration began to pay closer attention. On July 25 Charles Allen, the national intelligence officer for warning, placed a 60 percent warn-ing-of-war probability on Saddam invading Kuwait. The Pentagon's top Iraq analyst also stepped up warnings, but his calls did not resonate with his Pentagon superiors. Diplomatic signals went the other way—Egypt, Saudi Arabia, and other Arab states assured Washington that Arab di-plomacy would resolve the crisis. The U.S. dispatched two tankers and a transport plane to the United Arab Emirates, just in case.

With his troops massed and ready on the Iraqi-Kuwait border, Saddam summoned America's ambassador to Iraq, April Glaspie, to a midnight meeting late that July. She assured Saddam Hussein that our military deployment to the United Arab Emirates was not intended as a threat to Iraq, and that the U.S. had peaceful intentions. Saddam disclaimed any intent to invade but warned Glaspie: "Do not push us to it; do not make it the only option left with which we can protect our dignity." Her secret diplomatic post-meeting cable to senior U.S. offi-cials concluded that Saddam, "is worried.... He does not want to further antagonize us. With the UAE maneuvers we have finally caught his at-tention.... I believe we would now be well-advised to ease off on public criticism of Iraq until we see how the negotiations develop."

Senior Bush officials were split as to Saddam's likely next moves. President Bush sent a message to Saddam asserting that everyone had "a strong interest in preserving the peace and stability of the Middle East," while expressing "fundamental concerns about certain Iraqi policies and activities." He called for both countries to "maintain open channels of communication to avoid misunderstanding and in order to build a more durable foundation for improving our relations." Bush sent the message on July 28 for Glaspie to deliver to Saddam before she departed Bagh-dad on July 30 for vacation.

By August 1 intel warning chief Allen raised his war probability to 70 percent. But military analysts and commanders thought that even if Saddam moved he would only perhaps seize the northern Kuwaiti oil fields and occupy Kuwait's offshore islands. Even while realizing that

Iraq's land force was large enough not only to overrun Kuwait but also to seize Saudi Arabia's Eastern Province, the Bush administration did not make a single consequential military move prior to Saddam's August 2 invasion.

Gordon and Trainor flag several reasons for the intelligence failure: a tendency to take the most benign interpretation of ambiguous events, a trust in Arab allies' ability to mediate the crisis by diplomacy, and a desire not to anger these allies by acting in a way they might perceive as rash. The authors note that the U.S. misreading of Baghdad was matched by Baghdad's misreading of Washington's intentions, for which they blame not only Glaspie but also her superiors.

A five-week aerial blitzkrieg followed by a 100-hour ground war defeated Saddam in the first two months of 1991. International inspectors then entered Iraq to search for weapons of mass destruction, which Saddam had used against Iran and his own people (Kurds in the north). The allies discovered that Saddam was far closer to a nuclear bomb than had been thought possible—at most, a year or two away. But for Israel's 1981 bombing of the Osirak reactor, Iraq would have been a nuclear power in 1990. In the face of Saddam's nuclear threats, neither Saudi Arabia nor Turkey could have safely hosted American forces—and without such access the allies could not have ejected Saddam's occupying army from Kuwait.

Just before the Gulf War, Secretary of State James Baker handed Iraqi foreign minister Tariq Aziz a letter from President Bush warning Iraq to refrain from using chemical weapons against coalition forces. Were Iraq to do so, the letter stated, "[t]he American people would demand the strongest possible response" [and] Iraq "will pay a terrible price [for] such unconscionable acts." The evident import of Bush's letter was to suggest to Saddam that any use of chemical weapons in the war might be answered with nuclear weapons.

In the wake of this experience it was natural to try to avoid making the same error—underestimating Saddam—again. The pendulum swung in the reverse direction: *in 2003 we made the opposite error of overestimation,* remembering not only our failure in 1990 but also Iraq's serial lies and evasions when UN inspectors diligently tried to uncover WMD facilities in the ensuing decade.

In retrospect it is astonishing that we relied on sparse and stale intelligence—some of it from a single source of dubious reliability—to launch a major war. Yet "everyone knew" that CIA director George Tenet's "slam dunk"—the assertion that Iraq still had WMD stockpiles in 2002—was correct. Only *six* senators asked to review the full intelligence assessment, which contained caveats not stressed in the summary document, before casting a vote to go to war. That our belief was sincere is established by our troops bringing cumbersome protective gear into Iraq, which hampered their movements.

After taking Baghdad on April 9, 2003, we did discover suspended programs for chemical and biological weapons. Lost in the furor over missing stockpiles was the distinction that the weapons programs were not terminated, and were capable of being restarted on short notice. Years after the war—after the WMD mess had done immense and irreparable political damage to the Bush administration—the interrogator who had debriefed the captured Iraqi dictator for months told *60 Minutes* that Saddam admitted intending to restart his WMD programs once inspectors declared him fully disarmed.

A vast cultural gulf yawns between the point of view of the West and that of Saddam—his was the overwhelming desire of a Stalinist tyrant not to be seen as caving in to demands made by America. Even knowing that a second war was inevitable and that his regime would be toppled Saddam preferred such a fate to the humiliation of backing down. Mideast cultures, many of which stress the importance of not losing face, seem also to have played a role in Saddam's actions—and the U.S. failure to predict them.

This cultural gap can result—and did in the Iraqi case—in behavior that to us seems spectacularly irrational. After all, Saddam need merely have complied with the United Nations Security Council's unanimous request to let in the inspectors and fully cooperate—after destroying his stockpile. He would have faced a UN inspector markedly less aggressive than his two 1990s predecessors and with far more limited powers that required UN approval. Saddam could have slipped out of the sanctions regime with help from his two protectors on the Security Council, Russia and France.

The potential damage from the human tendency to overcorrect can spread far. In his memoir, former vice president Dick Cheney describes recommending in 2007 that the United States bomb Syria's reactor; all President Bush's other advisers argued against the bombing, citing the massive 2003 intelligence failure in Iraq. It was left to Israel to do the job. U.S. intelligence later concluded that Syria had been within at most months of starting the reactor, which then would have been able to produce enough nuclear fuel to make one or two atom bombs per year.

A Look at Nuclear Surprise

THERE ARE numerous examples of nuclear intelligence failures; successful predictions are rare. Russia's first nuclear explosion, in 1949, caught the United States by surprise—intelligence estimates published days *after* the blast placed the probable Russian A-bomb test date five years later. Similarly unexpected were China's 1964 blast and India's 1974 "peaceful" nuclear explosion. As to the latter the consensus among U.S. intelligence experts—in 1973—was that India would not explode a nuclear device. And in 1981—even after Israel had destroyed the Iraqi reactor that was to be loaded with weapons-grade fuel—U.S. intelligence and diplomatic officials refused to concede that Saddam had been running a nuclear weapons program.

Western observers had noted Pakistan's nuclear progress since the 1970s, but had not predicted the timing of its actual manufacture of a nuclear weapon. But analysts were caught by surprise when Pakistan conducted its first test in 1998, after India's second test (also unexpected by U.S. intelligence)—this time, of a weaponized bomb (a missile war-head).

South Africa clandestinely developed a nuclear weapon in the 1970s and 1980s with Israeli assistance. North Korea's clandestine nuclear program, begun in 1981, was only unmasked more than a decade later. In 2002 North Korean diplomats told the U.S. that it had built a nuclear device, but no one in the West knew the assertion to be true until Pyongyang's underground test in 2006.

The summer of 1998 was not a felicitous one for U.S. intelligence officials. In July Iran tested its first intermediate-range ballistic missile, a step CIA director George Tenet had told Congress months earlier was 5 to 10 years away. Weeks later officials were sandbagged again. On August 24 witnesses from the U.S. intelligence community told Oklahoma Republican Senator James Inhofe that North Korea was an estimated two to three years from acquiring a multistage rocket capability. *Just seven days later* North Korea test-fired a multistage rocket. Another possible nuclear intelligence surprise was reported in 2012 by a leading German newspaper: that our intelligence agencies cannot definitively decide whether North Korea conducted two low-yield nuclear tests in 2010.

If Roberta Wohlstetter's work teaches policy makers today anything, it is to be modest—very modest—about what intelligence can reveal. Getting reliable intelligence from a closed society is extremely difficult under the best of circumstances. Given the blizzard of intelligence signals from all over the globe pouring into our capacious collection centers 24 hours a day, separating signals from noise—and assembling them into a coherent whole—is even harder. Actually making decisions that incorporate inconvenient and uncomfortable assumptions is always a daunting task.

More often than not, on major strategic intelligence issues, our guesses will likely be wrong. This is especially true as to pendulum swings—the United States is focused on not repeating Iraq II while forgetting Iraq I, inevitably interpreting intelligence through the lenses of its own biases. Thus the United States is probably being too optimistic as to Iran's likely milestone dates en route to nuclear weapons capability.

It is no criticism of intelligence officials as such to observe this. The human tendencies Roberta Wohlstetter identified behind Pearl Harbor's intelligence failure persist in every generation. To date, only Israel has shown the fortitude to act far enough in advance to prevent certain Mideast nuclear efforts from bearing fruit. Perhaps this is because Israelis consider action a matter of elemental survival. The United States sees it as a matter of regional foreign policy—a viewpoint we may come to deeply regret.

The Seventh Lesson of nuclear-age history—INTELLIGENCE CANNOT RELIABLY PREDICT WHEN CLOSED SOCIETIES GO NUCLEAR—may be the hardest to absorb. As the UN concludes that Iran pursues nuclear-weapon-related activities, the official U.S. position remains that Iran does not have a weapons program. This likely is policy driving intelligence, else the U.S. could face irresistible pressure to act militarily, having promised that Iran will not get a nuclear weapon.

Ironically, deeply flawed intelligence drove Iraq policy in 2003. There the reliance was on prior evidence that was years out of date, thought compelling at the time. In that case, past history drove assumptions among analysts and policymakers alike. "Everyone knew" it was a "slam dunk" that Saddam still had WMD stockpiles. In fact, he had chemical and biological WMD programs that had been suspended, but could have been rapidly restarted.

This time the evidence is current and, if not conclusive, is very strongly indicative. The converse intelligence failure—a wrong conclusion that Iran is not pursuing a nuclear weapon—may come to pass, driven by mistaken assumptions opposite to those regarding Iraq the second time around. Everyone wants to be sure not to make the mistakes we made in 2003, just as then no one wanted to repeat the mistakes of 1990. This time there could well be nuclear consequences, ranging from blackmail to war.

10:

ALLIES: WHY FRIENDS PROLIFERATE

*We cannot live in a situation where Iran has nuclear weapons and
we don't. It's as simple as that. If Iran develops a nuclear weapon,
that will be unacceptable to us and we will have to follow suit.*
UNNAMED SAUDI ARABIAN SENIOR OFFICIAL,
QUOTED IN GUARDIAN.CO.UK, JUNE 29, 2011

WHAT TURNS AN ALLY INTO A NUCLEAR PROLIFERATOR? THE COMmon denominator in every single ally proliferation case since the United States ushered in the nuclear age in 1945 is this: the proliferator judged that its superpower ally's guarantee to protect it—and its own fundamental national security interests—was no longer ironclad. Thus the stark Eighth Lesson of nuclear-age history: ALLY PROLIFERATION CAN BE PREVENTED ONLY BY SUPERPOWER CONSTANCY.

In his 1989 memoir, *From Hiroshima to Glasnost,* Paul Nitze offers a striking historical example of how important America's nuclear umbrella is to those it shelters. During the Cuban Missile Crisis President Kennedy decided to secretly remove highly vulnerable, obsolete Jupiter intermediate-range missiles from Turkey, in order to give the Soviets a consolation prize in return for withdrawing their nuclear missiles from Cuba. The Jupiter missiles were based above ground, in range of Soviet medium-range missiles and bombers. They were liquid-fueled, meaning that getting them ready for launch took hours. Yet the Turks still wanted the missiles, to "couple" their strategic fate to America's. Turkey was a vital ally, having joined NATO in 1952. It was a key base for intelligence missions, including reconnaissance flights over the Soviet Union.

This chapter looks at three wartime allies of the United States—the USSR, the UK, and France, which in vastly different ways started nuclear programs before World War II was over. It looks at Israel's unacknowledged but widely known nuclear program. It looks at the Suez crisis of 1956, and specifically the U.S. response to it, to suggest how America's actions led its allies to believe they needed nuclear weapons of their own.

World War II: Our Russian Wartime Ally of Convenience

THE SOVIET bomb is a partial exception to the ally proliferation rule articulated above. Russia was a wartime ally of the United States when it stole U.S. atomic secrets, but hardly a true ally. Stalin knew, long before we did, how vastly the Soviet postwar interests would differ from ours. He was clandestinely planning to ingest Eastern Europe while we were demobilizing our armed forces in anticipation of peaceful coexistence and a world order organized via the United Nations. Sentiment for our Russian ally was buoyed by knowledge of its staggering wartime death toll of 20 to 25 million, plus vast land and city devastation—a human tragedy on a grand scale to which Stalin, mass murderer of a comparable number of his subjects plus jailer of a second comparable number, was considerably less moved than we. By the time of "Joe-1," the U.S. nickname for Russia's August 1949 atomic bomb test, Americans had received a painful education as to Stalin's intentions, courtesy of the Soviet subjugation of Eastern Europe and the subsequent 1948–1949 Berlin airlift that saved West Berlin from a Communist blockade.

The Soviet "ally" case was one of self-delusion on the part of the United States, which invested the man FDR called "Uncle Joe" with personal qualities and policy aims that simply did not fit the real person. Thus Truman at first considered Stalin "a moderating influence in the present Russian government." During the 1948 presidential campaign Truman said, "I like Old Joe" and called him "a prisoner of the Politburo." In fact, Stalin was a paranoid, genocidal monster who never intended his alliance with America and the West to be anything but a necessary expediency in order to survive the Nazi onslaught. Thus a Soviet nuclear weapon program was inevitable, given Stalin's intent to pursue world domination by launching the Cold War. The next three cases, however, involved real allies.

United Kingdom

THE FOUNDATIONAL work and leadership of, among others, Ernest Rutherford meant that Britain scientifically led atomic studies for 30 years. Rutherford died unexpectedly before the war began, but his colleagues and students, as well as British officials, were involved in the pre–Manhattan Project research stages. In 1943, the U.S., UK, and Canada signed the Quebec Agreement, which governed atomic research and development between the three allies and also made use of the bomb contingent on the consent of all signatories. The 1944 Hyde Park Agreement further detailed U.S.-UK cooperation. The British contribution—code-named Tube Alloys—to the huge 1942–1945 operation at Los Alamos was notable. By the end of 1945 the British had plans to make enough plutonium for 15 bombs per year.

In 1946, the United States passed the Atomic Energy Act (also known as the McMahon Act after its senatorial sponsor, Connecticut Democrat Brien McMahon). It placed harsh restrictions on sharing of atomic information with other countries, none excepted. The law also established the Atomic Energy Commission to provide civilian control of nuclear matters. The Senate passed the data-sharing restrictions unaware of the secret wartime agreements. In 1958 the McMahon Act was modified to restore data sharing with the UK, Canada having decided not to pursue nuclear weapons development.

But even before the 1958 modification the act could hardly stop America's main Manhattan Project ally. In 1946 Britain launched a program that brought a nuclear reactor online in four years and produced enough plutonium by 1952 to enable an October test near Australia. Britain's leadership pushed nuclear programs partly to give Britain's word greater weight in world affairs, but mainly because during the first decade after the Cold War the major allied effort to launch planes targeting the Soviet Union would come from bases in Britain. This made Britain the top target for a Soviet attack. Even before the United States, total war would mean the Soviets' utter destruction of England. Only after the advent of the intercontinental-range B-52 (1955) and U.S. ICBM (1958) did America become the number-one threat to the USSR.

The British A-bomb was followed in 1954 by a decision to build an H-bomb. Britain wanted this second bomb for much the same reasons it had wanted the first. The H-bomb, the British believed, would give strategic weight to what Britain did on the international scene and help keep Britain a world power. It would also deter against a Soviet first strike— or a retaliatory Soviet strike against Britain if the U.S. struck the Soviets preemptively. British leaders knew that a five-megaton H-bomb dropped on London would incinerate everything within a two-mile radius, dig a crater three-quarters of a mile across and 150 feet deep, destroy all housing within a three-mile radius, and badly damage structures within a radius of three to seven miles.[37] The British detonated their first H-bomb in 1957.

On June 26, 1954, Churchill told President Eisenhower about the British H-bomb program. Just weeks earlier, on June 1, the Chiefs of Staff advised the prime minister that in event of war, 10 H-bombs of 2 to 20 megaton yield would kill 5 to 12 million people—this in a country whose 1954 population was some 52 million. While the two discussed a nuclear-armed Russia at a White House luncheon, Churchill quipped: "Meeting jaw to jaw is better than war." (The quote is frequently presented as "jaw-jaw beats war-war.") It should be noted that Churchill felt very differently in the middle and late 1930s, repeatedly calling for Allied military action against Hitler's legions before they gained greater strength than Allied units. The hydrogen changed his assessment.

Prime Minister Harold Macmillan made restoration of Anglo-American nuclear cooperation a top priority. When in 1962 the Kennedy administration peremptorily cancelled the joint U.S.-UK Skybolt air-to-ground nuclear missile project, Macmillan met with Kennedy at

---

37. Future prime minister Harold Macmillan also stated during the 1955 debate in the House of Commons that Britain might wish to use tactical nuclear weapons in the Middle East or in Asia.

the hastily convened Nassau Summit to discuss a replacement. The result was that Britain got American Polaris undersea-launched ballistic missiles for its own ballistic missile submarines. As of 2010, the British had deployed some 160 to 200 nuclear warheads, all carried on nuclear subs.

France

WITH ITS three Nobel Prize winners of 1903—Henri Becquerel and the Curies, Marie and Pierre—France, like Britain, was a pioneer in nuclear research. Under Frederic Joliot-Curie, its nuclear program started almost immediately after the Battle of Normandy and the Allies' August 1944 liberation of Paris from the Nazis. General Charles de Gaulle (still exiled in England) ordered French scientists working in the U.S. nuclear program to return to France even before the Germans surrendered. In his memoir, Manhattan Project chief General Leslie Groves recounts how Joliot-Curie, an ardent Communist, refused to help the Americans, and also helped France obtain access to American nuclear know-how by blackmail. Unless the U.S. helped France, Joliot-Curie would get France to turn to the Russians. The October 1945 elections brought in a government that abandoned the project, but it resumed in 1952, with a nuclear reactor program.

Then, in 1954, the Vietminh Communists defeated the French at Dien Bien Phu. The French had asked President Eisenhower to drop atomic bombs on the insurgents. His refusal made a French weapon inevitable.[38]

A month and a half after the defeat at Dien Bien Phu, anti-colonialist Pierre Mendes-France came to power. His government would not last a year, but while in office, he took the decision to build an independent nuclear weapon. Back under the leadership of de Gaulle, France tested its first A-bomb on February 13, 1960, in the Algerian desert (U.S.

---

38. However, it is far from clear that nuclear bombs would have been effective against widely dispersed forces. Like Afghanistan today, Vietnam simply did not have the kind of concentrated targets that make nuclear weapons effective.

code-name BB-1, the BB for French sex siren Brigitte Bardot).[39] Shortly after the test de Gaulle exclaimed: "If France must have allies, she has no need of a protector!" Ironically, none other than A-bomb father J. Robert Oppenheimer had told French nuclear scientist Francis Perrin that France should make an atom bomb: "It would be good for France. And it isn't very difficult. All you need is a metallurgist endowed with a little imagination."

De Gaulle was the prime guiding spirit of France's bomb program. De Gaulle believed that a nuclear program conferred technology leadership valuable in world markets. He also believed a third world war to be imminent—and he was reluctant to rely on the American nuclear umbrella to deter Soviet aggression. As he explained to Eisenhower in a summit meeting in 1959:

> You, Eisenhower, would wage nuclear war for Europe, because you know the interests that are at stake. But as the Soviet Union develops its capacity to strike the cities of North America, one of your successors will agree to wage nuclear war only [in Europe]. When that time comes, I or my successor will have to possess the necessary means to change into nuclear war what the Soviets would have liked to have remained a classic war.

De Gaulle's quest for nuclear independence reflected his World War II experience: British troops leaving European soil at Dunkirk in June 1940, American officials hesitating to send troops into combat in Europe until Hitler declared war on America, America's delaying the Normandy landing until 1944, and de Gaulle's exclusion from major Allied strategic decisions, despite his being commander (in exile) of the Free French Forces. De Gaulle also made the point that no one could foresee how the world would look in 20 years. (In that he was guilty of gross understatement.)

Even before his meeting with Eisenhower and France's 1960 atomic bomb test, de Gaulle had decided to push research on a hydrogen bomb.

---

39. France tested its last weapon in 1996 in the final series by a Western country.

De Gaulle considered full nuclear-club membership to require development and deployment of thermonuclear bombs and believed that only
with such an arsenal could a nation truly be fully independent in the
nuclear age. France exploded its first two thermonuclear devices in August 1968.

De Gaulle was taken aback when the Kennedy administration
changed American deterrence policy from "massive retaliation" to "flexible response" without consulting Europe, and when Kennedy used the
adjective "unfriendly" to describe the French nuclear program. Guided
by his imperial, intensely patriotic vision of France standing alone, de
Gaulle withdrew France from the NATO defense command structure
in 1966, because NATO weapons require American approval as part
of their release. (France rejoined that structure only in 1996, well after
the Cold War had ended.) De Gaulle's concerns about American willingness to use nuclear weapons to defend France were not unjustified.
When Secretary of State Dean Rusk was told by a French officer that
France would use nuclear weapons to force America to "go to extremes"
in the event of a Soviet invasion, Rusk answered that in such event
America would tell the Soviets that America had nothing to do with
France's nuclear decision.

By 2010, France had an estimated arsenal of 300 nuclear weapons,
based on bombers, land, and sea, but equally fateful was France's decision to help Israel build a nuclear bomb.

Britain, France, and Israel in Suez

PRESIDENT TRUMAN recognized Israel upon its May 14, 1948, founding.
But when Egypt, Syria, Lebanon, and Iraq invaded the next day (joining Palestinian guerillas, who had attacked Israel the day after the UN
passed its November 29, 1947, resolution partitioning Palestine), Israel's
main help came from private sources. The U.S. government subsequently remained neutral, and British sentiment tilted towards the Arabs. The

USSR, though not allied with Israel, allowed Czech arms dealers to sell their wares to the Israelis.

After Israel won its initial war of survival in 1949, Israel's first prime minister, David Ben-Gurion, began thinking about developing nuclear weapons. Before he left office, a tectonic political event occurred to make the question of nuclear weapons more urgent: the 1952 Free Officers coup in Egypt, which brought the charismatic pan-Arabist, pro-Soviet Gamal Abdel Nasser to power.

After a botched covert operation discredited the Israeli government (the affair, which partly aimed at getting rid of Nasser, involved Israeli agents clandestinely bombing *two U.S. buildings in Cairo*), the 69-year-old Ben-Gurion took up office again in late 1955. He entered into the Atoms for Peace commercial nuclear program, but also began a clandestine effort to develop a weapon.

On July 26, 1956, Nasser nationalized the Suez Canal and closed it, cutting off the only short sea transit route from Europe to Asia. Britain and France, among those who relied on the canal to save months of shipping transit time for cargo from Asia, allied themselves with Israel to topple Nasser. Their plan was to invade the Sinai Desert. British and French forces would seize the Suez waterway, blockade key Egyptian ports, and conduct aerial bombardment. They would give Nasser an ultimatum: withdraw from the Suez Canal Zone or lose power.

In too-clever-by-half timing, the momentous, ill-starred operation began October 29, one week before the American presidential election. America was supposed to be distracted by its upcoming presidential election and surely would not oppose the takedown of a virulently anti-American, charismatic Arab demagogue and Soviet client. Instead, on November 6, the day of his landslide reelection, Eisenhower condemned the operation.

In a bizarre coincidence that compounded Eisenhower's fury at the three allies, Hungarians were in the midst of a revolt against Soviet rule.

Eisenhower was utterly impotent in the Hungarian crisis. Russian artillery took commanding heights and tanks rumbled in the streets of Budapest, against which Hungarians had small arms, virtually no artillery, no tanks, and at best "Molotov cocktails"—bottles filled with kerosene and lighted with a wick, tossed at Russian armor and Soviet buildings. Moscow brutally suppressed the revolt on November 10.

Eisenhower's impotence in Hungary was not replicated in the Mideast, and his decision to sandbag key allies was fateful and disastrous for the West. On November 8 the Soviets warned the British, French, and Israeli invaders to pull back or else face retaliation. Strategic bombers armed with nuclear weapons backed their threat. Had it been hit by three Russian hydrogen bombs, the State of Israel would have virtually ceased to exist. And the Soviets had the power to inflict upon England and France vastly greater devastation than did the Germans in World War II.

The three countries were left to fend for themselves against the Soviets because Eisenhower feared losing support in the Arab world if he allowed the invasion to proceed. And as superpower guarantor, via NATO membership, to Britain and France (it was not until 11 years later that America and Israel entered into a formal alliance), he did not want to be drawn into a possible nuclear confrontation with Russia.

Without U.S. support, and only Britain armed with nuclear bombs—few, at that—the three countries had no practical choice but to capitulate to the Soviets.

On November 30, 1956, the frustrated France and Israel made their first nuclear weapons development pact. The next year, the French agreed to help Israel build a nuclear plant at Dimona, in Israel's Negev Desert.

The French-Israeli nuclear collaboration lasted only until May 1960. Charles de Gaulle ended it shortly after he returned as president of what remains today France's Fifth Republic. But the work went on, and Israel made a clandestine deal for heavy water, used to produce nuclear fuel, from Norsk Hydro, a huge Norwegian company.[40] In December 1960, on the cusp of John F. Kennedy's inauguration, Israel's program became public knowledge. Kennedy pressed Israel hard to allow inspection of its Dimona facility, but Israel resisted. In an April 2, 1963, Oval Office meeting, Israel's then-Deputy Foreign Minister, Shimon Peres, offered Kennedy what was to become the permanent formulation for Israel as to its nuclear program: Israel would not be the first nation to introduce nuclear weapons into the Middle East. (The key word is *weapons*, which Israel clearly restricts to meaning a *fully assembled weapon*. Having components that can be rapidly assembled into a bomb does not qualify as actually introducing weapons under this formulation.)

The Dimona reactor began operation—in nuclear parlance "went critical"—in December 1963. Ironically that same year Nasser was helping to midwife the Palestine Liberation Organization, which would come to pose an existential terrorist threat to Israel's future, one not anticipated by Israel's focus on a nuclear deterrent.

Sometime between December 1963 and the June 1967 start of the Six-Day War, Israel completed all the steps necessary to rapidly assemble a nuclear device. (The time needed to assemble a usable bomb is short. Final assembly of the primitive Nagasaki implosion A-bomb in August 1945 took less than one day. Assembling a gun-trigger device would be even quicker.) Two prototype devices may have been ready for use in 1967, during the Six-Day War. By then Lyndon Johnson was president and looking to run again in 1968. With a close election expected in the fall, the Jewish vote took center stage, and New York's then-45 electoral votes were crucial. Johnson told his staff with the plain-speak he was known for: "Good nonproliferation policies lead to bad politics." [41]

---

40. It was Norsk Hydro that during World War II manufactured heavy water for the Nazis. The Allies so feared the prospect of a Nazi bomb that they destroyed the factory and later, after centrifuges were replaced, sank a ferry carrying heavy water as it began a journey to Germany. Fifty-three civilians were on the ferry, some of whom drowned. The story is told in the suspenseful 1965 action film *The Heroes of Telemark*.

41. Ultimately Johnson decided not to run again, but in any case, his warm support for Israel went beyond politics to religious identity. LBJ was a Christadelphian; the sect

The Fallout from Suez

THE TURN at Suez proved among the most catastrophic miscalculations in American foreign policy history. In condemning Nasser's enemies and allowing Nasser to proceed unchecked, the United States tossed away the chance to crush Nasser and nip pan-Arabism in the bud. In 1958, the radical passions Nasser stirred up in the Arab world bore ugly fruit, with Egypt-sponsored revolution in Iraq, soon followed by revolution in Syria. These uprisings brought a pair of secular militarist tyrannies to power and destroyed French and British influence there.

These revolutions destroyed what was left of the power of pro-Western moderates. Along with the 1963 founding of the Palestine Liberation Organization, these events set in motion a cascade of Mideast calamities over the ensuing decades. Had the United States used its superpower status to protect the interests of its close allies in 1956, these calamities—briefly described below—might have been avoided entirely, or at least, their impact blunted.

On New Year's Day 1965 the PLO launched its first attack against the Jewish state—one aimed at "liberating" not the West Bank, then occupied by Jordan, or Gaza, then under Egyptian suzerainty, but Israel, from democratic Jewish status. While the Palestinians had chafed under Arab rule few outside the region had cared. Nor had there been serious international talk about their "national historic rights."[42]

But Nasser's post-Suez decade of agitation against Israel's right to exist (a point of view then held unanimously by Mideast Arab countries) led to the Six Day War, and that changed Palestinian politics. It was only

---

believes that the Kingdom of God will be seated on Earth in Jerusalem. LBJ also forged a warm bond with fellow farmer Levi Eshkol, Israel's Prime Minister.

42. Indeed, in September 1970 Jordan's King Hussein (whose son Abdullah now rules the kingdom) decided to end Palestinian unrest inside Jordan by driving the Palestinian Liberation Organization military units out of the West Bank and into Lebanon. Jordan's British-trained army slaughtered thousands of PLO fighters and West Bank civilians. One of the terrorist groups took the name "Black September" after the debacle. The world stood mute. Israel warned off Syria and Iraq.

when Israel occupied the West Bank and Gaza after the 1967 war that the plight of the Palestinians became a staple of international politics.

Suez ended the brief alignment between Britain, France, and Israel.[43] Britain and France never fully recovered from their shattering defeat at Suez. Britain, pro-Arab, rarely was a close ally of the Jewish state, and France became beholden to Arab oil until nuclear power changed its energy equation.

France also allowed a refugee from Iran, one Ayatollah Ruhollah Khomeini, to take shelter in the late 1970s. From there he sent audiotapes into Iran to supporters. They were played to public audiences in mosques, urging revolution against the Shah. Syria, after a 1970 coup, turned more extreme under Hafez al-Assad. The Assad family was to become radical Iran's prime surrogate ally in Mideast politics, and a client of the Russians. A Mideast Stalin, Saddam Hussein, brutally seized power in Iraq in 1976.

Then came the fateful year of 1979, when Khomeini established his fascist clerical regime with global revolutionary aspiration, and the Great Mosque seizure led the Saudis to start surreptitiously subsidizing Sunni Islamic extremists around the globe. Islamic Jihad, an al-Qaeda precursor, assassinated pro-Western Egyptian reformer and Arab-Israeli peacemaker Anwar el-Sadat in 1981. Financing the spread of radicalism were petrodollars taken from the West, at grossly inflated cartel prices. Iran, for its part, used petrodollars in 1982 to found Hezbollah, as formidable as any terrorist group in the world today. Iran also funded terror attacks by various Palestinian groups around the globe. And as the Soviet Union's decade-long Afghan war wound down in 1989, Osama bin Laden founded al-Qaeda.

---

43. Note that in the decades before Suez, Britain and France had combined to give the Mideast the grim gift of the Grand Mufti. In 1922, early in its 30-year Palestine Mandate, Britain revived the office of Grand Mufti of Jerusalem. The apointee, Amin el-Husseini proved a vile anti-Semitic demagogue who conspired with Hitler to kill Jews. The French held him as a war criminal at war's end, but in 1946 let him escape to Egypt, and he fomented hatred of Jews and preached radical politics until his death, at age 80, in 1974.

Thus did the events of 1954–1967 set in motion a cascade of calamities for the West, with a nuclearizing Iran now poised to become the greatest catastrophe of all in the world's most volatile region, one riven with instability, violence, tyranny, and terror, and seated astride the economic lifeline of the West.

The post-Suez disasters came from a common predicate: America's failure to use its superpower status to protect the interests of its close allies—interests the U.S. shared, had its leaders grasped the stakes. An American failure to prevent Iran from joining the nuclear club will pose similar dangers. Those who believe we can rely on traditional deterrence are wrong. America's allies in the Mideast are not confident that the United States can protect them from a nuclear Iran.

As former Saudi intelligence chief Prince Turki al-Feisal has strongly hinted, Saudi Arabia will pursue nuclear weapons if Iran goes nuclear—that is, Iran's crossing the nuclear weapon threshold "would compel Saudi Arabia... to pursue policies which could lead to untold and possibly dramatic consequences." Under the circumstances, pursuit of nuclear weapons is understandable, just as it was understandable when David Ben-Gurion decided that only Israel could be trusted to safeguard its own security, a principle to which Israel has adhered ever since.

The latest manifestation of this principle is Israel's refusal to bow to pressure from the Obama administration concerning a strike on Iran's nuclear facilities. Israel has refused to accept that it requires American approval for such a strike, partly because it reserves, as does any sovereign nation, the strategic prerogatives of *raison d'etât* ("reason of state") and *ultima ratio* ("last resort"); President Obama recognized these prerogatives in public. But his administration serially leaked information, some of it classified, in a transparent effort to undermine Israel's case for striking, and to raise the political cost to Israel of acting without administration approval. Thus Israel does not trust the U.S. to back it up diplomatically in the aftermath of a strike, let alone believe that the Obama administration is truthful in asserting that the military option is on the table.

Whether Israel's viewpoint is correct is beside the point. Because Israel believes that it cannot fully trust its ally to give full diplomatic support, it cannot commit to informing its superpower ally before acting.

A similar solicitude for Western security interests would have led the United States to back the Suez operation, bring down a tyrant aiming to upend all pro-U.S. regimes, and hand the Soviets a major regional defeat. To this day we are suffering the baleful foreign policy fallout from the debacle at Suez.

And thus the Eighth Lesson of nuclear-age history: ALLY PROLIFERATION CAN BE PREVENTED ONLY BY SUPERPOWER CONSTANCY. This lesson applies not only to America's allies, but to other present, former, and aspiring nuclear-club powers. China did not fully trust its superpower guarantor, the USSR, even before their 1962 split made China's crash nuclear weapon program inevitable. Neither India nor Pakistan had a superpower guarantor, nor, truly, does nuclear aspirant Iran. (South Africa and Libya were pariahs, and North Korea remains one.)

A continued restraining influence upon prospective proliferators can only be effectively exercised by a nuclear ally. Such a partnership extends a nuclear guarantor's deterrence umbrella to cover states considering an independent deterrent. An American failure to sustain extended deterrence on behalf of its allies in the Mideast will reverberate around the globe. It will not be lost on nuclear-capable allies of the U.S. such as Australia, Japan, South Korea, and Taiwan. Burgeoning regional arms races are a recipe for accelerating the advent of nuclear conflict.

11.
DISARMAMENT I: SUPERPOWER ARMAMENT, POPULAR DISARMAMENT

I thought the mushroom cloud had followed me from Hiroshima.
TSUTOMU YAMAGUCHI, SOLE OFFICIAL SURVIVOR OF BOTH HIROSHIMA AND NAGASAKI

IT IS ESTIMATED THAT 165 PEOPLE SURVIVED BOTH BOMBS DROPPED on Japan, but Tsutomu Yamaguchi was the only one officially recognized by the Japanese government to have done so. The 2010 *New York Times* obituary of the 93-year-old survivor reported that Yamaguchi had been in Hiroshima on a business trip, and then returned home to Nagasaki the next day. Though his eardrums were ruptured and upper torso burned by Hiroshima's "Little Boy" explosion, he went to the office. He was telling his boss about Little Boy two days later when "Fat Man" lit up the room—and all of Nagasaki—with blinding white light.

The unspeakable human misery and horrific carnage of Hiroshima and Nagasaki, and fears of generations of genetic mutants, gave birth to a vigorous popular disarmament movement. Stalin's refusal to play along, even while he had no nuclear bomb himself, in no way deterred disarmament dreams. Focusing first on superpower arsenals, disarmament advocates pressed for a "nuclear-free" world. This chapter looks closely at popular movements to disarm and offers the Ninth Lesson of nuclear-age history: POPULAR PRESSURE FOR UNILATERAL DISARMAMENT CAN PREVAIL UNLESS WESTERN GOVERNMENTS EXPLAIN ITS HIDDEN, GRAVE DANGERS.

The Bombings

THE BOMBS dropped on Japan in August 1945 finally ended a world conflagration that had already claimed 50 million lives. It is not hard to understand, however, why they were the beginning of massive public revulsion against nuclear weapons.

The raids were conducted by the Boeing B-29 Superfortress, the world's finest strategic bomber, whose $3 billion development cost exceeded the cost of the Manhattan Project. In the predawn darkness of August 6, a B-29 nicknamed Enola Gay (after the pilot's mother) barely cleared the end of the runway on the tiny Pacific island of Tinian, its ungainly five-ton payload still unarmed in case of a crash. From the runway plateau it dipped towards the sea and then climbed to cruising altitude.

Upon reaching Hiroshima, Enola Gay released the A-bomb at 31,600 feet. It took 45.5 seconds for the bomb to fall to the detonation altitude of 1,900 feet, selected to be high enough so that the fireball would not touch the ground and the radius of total destruction would be maximal: 3,000 feet. The uranium-fueled bomb detonated at 8:15 a.m., right on target in the center of the city, killing some one-third of the city's 365,000 inhabitants, many within minutes. Only 1.4 percent of the bomb's 140 pounds of uranium fissioned before the assembly blew apart and its mass became instantaneously subcritical, ending further chain reaction. The estimated yield for Little Boy was 14 kilotons, equivalent to 14,000 tons of TNT. This was 2,300 times the explosive power of the six-ton "Tallboy" bombs the British used to sink the super-battleship *Tirpitz*. Enola Gay's crew could still see the mushroom cloud from 360 miles away, looking back while returning to base.[44]

Three days later another B-29, *Bock's Car*, took off from Tinian. It dropped the plutonium-fueled 10,800-pound Fat Man on Nagasaki, struck because primary target Kokura was closed in by cloud cover. The bomb detonated 1,800 feet above ground. It was more powerful due to the greater efficiency of plutonium fission: 17 percent of its 13.6 pounds of plutonium fissioned, giving it 12 times the efficiency of Little Boy. It yielded some 21 kilotons. Nearly half—5,300 pounds—of its weight was conventional high explosive encircling the plutonium; it would com-

---

44. The Hiroshima bomb was originally dubbed "Thin Man" after the Dashiell Hammett fictional detective, while "Fat Man" was the nickname of the Caspar Gutman character played by Sydney Greenstreet in the film of Hammett's novel *The Maltese Falcon*; Thin Man was shortened and then renamed Little Boy.

press the dense plutonium into the size of a tennis ball—about the size of the orange-sized bomb Winston Churchill envisioned in 1924 someday destroying a city.[45]

While many scientists who worked on the bomb expressed regret later, President Truman never looked back. Once, Oppenheimer met with President Truman and told him: "I feel I have blood on my hands." To which Truman was later heard to mutter: "Blood on his hands! Dammit, he hasn't half as much blood on his hands as I have. You just don't go around bellyaching about it."

Already in 1944, the U.S. had begun the landmark Strategic Bombing Survey to assess the effects of long-range bombing on Germany. The survey found that bombing Germany would in many respects be ineffective. Targets like ball-bearing plants proved easy for the Germans to rebuild. The Allies had ignored hard-to-replace transportation and electric grid networks until late in the war. Their early destruction would have accelerated the war's end.

When it went to Japan, the survey's findings were far different. The intense bombing campaign inaugurated by General Curtis LeMay began with the Tokyo raid of March 9–10, 1945. It killed over 100,000 people and erased one-quarter of the city. Fire bombings claimed far more total lives than the two atomic bombs. In all, 600,000 Japanese were killed in the B-29 raids during the last five months of the war. The survey noted that with enough incendiary bombs LeMay's B-29 armada could have destroyed every city in Japan with a population of more than 30,000 people.

The survey reached three important conclusions as to atomic weapons. First, the firebombing aerial campaign alone—without atomic bombs—would have forced Japan's leaders to accept unconditional sur-

---

45. Because Fat Man missed its aim point by over two miles the death toll was about half that for Hiroshima. This dramatically taught the first nuclear-age targeting lesson: *accuracy is a greater factor in a nuclear weapon's overall destructiveness than is yield.* It is for that precise reason that as missiles became far more accurate their warhead yields even more dramatically declined.

render. (This conclusion was disputed by many commanders and by President Truman—diehards in the militarist Japanese cabinet wanted to fight on, even after the A-bomb dropped. Only the intervention of Emperor Hirohito, then still regarded as divine, tilted the balance towards surrender.) Second, the atomic bomb multiplied a bomber's destructive power by 50 to 250 times, depending upon the nature and size of the target. Third, while the basic principles of war (unstated in the report), and units such as ships and infantry, would remain in use, atomic weapons would force radical alteration in tactics.

Strategically, on the other hand, the surveyors thought the impact of the atomic bomb would be modest. Only the advent of a practical, deliverable hydrogen bomb, with its thousand-fold increase over the atom bomb's destructive power, convinced planners and commanders that the strategic world had fundamentally changed too.

President Truman decided to drop the bomb to bring the quickest possible end to what had been nearly four years of sanguinary conflict in the Pacific. He had been advised that troops invading the Japanese Home Islands would suffer roughly the 35 percent casualty rate that had proven the case during the spring 1945 Okinawa campaign. With 750,000 troops slated to land on the largest island, Kyushu, that likely meant more than a quarter-million Allied toll for taking a single one of Japan's four Home Islands. Indeed, fear of mass troop carnage led FDR's chief of staff, General George C. Marshall, to inquire of Manhattan Project chief General Leslie Groves if atom bombs could be used as tactical weapons to drop on Japanese defenders in event of a Kyushu landing.

To forestall such a landing Truman warned after Hiroshima: "If [Japanese leaders] do not now accept our terms they may expect a rain of ruin from the air, the likes of which has never been seen on this Earth." Truman was relieved when the Japanese surrendered, because of Allied lives thus saved, and because he had planned to drop the third atom bomb on Tokyo (already ravaged by the March 1945 fire raid). Yet Truman said in his 1953 farewell address that "starting an atomic war is totally unthinkable for rational men."

The Disarmers

CALLS FOR world disarmament began almost immediately after General Douglas MacArthur accepted Japan's surrender on the deck of the battleship *Missouri* on September 2, 1945. But as noted in chapter 4, the movement for world disarmament dates back to the late nineteenth century. Utopian views became commonplace among disarmers in the run-up to World War I.

In his 1914 novel *The World Set Free*, H. G. Wells foresaw a war with "atomic bombs" releasing the energy of the sun, followed by total disarmament and world peace. Wells offered a vision of World War I biplanes carrying small bombs that an aviator could push out. Derived from a fictional element called "carolinum," the devices did not simply explode, but burned for a month, releasing toxic elements and fire. Targets hit during the imaginary conflict included London, Berlin, Paris, and the dikes that protect Holland from the sea, causing that country to be submerged. Following a series of intrigues, the heroes stop the secret plot of a small cabal of evil leaders and, as a result, world peace blossoms and wars end.

The real world challenge was, however, to prove far more complex and less amenable to utopian solutions. On June 11, 1945, a group of scientists led by physicist Leo Szilard called for demonstrating the bomb's power but urged it not be used against Japan:

> If the United States would be the first to release this new means of indiscriminate destruction upon mankind, she would sacrifice public support throughout the world, precipitate the race of armaments, and prejudice the possibility of reaching an international agreement on the future control of such weapons.

But such predictions proved mainly wrong. As noted earlier Andrei Sakharov, the father of the Soviet H-bomb, made clear in his memoirs that Joseph Stalin would have gone ahead with his nuclear program—

having already gotten the secrets well before the July Trinity test—even if America did not. In 1946 America did offer to give up its small nuclear arsenal to international control by the United Nations. But Stalin rejected the proposal in 1948—even *before* the first Soviet atomic bomb was tested. On the fair evidence of it, nothing like the future envisioned by Szilard and his fellow signatories came to pass.

Public support for America was strong in many allied countries. The captive peoples enslaved by the Soviet Union regarded America as the "last, best hope on earth," in Abraham Lincoln's famous words. Thus Soviet dissident Natan Sharansky, released in 1986, reported that he and fellow prisoners had been thrilled to hear President Reagan use phrases like "locus of evil" and "evil empire" in describing the USSR, because they told them America would not give up. The people of Eastern Europe were then and remain today among America's finest friends on the planet.

But the public, as well as prominent public figures, were galvanized by the bombings. In 1949 Indian Prime Minster Jawaharlal Nehru said his countrymen "exulted" at not having the bomb, which he called "the symbol of incarnate evil." (Despite this, Nehru enrolled India in the Atoms for Peace program, putting in his country's hand the material to make nuclear bombs, as his successors were to do.)

Nehru's phrase—as opposed to Reagan's—calls to mind an enduring difference between disarmament advocates and skeptics: Advocates ascribe evil to inanimate, weaponized objects, drawing no moral distinction between civilized and uncivilized leaders possessing such weapons. Skeptics ascribe evil to human actors and argue that it makes a huge difference which country has the bomb. The latter view is more credible. During the Cold War, most Americans were worried about Russia's arsenal, while few were worried about Britain's. Today many more Americans fear an Iranian bomb, while few fear a nuclear Israel. The Arab states agree, as WikiLeaks cables showed.

The "Ban the Bomb!" movement gathered real steam when in 1954 the U.S. conducted its Castle Bravo H-bomb test, whose 15 megatons released three times the total energy released by all bombs dropped during World War II. In fact, the test was designed to yield five megatons, but a subtle error in calculation caused the vast underestimate. It was discovered before the test, but the message did not reach the test site in time. The permanent atmospheric test ban finally enacted in 1963 was the culmination of public alarm in the wake of Castle Bravo. The vast majority of citizens opposing the bomb were patriotic people who feared the destruction atomic war would bring. It was a perfectly reasonable fear, and one shared by those who supported the bomb programs as necessary. (Not everyone protested. In the late 1950s Las Vegas hotels ran bus tours to viewing vantage points for atomic tests. Viewers could sip "atomic cocktails" but were warned to protect their eyes, lest their macabre fascination prove injurious.)

Popular protests bore fruit in 1958: in March, the Soviet Union announced a moratorium on nuclear testing, and five months later President Eisenhower declared a U.S. moratorium to begin at the end of October. France—not a signatory to the treaty ban—ignored the superpower moratorium and tested in the atmosphere after the 1963 ban, as did China.

The Bomb to End All Bombs

THEN, IN September 1961, the Soviets ended their three-and-a-half-year hiatus. They began a series of tests, culminating in the largest man-made nuclear explosion ever, the Tsar Bomba, tested in the Arctic Ocean archipelago of Novaya Zemlya.[46]

The 1961 Tsar Bomba test yielded 50 megatons, equal to a magnitude 7 earthquake like the one that devastated Haiti in 2010. It released one-quarter the explosive force of the 1883 Krakatoa island eruption

46. Manhattan Project physicist Hans Bethe opined at the time that the Soviets must have begun their extensive preparations by March 1961, just as the Geneva test ban talks resumed. Half a year before they announced it, the Soviets already had begun planning to end their moratorium.

that created a 135-foot tsunami, sent a huge layer of dust around the world, and was heard thousands of miles away. The 27-ton monster bomb created a fireball that reached almost as high as the 6.5-mile altitude from which the Russian TU-95 bomber dropped it, and generated a mushroom cloud that rose 40 miles, seven times the height of Mount Everest. Because it detonated at 12,000 feet, far too low for a bomb this size, it hurled highly radioactive debris that spread all over the globe via jet-stream winds.[47] The radius of *total destruction* was 34 miles, the third-degree burn radius was over 60 miles, the blast shock wave reached 430 miles, and windows broke as far away as Norway and Finland, over 600 miles away.

The bomb's energy was 97 percent fusion energy, which does not produce the poisonous radioactive by-products that fission does—only the 3 percent from the fission first-stage A-bomb trigger (which ignited the fusion H-bomb "secondary" stage) released radioactivity. The Soviet bomb designers could have used fission boosting—surrounding the fissile plutonium core with uranium-238 as a fissionable third stage, as originally planned. Instead they used a tamper of nonfissionable lead. A 3-stage bomb would have yielded 100 megatons, and all the extra energy release would have sent vast quantities of highly toxic by-products into the atmosphere to circle the globe. But Sakharov convinced Khrushchev that a 100-megaton blast would increase total radiation in the atmosphere by 25 percent over that released by all previous tests combined.

---

47. A rule of thumb for blast effect: each ton of nuclear yield vaporizes one ton of debris at ground level. Because the Tsar Bomba's 50-megaton blast was an airburst, but too low, it vaporized earth at ground zero. A pure ground-level Tsar Bomba burst would have thrown skyward 50 million tons of debris. (The U.S. Air Force nixed a Strategic Air Command request for a 60-megaton H-bomb; in the event, President Eisenhower refused to allow an atmospheric test in the Pacific.)

Far-flung radiation effects began with the 1945 Trinity test, which transmuted cerium-140 (a stable rare-earth element of the soil in the western continental U.S.) into intensely radioactive cerium-141. Winds carried it across the United States, where it ruined film at the Eastman Kodak factory in Rochester, New York. Another odd example: on May 25, 1953, a shell from the Army's atomic cannon exploded in the Nevada desert with a 15-kiloton yield (slightly greater than the Hiroshima bomb), sending a radioactive cloud east that contaminated hail falling in a thunderstorm over Washington, D.C.

The Tsar Bomba, even at 50 megatons, was in fact not a deliverable weapon—it was far too large to fit in any bomber's bomb bay. It was suspended underneath the plane's fuselage and dropped with a parachute that slowed its descent, so that the lumbering TU-95—whose top speed is roughly that of civilian airliners—could get far enough away to withstand the severe blast shock wave and intense heat.

The largest deliverable weapons known to have been deployed were 25-megaton warheads (deployed by both superpowers). We do not know for sure the largest remaining from the Soviet arsenal, but there are few U.S. weapons today with yields above one megaton. Yet a one-megaton weapon is 70 times as powerful as the Hiroshima uranium bomb and 50 times as powerful as the Nagasaki plutonium bomb. (The largest A-bomb ever detonated was a 500-kiloton U.S. A-test.) Britain, France, and China have tested in the megaton range. Israel is believed to have such an H-bomb capability, and Pakistan reportedly is working on it.

The Bomb Goes Underground

AN EXPLOSION the Soviets conducted on Christmas Day 1962 marked the last superpower atmospheric test. July 1963 was the "hottest" radioactive month in U.S. history, as debris continued to fall from the atmosphere. On August 5 the U.S., USSR, and UK signed the Limited Test Ban Treaty, which ended atmospheric, surface, and underwater tests.[48] The U.S. Senate ratified it later that year.

A decade later, in July 1974, President Nixon signed two treaties—the Threshold Test Ban Treaty and the Peaceful Nuclear Explosives Treaty (which dealt with excavation)—limiting underground nuclear explosions to 150 kilotons (roughly 10 times the Hiroshima bomb's yield). The yield limitation was important. Scientists found that in principle, the potential yield of the H-bomb is without limit.

The disarmament movement's revival began with another success, but this time, it was Western activists collaborating with the Soviets

---

48. Paul Nitze points out that the Soviets gathered more detailed information than did the U.S. on atmospheric tests and by signing the treaty locked in a knowledge edge.

to undermine support for deployment of the neutron bomb, as noted in chapter 4. The Soviets concocted a brilliant propaganda campaign, labeling the neutron weapon "the capitalist bomb" because it killed people while preserving property. The claim was laughable, as property within range of the lethal dose of neutron radiation would be contaminated for years, and thus rendered unusable. West German Chancellor Helmut Schmidt staked his prestige on neutron deployment, only to see President Jimmy Carter unilaterally cancel the weapon. For the Soviets it was a twofer: getting an effective battlefield weapon cancelled and creating a fissure within the NATO alliance.

During the 1980s the movement was considerably less successful than it had previously been. Activists hampered but did not prevent NATO's efforts to counter Moscow's aggressive deployment of nuclear missiles in Europe. They pressed for a nuclear freeze, which would in actual practice have been utterly unenforceable against Moscow, while enforced against the West by public opinion. Key hardcore activists were working hand in glove with "peace groups" like the World Peace Council, which the Soviet Union created to hinder Western nuclear programs. The vast majority of freeze supporters among the general public had no inkling of the shadowy connections between phony peace groups and the Soviet KGB (secret police), but Western intelligence agencies knew.

A nuclear freeze also would have eliminated Moscow's fear that it could not keep up with emerging American nuclear strategic developments. It was narrowly defeated by the steely resolve of Western leaders, above all Ronald Reagan and Margaret Thatcher, who surely understood that once a freeze is signed, it for practical purposes binds Western nations far more firmly than their adversaries.

In 1983 a highly touted film about nuclear war between the U.S. and USSR, *The Day After*, was shown on ABC. The film was clearly aimed at pushing public sentiment towards abolition of nuclear weapons. It presented a scenario in which a crisis ensues when the Soviets blockade Berlin. The U.S. sends forces to re-open the city, and a shooting war begins. NATO forces use tactical nuclear weapons first, and Moscow responds. Then one of the sides—which is left unclear—escalates to use of strategic weapons against cities. Shortly thereafter an all-out nuclear exchange results, with countless millions killed on each side, plus vast physical devastation.

The Reagan administration feared that the movie's graphic depictions of the horrific devastation and loss of life caused by a nuclear exchange would stampede public opinion. It requested airtime after the movie to respond to it, and ABC assented. Secretary of State George Shultz appeared, and declared nuclear war "unacceptable." The movie did not noticeably shift public attitudes.

The Cold War triumvirate of Ronald Reagan, Margaret Thatcher, and West German chancellor Helmut Kohl held the line against the nuclear freeze movement, a critical psychological factor in preserving the Western alliance and convincing the Soviet Union that the West would not crumble from within. Earlier, however, disarmament movements had driven government policy—for the better with the ban on above ground and underwater tests, but for the worse with NATO's unilateral scrapping of the neutron bomb.

How popular pressure will weigh in the new push for nuclear abolition remains to be seen, but whatever happens will confirm the Ninth Lesson of nuclear-age history: POPULAR PRESSURE FOR UNILATERAL DISARMAMENT CAN PREVAIL UNLESS WESTERN GOVERNMENTS EXPLAIN ITS HIDDEN, GRAVE DANGERS. One major step is pending: the Comprehensive Nuclear Test Ban Treaty, to ban all nuclear weapon testing.[49] The challenge skeptical governments must meet is to educate their publics about the risks of precipitous disarmament, which could lead to, rather than prevent, nuclear blackmail.

---

49. Through January 2012, 182 countries had signed and 156 had ratified the treaty. It will enter into force once 44 nuclear-energy countries that helped negotiate have ratified it. Eight countries remain on this list: China, Egypt, India, Iran, Israel, North Korea, Pakistan, and the U. S. The U.S. has signed, but not ratified, the treaty.

12.

DISARMAMENT II: SOME DISARM, OTHERS MUST BE DISARMED

You don't want a messianic apocalyptic cult controlling atomic bombs. When the wide-eyed believer gets hold of the reins of power and the weapons of mass death, then the entire world should start worrying, and that is what is happening in Iran.

Israeli Prime Minister Binyamin Netanyahu to Jeffrey Goldberg, The Atlantic, March 2009

COUNTRIES DISARM FOR THE SAME REASON THAT THEY ORIGINALLY arm: because they judge it to be in their supreme national interest. They do not disarm because America or anyone else is "setting an example." Nor do they do so because they wish to earn the goodwill of the (largely fictive) "international community," unless the step is tied to a specific benefit such as the lifting of economic and political sanctions (South Africa), or winning political autonomy (former Soviet republics).

About hostile nations in particular—rogues like North Korea and revolutionaries like Iran—we can say that they do not disarm if they think they can get away with not doing so. Given sufficient national security reason to retain a clandestine cache of nuclear weapons, they will retain it, even if other nations are reducing. For them, some combination of sanctions, credible threats, or military action is necessary to derail their programs. Thus the Tenth Lesson of nuclear-age history: DISARMING HOSTILE POWERS CANNOT BE DONE BY NEGOTIATIONS ALONE.

This lesson has been behind various efforts to disarm recalcitrant nascent nuclear powers by force, before they produce weapons. These efforts include Israel's 1981 raid on Iraq's Osirak reactor, its 2007 raid on a partially finished Syrian nuclear reactor, and the allied coalition's 2003 decision to invade Iraq and end any possibility of Saddam Hussein becoming head of a nuclear state. America and Israel have contemplated a preemptive strike against Iran's nuclear facilities, to prevent or at least delay Iran's ability to produce nuclear weapons.

In considering a variety of cases of disarmament, this chapter makes clear that when leaders deem it in their country's best interest to disarm, they will do so. But hostile powers must be disarmed by force.

Latin America

BROAD-SCALE DISARMAMENT efforts first bore fruit in Latin America. Brazil floated the first proposal for a Latin American nuclear-free zone in 1962—even before the Cuban Missile Crisis brought nuclear missiles to America's neighbor. Just five years later, in 1967, five Latin American countries—Bolivia, Brazil, Chile, Ecuador, and Mexico—signed the Treaty for the Prohibition of Nuclear Weapons in Latin America (known as the Treaty of Tlatelolco, after the part of Mexico City where the signing ceremony happened). The treaty came into force just over a year later, and by 2002 all 33 Latin American countries had signed and ratified it.[50]

The treaty prohibits the "testing, use, manufacture, production or acquisition by any means whatsoever of any nuclear weapons" and the "receipt, storage, installation, deployment and any form of possession of any nuclear weapons." Cuba's compliance is conditioned on reaching a satisfactory agreement with the U.S. over Guantanamo Bay—which makes its compliance essentially illusory. There is no prospect of the U.S. ceding Guantanamo any time soon, even if eventually all terror detainees are transferred elsewhere.

The United States, ever ardent for disarmament treaties, signed both protocols (supplemental agreements) to the Tlatelolco treaty. Protocol I requires outside powers retaining territories in the zone (U.S., UK, France, and the Netherlands) to adhere to the treaty and not bring

---

50. Two other notable nuclear-free-zone treaties are the Treaty of Rarotonga covering the South Pacific, which came into force in 1986; and the African Nuclear-Free Weapon Zone Treaty, which came into force in 2009.

nuclear weapons into the zone. Protocol II requires all declared nuclear weapons states to respect the nuclear-free status of the zone. It has been signed by all five Security Council nuclear powers (the five permanent members: U.S., UK, France, Russia, China). Israel, which is unlikely to import nuclear materials into the region, has not signed because it is not a declared nuclear power. India and Pakistan are not parties to nonproliferation treaties.[51]

The Latin American equation could be radically altered by Venezuelan strongman Hugo Chavez—an aspiring Fidel Castro seeking to lead all Latin American countries in revolution against American influence in the region and against governments allied with the U.S.—provided he survives his bout with cancer. Chavez desires to send uranium ore to Iran for its nuclear program. Eventually, he might seek Iran's aid in launching a nuclear weapons program for Venezuela, in violation of Tlatelolco's nonproliferation norms. Assuredly Chavez would follow North Korea's example of blithely ignoring signed agreements if they interfere with his plans.

Africa: Libya and South Africa

SINCE THE mid-1970s, Libyan dictator Muammar Qaddafi had a standing offer to purchase nuclear weapons from any seller. He was an eager supporter of terrorism against the West—worrying, among others, Reagan, who wrote in his diary in 1987, "Someone like Qaddafi could develop nuclear weapons and perhaps smuggle them into the United States."

---

51. Argentina did not accede to the treaty until 1994, which meant that in the spring of 1982, during the Falklands War with Britain, the Argentines had no legal grounds to object to Britain's using nuclear submarines or other nuclear-armed platforms during the conflict. On May 2, 1982, the UK nuclear submarine *Conqueror* sank the Argentine cruiser *General Belgrano*, causing the largest loss of life (323 of 993 on board) during the war. As Argentina still claims the Falkland Islands, located in the southern Atlantic Ocean about 300 miles off its eastern coast, in event of a future conflict Britain would be violating the Tlatelolco Protocols if it sent nuclear-powered, let alone, nuclear-armed, ships into the conflict. In February 2012 Britain sent a nuclear sub to the area; Argentina claimed this violated the protocols; Britain denied the charge but refused to reveal the sub's location.

In 1986, Libyan terrorists had bombed a West German disco-theque, killing a U.S. soldier and a Turkish woman and injuring over 120 (40 of them Americans). In response, Reagan ordered the bombing of Libyan barracks and airfields, just missing Qaddafi himself. Qaddafi answered that bombing by downing Pan Am flight 103 on December 21, 1988, days before the end of Reagan's term of office. After these violent interchanges and sponsorship of terrorism worldwide, what made Libya decide to abandon its nascent nuclear program in 2003?

Though negotiations had been going on for years, and were tied to a settlement of Libyan liability for the Pan Am bombing, it seems clear that the factor uppermost in Qaddafi's decision was fear that his country would be next after Iraq on the allied coalition target list. Libya committed to dismantling its WMD programs within days of America's "shock and awe" air assault on Iraq in March 2003. As Dr. Johnson famously quipped, "Depend upon it, sir, when a man knows he is to be hanged in a fortnight, it concentrates his mind wonderfully."

South Africa, on the other hand, already was a nuclear-weapon state when it voluntarily disarmed. It began a commercial nuclear program in the 1950s under Atoms for Peace, and by 1965 could produce enriched uranium for a bomb. South Africa's military nuclear program began in 1974, following the Carnation Revolution in Portugal that brought de-colonization—and with it, instability—to the region. With Marxist dictators seizing power in neighboring countries in the years following—in Mozambique and Zimbabwe (formerly Rhodesia)—South Africa had no incentive to disarm.

Also significant for South Africa's nuclear weapons program was its relationship with Israel. After the 1973 Yom Kippur War, when Israel's formerly warm relations with pro-Arab African nations came unglued, Israel turned to South Africa as its supplier of uranium ore, which it is unable to mine domestically. Israel reportedly traded its design expertise to enable the South Africans to build gun-type uranium A-bombs in return for uranium to make atomic bomb "primary" triggers for "secondary" hydrogen bombs.

Weapons designers Thomas Reed and Danny Stillman (*The Nuclear Express*) believe that Israel also wanted from South Africa a clandestine site to test a neutron bomb, presumably for use against Egyptian and Syrian tank assault in event of a repeat of their 1973 surprise attack. They note that it took China, a sophisticated nuclear-club member, five tests to get a working neutron bomb. They conclude that Israel tested a neutron bomb 1,500 miles southeast of Cape Town on September 22, 1979, to make it appear to outside observers as a South African test. The signals matched French weapons, but Israel, as noted earlier, obtained weapons expertise from France.[52]

The Soviets were energetically backing Communist "liberation" movements in Africa, all of which South Africa adamantly opposed. Evidence of a South African nuclear test would have strengthened South Africa's hand in supporting regional allies against Russia's Marxist proxies. In 1976 the Soviets persuaded the U.S. to cooperate in pressuring South Africa not to conduct a nuclear test at its Valindaba site. (Reed and Stillman drily note that in Zulu the word means, "We do not talk about this at all.") By 1978 Valindaba was producing enough highly enriched uranium to make one bomb per year, and when P. W. Botha succeeded John Vorster that year as prime minister, he pressed for more. In the 1980s South Africa produced six uranium gun-trigger devices. Needing no testing, these enabled South Africa to go nuclear without alerting the world and risking nonproliferation blowback.

By the mid-1980s the Cuban-backed Marxist rebels were making progress in the ex-Portuguese colony Angola—just north of the guerrillas fighting South African control of South West Africa (now Namibia).

---

52. For more on the detective work that found Israel the likely candidate responsible for the test, see source notes at www.SleepwalkBomb.com. Reed and Stillman argue that the Carter administration—to avoid roiling the political climate in the Mideast after the Camp David Accords between Israel and Egypt were signed in 1978—whitewashed the 1979 nuclear test event and produced a finding of no nuclear test.

South Africa reportedly had contingency plans to use a uranium bomb on Luanda, the Angolan capital, in event of war.

In 1989 F. W. De Klerk became South African head of state, and oversaw the end of apartheid. In November 1989 he ordered Valindaba to be closed and his country's half-dozen uranium bombs dismantled. By September 1991 the task was done. His apparent motivations were to end international isolation and to prevent nuclear weapons from falling under control of a black African leader. This despite the evident fact that the new South African leader, Nelson Mandela, was as unlikely as anyone on the planet to use nuclear weapons.

South Africa's decision had two real-world impacts: it reduced weapons-grade nuclear material suitable for theft, and it was a political symbol of voluntary nuclear disarmament as the Cold War ended. But several thousand South African nuclear scientists were now seeking new employment, joining thousands of jobless Russian scientists. They were ripe for picking by nuclear aspirants.

Former Russian Republics: Ukraine, Belarus, Kazakhstan

THE MOST significant voluntary disarmament moves were made in three republics formerly part of the Soviet Union: Ukraine, Belarus, and Muslim-majority Kazakhstan. The prime incentive these nascent countries had for surrendering their arsenals was that it would facilitate separation from post-Soviet Russia. They had no great incentive to keep them—using them against the West or against Russia would surely have resulted in their own destruction.

Securing their nuclear material against diversion by hostile states or sophisticated terrorist groups proved a grand challenge. Once again, *The Nuclear Express* provides unmatched narrative detail, in this case, on the technology and logistics of securing nuclear material in the former Soviet Union. The scale of the problem was breathtaking.

Between entering the atomic age in 1949 and its year-end breakup in 1991, the USSR produced 1,200 metric tons of highly enriched uranium and 140 to 162 metric tons of plutonium reprocessed from nuclear reactor waste. If a tenth of a percent of the material went missing, there would be 1.3 tons of weapons-grade uranium and 310–360 pounds of weapons-grade plutonium loose in the world, enough for dozens of nuclear bombs.

Further, as the Soviet Union dissolved there were still some 27,000 Soviet nuclear weapons—including 11,000 thermonuclear ones—to be dismantled, much of this arsenal located in the three former Soviet republics. Having been part of the former Soviet Union, and thus parties to the 1991 START I Treaty, they agreed to transfer their entire arsenals to Russia. Of the three, Belarus had the fewest weapons—81 warheads on mobile ICBMs (an arsenal nearly as large as that of India or Pakistan). Ukraine's immense arsenal of 5,000 nuclear warheads—several times larger than the arsenals of Great Britain and France *combined*—made it the *world's third-largest* nuclear power. And Kazakhstan had nearly 2,000 warheads—including an estimated 1,000 multi-megaton warheads sitting on the monster SS-18, the largest ICBM ever built.

Kazakhstan faced even thornier problems than disposing of weapons. Its nuclear test area underwent 456 tests in 41 years, the highest number of tests for one test site, massively contaminating the test site soil. Worse, Kazakhstan had to find a way to rid itself of its weapons-grade uranium used in Russian nuclear submarines. In late 1994 the U.S. sent massive military cargo planes on a secret airlift mission to Kazakhstan to pack up and remove the fuel. In an operation that equaled anything Hollywood could serve up, they succeeded in getting their cargo out just before Iranian buyers could get their hands on the stuff for use in crude uranium "gun-trigger" devices.

Amazingly, by 1996 all three former Soviet republics were nuclear weapon free. In 2012 Ukraine's final shipment of weapon-grade uranium was sent to Russia.

Pseudo-Disarmers: North Korea and Iran

HOSTILE STATES manipulate the international community to frustrate nonproliferation enforcement. North Korea and Iran have been following the same playbook, with North Korea having already crossed the finish line and Iran rapidly approaching it. They use dummy firms to purchase prohibited items; they launder money to fund their program; they make serial offers of pseudo-concessions to curry goodwill; and they use negotiations to stall.

When nice does not work they use not-nice: threats of war, or other forms of intimidation—terrorism, hostage taking, etc. They use elaborate schemes to evade inspection regimes—phony accounting, commercial use, and materials unaccounted for.

North Korea, to put it gently, has played U.S. diplomats—and several presidents—like the proverbial violin. Former president Jimmy Carter's 1994 visit to Pyongyang is just one of these cases. Traveling there against the wishes of President Clinton, Carter came back with news that the North was ready to make a deal, and would stay within the Nonproliferation Treaty. Indeed—but on its terms, not ours.

When State Department diplomat Robert Gallucci returned to the U.S. after signing the Agreed Framework that laid out the U.S.-North Korea deal President Carter had worked out, the Americans assumed that the crisis had passed. After all, North Korea had committed to shut down its Yongbyon facility, whose design and operation facilitated production of weapons-grade plutonium. Pyongyang also agreed to use plutonium fuel for commercial reactor production only. In return the U.S. agreed to supply the North with two light-water nuclear reactors designed to be less usable for proliferation (that is, plutonium production). The U.S. also threw in fuel oil to help the North meet its domestic energy need.

Needless to say, North Korea deceived inspectors over the next eight years, as it clandestinely diverted fuel for a bomb. Its October 4, 2002, statement to U.S. diplomats that it had developed a uranium-enrichment capability for a bomb was not sufficient to convince the Bush administration that the North had in fact joined the nuclear club, but it led to the suspension of nuclear cooperation on November 21.

Less than a month later, the North announced it would restart its Yongbyon facility, and it formally announced its withdrawal from the Nonproliferation Treaty at the start of 2003. Its underground atomic test in October 2006 proved that the world's nuclear club had a new member.

Yet this reality only intensified U.S. diplomatic efforts—at times via the "six-party talks" that added South Korea, Japan, China, and Russia as parties—to tame the North's nuclear program. Carrot and stick diplomacy followed, with, as ever in such talks with bad guys, more carrot than stick. In 2007 the U.S. unfroze $25 million of assets on Pyongyang's promise that the money would be used for humanitarian purposes. In 2007 North and South Korea agreed to hold talks aimed at a final formal peace treaty to officially end the Korean War.[53] On October 11, 2008, the Bush State Department took North Korea off the terrorism list, making it eligible for more aid.

The North responded to these gracious gestures early in 2009, conducting a series of long-range missile tests of multistage missiles, including one shot fired over Japan, towards Hawaii (though landing short of it). Pyongyang also seized two journalists who had wandered over the 38th parallel dividing the two Koreas, holding them for 140 days. It took a personal visit from former president Clinton to obtain their release, thus saving them from a show trial and many years in prison. And in May 2009 it conducted a second underground nuclear test, one more powerful than its first, though generally believed to be less powerful than the 14-kiloton Hiroshima blast—the North's designs remain rudimentary.

---

53. The 1953 armistice merely withdrew forces 2,000 meters (2,200 yards, 1-1/4 miles) from the 1953 front lines. Since 1953, North Korea has repeatedly violated the border, sometime even killing military personnel working in the demilitarized Joint Security Area (JSA), a four-kilometer-wide zone with one half in each Korea; the 38th parallel literally bisects the conference table within the JSA that is used for negotiations.

As this book went to press the North was preparing to conduct its third nuclear test. Or it may be a fifth test, given that monitoring equipment has suggested, though analysts have been unable to confirm, that tests have taken place twice since its second test. This uncertainty shows that nuclear forensic detection is far from guaranteed to detect clandestine activity.

In 2010 things got even worse. On March 26 the North torpedoed a South Korean ship, the Cheonan; the ship sank with all hands. On November 12, the North unveiled its pilot uranium enrichment facility to a group of U.S. officials and scientists. Thus in addition to its ability to divert spent plutonium from spent nuclear fuel (the method used to fuel its two nuclear tests) Pyongyang now has the ability to fuel bombs with enriched uranium.

In sum, having never once since its 1948 creation honored a commitment in full, the North is, if nothing else, consistent. Its ace of trumps is duplicity, its ability to manipulate Western hopes that bad guys will become good. In the real world, for good things to take place there must be positive regime change, as happened in the former Soviet Union when Mikhail Gorbachev came to power.

The experience with North Korea repeated itself with Iran. After UN inspectors revealed Iran's clandestine nuclear program in August 2002, a familiar drama unfolded. In 2003 the EU3 (Britain, France, and Germany) began three years of negotiations with Iran, seeking to confine it to commercial nuclear use. This effort went on despite the evident reality that Iran sits on immense oil and natural gas reserves (its energy dependency comes from lack of refining capacity, requiring it to ship some three-fifths of its oil elsewhere to be refined and returned for domestic consumption). In 2006 the U.S., Russia, and China joined the negotiations.

On November 30, 2007, U.S. officials released a new National Intelligence Estimate—reversing their position of two years earlier—concluding "with high confidence" that Iran had abandoned covert uranium enrichment four years earlier, in 2003, and also abandoned efforts to produce a nuclear weapon. But the estimate treated uranium enrichment, which is by far the main event in terms of going nuclear rogue, as commercial. As Vice President Cheney noted in his memoir, weaponization can be rapidly resumed.

In September 2009, on the eve of the annual UN General Assembly session in New York, in order to preempt a disclosure of the facility by the U.S., Iran revealed a new, hitherto undisclosed uranium enrichment facility near the holy city of Qom. The facility, which the U.S. had monitored for several years, has a 3,000-centrifuge capacity—far too small to be useful for a commercial program.

Instead of acknowledging the danger posed by Iran, President Obama's response was to talk at the UN session about negotiating a new superpower arms treaty with the Russians, thus "setting an example" for other nuclear powers to reduce—and, eventually, eliminate—their own nuclear arsenals. It was left to French president Nicholas Sarkozy to point out that there were two present nuclear dangers—North Korea and Iran—that deserved prompt attention. The president went on in April 2010 to sign New START with Russia, and a month later presided over a two-day international nuclear proliferation summit in Washington, talking anew about moving towards a "nuclear-free" world.

Iran continues to proceed with open contempt for the U.S. and others, steadily increasing its military capabilities—testing longer-ranger multistage ballistic missiles, and launching a satellite. It continues working on advanced warhead design (necessary to build a compact nuclear warhead to sit atop a missile), including specialized devices with no civilian application, such as a neutron initiator, part of the triggering mechanism for a bomb. It has installed newer, faster centrifuges at its Fordo facility near Qom, aiming to speed up uranium enrichment to produce fuel for a uranium bomb.

Iran took British hostages (released after the British government groveled publicly) and arrested three American hikers who Iran asserted strayed over the Iraq-Iran border, ostensibly to spy on Iran. One was released by Iran as a "humanitarian" gesture, but the other two were convicted in a carnival show trial on ludicrously trumped-up charges. (They were eventually released.) In January 2012 Iran (falsely) charged an American with being a CIA spy—an action taken immediately after the U.S. Navy rescued Iranians from the Persian Gulf waters and immediately before the Navy rescued a second group of wayward seafarers.

Particularly disturbing was the supine reaction of the Obama administration to the rebellion that erupted in Iran on June 9, 2009, after a patently fraudulent election returned Iran's firebrand Islamist president Mahmoud Ahmadinejad for a second four-year term. Brutal street shootings—plus mass arrests with beating and rape used as intimidation tactics against detainees—quelled the protests after several weeks. President Obama's response was tepid because he held out quixotic hopes that he could somehow persuade Iran—which had spent 25 years developing its nuclear program and building a massive human and physical infrastructure—to abandon nuclear weapons on the cusp of successfully producing them.

At the end of 2011 the U.S. and Europe finally imposed strong sanctions, targeting Iran's central bank and embargoing the import of Iranian oil. Had this been done in June 2009 the Iranian threat already might have been ended via positive regime change. Yet Iran's nuclear march continues despite sanctions.

Preventing Nuclear Armament

WHEN NEGOTIATIONS fail or are used to run out the nuclear clock (as with Iran and North Korea), and when sanctions fail (as frequently they do), the remaining options are aiding the opposition and taking military action. The former was not viable in Saddam's Iraq—save after the Gulf War, when a countrywide popular uprising was on the verge of dethroning Saddam. But the U.S. stood down, and Saddam crushed the rebellion. As for Syria, it was only the Arab Spring of 2011 that galvanized popular revolt there, its fate uncertain at this writing.

As for the latter option, twice Israel has destroyed unloaded nuclear reactors, both times with complete mission success. Israel's demolition of Saddam's above ground reactor in 1981 was a textbook armament-prevention operation. Eight planes—F-15s for escort and F-16s to bomb—flew over the desert for two hours a few hundred feet off the ground, emerging at sunset to drop unguided gravity bombs on the exposed Osirak reactor. One 2,000-pound bomb landed squarely inside the reactor. Though publicly the U.S. joined a UN condemnation of the raid, privately President Reagan chuckled: "Boys will be boys."

The raid was launched because the Israelis knew that the reactor would soon be loaded with nuclear fuel. Once it had gone critical the consequences of scattering highly radioactive material over several countries made a raid untenable. On the advice of most of his top advisors, who wanted to assuage anger in the Arab world, President Reagan allowed the UN Security Council resolution condemning the measure to pass, instead of ordering a U.S. veto.

There was no serious doubt that Iraq's program was aimed at obtaining a nuclear weapon. While Iraq's program started in 1959 as a commercial venture under Atoms for Peace, in the late 1970s Saddam Hussein signed contracts to purchase weapons-grade uranium from France and reprocessing equipment from Italy, the latter to separate plutonium from spent reactor fuel. France offered its newly developed, 7 percent enriched "caramel" fuel, which would have substantially cut Iraq's operating costs but is not suitable for use as the core of a uranium bomb and does not allow easy separation of plutonium from spent fuel. Saddam turned down France's offer.

Saddam preferred 93 percent enriched uranium for the reactor core—vastly higher than needed for commercial or research purposes. In November 1980, two months after invading Iran, Iraq ended international inspections of its reactor. In January it permitted one visit, but the reactor was not yet operational, so inspection was all for show. After Israeli's June 1981 strike, condemnation was nearly unanimous. As noted earlier, American intelligence still refused to concede that Iraq had been seeking nuclear weapons, and only two of President Reagan's senior advisers, Secretary of State Alexander Haig and National Security Adviser Richard Allen, backed Israel. Incredibly, Secretary of Defense Caspar Weinberger accused the Israelis of violating international law by committing an act of war. It took retired Supreme Court justice Arthur Goldberg to answer: as Iraq had attacked Israel in 1948, never recognized what it continued to call "the Zionist entity," and never signed a peace treaty, the two nations were still legally at war. Israel's precision strike was thus entirely lawful.

Saddam likely would have had the bomb well before launching his August 1990 invasion of Kuwait had Israel not moved. After the Gulf War, arms inspectors discovered that Iraq was at most a year or two away from having a bomb.

Israel repeated this strategy in destroying Syria's nascent reactor in 2007. In his memoir former President George W. Bush recounted how Israel's then–prime minister, Ehud Olmert, telephoned and asked him to have the U.S. Air Force bomb the Syrian facility. Bush declined, preferring to pursue a combination of diplomacy and threat of force, but kept mum while Israel acted. Bush said that the 2007 intelligence finding that Iran had suspended its nuclear weapons program undermined his military option.

Targeting Iran's underground facilities is far more complex. Conventional-warhead cruise missiles are accurate enough, but cannot penetrate the hundreds of feet of rock or concrete that shelter Iran's deepest facilities. Missile payloads likely would have to be nuclear to do the job, and neither the U.S. nor Israel is willing to resort to this choice, unless an Iranian nuclear attack takes place. Warplanes can achieve pinpoint accuracy, but in the absence of U.S. or Russian heavy bombers to carry massive penetrating bombs, smaller planes might have to drop several smart bombs into the same path to dig deep enough. An air attack would miss any undiscovered facilities. At best, the program could be delayed rather than ended. But on the other hand, a few years' delay can buy precious time for sanctions or aid to the opposition to sink the regime.

There is another option against deeply buried facilities that, due to the deeply-ingrained taboo against nuclear use, Israel will forgo: according to the late American bomb designer Ted Taylor, a one-kiloton bomb if properly molded into a shaped charge could bore a ten-foot wide hole 1,000 feet into solid rock.

One dangerous consequence of the 2003 WMD intelligence debacle is that it establishes (for practical political purposes) a de facto standard of proof beyond a shadow of a doubt before the world's governments might support military action. Closed societies conceal their programs and use periodic diplomatic "charm offensives" to cloak their intentions with ambiguity and raise hopes of peaceful resolution. Rejecting such hopes appears nearly impossible for Western societies, who value peace so highly that they assume all others must as well.

In effect, ruthless proliferators have taken Western societies hostage in the past, and continue to do so. In a diplomatic version of the Stockholm Syndrome—the condition of hostages who come to sympathetically identify with their captors—advanced societies reflexively shrink from the unpleasant task of confronting hostile states pursuing nuclear weapons.

Given how stark the military options are, and uncertain the prospects for success, it is understandable that the West recoils. But a nuclear Iran, even short of war, will ignite a nuclear arms race, shift the balance of power, and supplant the U.S. as potentially the preeminent Mideast regional player.

If Israel Strikes Iran

As THIS book goes to press the air is rife with speculation as to whether Israel will strike against Iran's nuclear facilities. It seems increasingly apparent that President Obama will not do so, unless one of two contingencies comes to pass: Iran mines the Strait of Hormuz, or Iran attacks America—either its interests abroad or the American homeland. Israel clearly understands that it is alone.

In an address to the American-Israeli Public Affairs Committee, Israeli prime minister Binyamin Netanyahu crisply summed up the absurdity of those questioning Iran's commitment to build a nuclear weapon, noting that underground facilities and ICBMs are not designed to deliver medical isotopes:

> The Jewish state will not allow those seeking our destruction to possess the means to achieve that goal. A nuclear-armed Iran must be stopped. Amazingly, some people refuse to acknowledge that Iran's goal is to develop nuclear weapons. You see, Iran claims that it's enriching uranium to develop medical research. Yeah, right. A country that builds underground nuclear facilities, develops intercontinental ballistic missiles, manufactures thousands of centrifuges, and absorbs crippling sanctions—is doing all that in order to advance... medical research. So you see, when that Iranian ICBM is flying through the air to a location near you, you've got nothing to worry about. It's only carrying medical isotopes.

The prime minster put his position plainly: "As prime minister of Israel, I will never let my people live in the shadow of annihilation."

As to the likelihood of Iranian retaliation, perhaps ironically the severe response that Iran's regime threatens is more likely if Israel fails than if Israel succeeds. In the Mideast, an adversary's strength is grudgingly respected, while weakness earns contempt and incites retaliatory violence.

The comparative histories of powers that choose to disarm versus those that scorn disarmament underscore the Tenth Lesson of nuclear-age history: DISARMING HOSTILE POWERS CANNOT BE DONE BY NEGOTIATIONS ALONE.

13.

INVITATION TO STRIKE: THE SMALL POWER'S NUCLEAR EQUALIZER

Should significant parts of the electrical power infrastructure be lost for any substantial period of time ... many people may ultimately die for lack of the basic elements necessary to sustain life in dense urban and suburban communities....

The Federal Government does not today have sufficiently robust capabilities for reliably assessing and managing EMP threats.

REPORT OF THE COMMISSION TO ASSESS THE THREAT TO THE UNITED STATES FROM ELECTROMAGNETIC PULSE (EMP) ATTACK, APRIL 2008

A WORST-CASE NUCLEAR NIGHTMARE SMALL-POWER ATTACK SCENARIO is not a terrorist nuke exploding in a big American city. Such an attack would be a catastrophic event, killing hundreds of thousands and erasing trillions of dollars in economic value, while undermining social cohesion and plunging the nation—and the world—into unprecedented crisis.

But there is a more devastating catastrophe, one that could end America's status as a world power: an esoteric phenomenon generated by a nuclear explosion, known as "electromagnetic pulse" (EMP). If an adversary *detonated a single nuclear warhead over the country's midpoint at high altitude,* the explosion would generate a series of powerful pulses that would break through surge protectors. In a worst case it could take down all or nearly all of America's electric grid and communications fabric. In a few days, as backup power ran out, America would be returned to its energy status of 1875, with several times as many people to support. The Eleventh Lesson of nuclear-age history, then, is this: NEVER ALLOW SINGLE OR LOW-NUMBER POINTS OF CATASTROPHIC VULNERABILITY.

Historical and Scientific Background

SHOULD AN EMP attack not only disable America's power grid but also, in parallel attacks, disable the grids of allies who might aid us, *in a worst case an estimated 90 percent of Americans could perish within one year*— mostly from starvation and disease. America could never recover, as William Fortschen vividly describes in his 2009 novel, *One Second After*.

Some scientists, among them physicist Howard Hayden, have sharply questioned the total-collapse scenario. They point to relatively limited damage suffered in early EMP incidents. Even if they are right, it does not take an attack of worst-case outcome to inflict horrific casualties and societal damage. Suppose that only 1 percent of Americans lose all vital life services for a year. In such event some 3 million people might perish within that period. That is roughly twice the 1.34 million total U.S. fatalities in all American wars from 1775 to mid-2012.

Knowledge of EMP dates back to the first nuclear explosion. Enrico Fermi shielded all nearby electronics before the Trinity test in 1945 in expectation of an electromagnetic pulse. When it came, it still knocked out data, despite the shielding. But the phenomenon was at first highly localized and dwarfed by blast, heat, and lethal radiation effects, and nuclear explosions in the 17 years afterwards were either surface bursts, like Trinity, or low-altitude air bursts, like Little Boy and Fat Man.

High-altitude EMP first revealed its surprising destructive potential in 1962, when the U.S. detonated its Starfish Prime 1.4 megaton H-bomb 250 miles over Johnston Island in the Pacific Ocean. The explosion occurred in the intense bands of radiation in the ionosphere known as the Van Allen radiation belts. Discovered by James Van Allen (from data collected by America's first successful satellite, Explorer I, launched in 1958), the belts interact with EMP and amplify its intensity. The pulse of electromagnetic energy from the test reached Honolulu, 900 miles to the east, and knocked out 300 streetlights, a telephone microwave radio link, and lots of burglar alarms.

Russia conducted atmospheric tests over land, its leaders secure in the knowledge that its citizens dared not protest. Russian Test 184, part of a series of detonations over Kazakhstan later in 1962 called the "K Project," knocked out a 625-mile underground electric power line, interfered with diesel generators, and started some electrical fires in damaged equipment. At 300 kilotons yield, Test 184 was one-fifth the power of Starfish Prime; it also was detonated at just over 70 miles up, less than one-third the American test's altitude. EMP effects are not overly sensitive to explosive yield, according to EMP expert Dr. William Graham, who chaired the congressional EMP panel. But effects are far more intense over land, because EMP perturbs the Earth's magnetic field, which is far stronger over land than water. The lower altitude of the Russian test limited EMP radius. But having been detonated over land, the Russian test caught more ground installations within reach of its footprint than did Starfish Prime.

A chain of events causes EMP. First come the intense gamma emissions from the fissioning atoms of the bomb. These ionize the air, knocking electrons out of atoms. When the electrons hit the earth's magnetic field, it knocks them sideways, and it is this interaction that generates the electromagnetic pulse.

Three successive, different pulses generate the EMP effect: E1 is the superfast high-voltage pulse that bypasses surge protectors (which are designed to stop pulses that build up less rapidly) and "fries" all affected electronics. E2 is akin to the electromagnetic charge emitted as lightning strikes. This pulse is low frequency and ordinarily would not get past surge protectors, except that if the first pulse has fried the protective equipment, then the second pulse, like a burglar who enters an open door, gets in. The third pulse, E3, is akin to the geomagnetic storms generated by solar flares. This pulse is the Earth's magnetic field being disturbed by the bomb, then settling back to normal—an extremely low frequency pulse that lasts tens, even hundreds of seconds. Though weak, because of its duration this third pulse builds up enough strength to knock out large components like electric grid power transformers, and reaches deep into the ground.

EMP confounds some common expectations of the relative dangers of different nuclear weapons. Aside from the displacement of the Earth's magnetic field (E3), the intensity of the phenomenon does not, as indicated above, scale with warhead yield. A Hiroshima-size blast (14 kilotons, less than 1/20th the K Project yields and 1/100th that of Starfish Prime) will do very nicely. Counter-intuitively, a hydrogen bomb with yields in the megaton range short-circuits EMP by the phenomenon of pre-ionization. The hydrogen bomb's trigger (an A-bomb) prematurely strips electrons from the atoms of the air, so that the later, larger quantity of electrons shorts out in the atmosphere rather than interacting with the Earth's magnetic field. H-bombs thus cause less EMP damage than A-bombs.

EMP means that a foe does not need the massive explosive yield of an H-bomb to inflict grave damage. An A-bomb will perform the EMP task with greater effect. North Korea already has an A-bomb, and Iran is getting tantalizingly closer to one.

Altitude is a critical factor in EMP effects—the bomb must go off at the right height to hit the Earth's magnetic field. Deep space detonations do not cause EMP effects on earth—the gamma ray emissions from the bomb dissipate long before reaching Earth's magnetic field. And low-altitude nuclear detonations, which generate vast blast, heat, and radiation damage, explode below most of Earth's magnetic field and hence generate less EMP.

An attacker could detonate an EMP weapon 300 miles over Kansas, and cover a 1,470-mile radius that would encompass the entire lower 48 states. On a smaller scale, even a ground burst weapon's EMP effects could devastate local electric power in a radius of roughly 6 to 12 miles, potentially hugely effective over a major metropolis. EMP can create imbalances within the grid that cause the system to shut down and inflict severe damage. Because newer infrastructures rely so much on digital technologies, far fewer people are required to run them; thus, in a crisis, there are far fewer workers available to rapidly reconstitute damaged parts of the system. Infrastructures driven by modern silicon computer chips are much more vulnerable to disruption via EMP than are infrastructures built with older-generation electric power technologies.

In 1998, Iran, which lacks strategic bombers and missile subs, test-fired a missile from a floating barge, validating its ability to launch a ballistic missile from a platform less stable than a ground launch (and thus more susceptible to inaccurate guidance). Barges could easily cruise offshore in international waters, i.e., outside the 12-mile limit.[54] Iran would have to launch its missiles a few hundred miles at sea, to limit the chance of detection. Reaching 1,500 miles inside the U.S. homeland would require a missile range of about 2,000 miles. New Iranian models are approaching this range. Such missiles could be launched from either the Atlantic or the Pacific Ocean, or from the Gulf of Mexico.

In 1999, Iran tested an armed ballistic missile in an "EMP mode": this means that the missile was fired in a steep trajectory whose angle of ascent matched that required for an EMP attack. The missile's conventional warhead detonated at high altitude. This test validated Iran's ability to carry out a coastal EMP strike. When newer, longer-range missiles enter service, Iran could target the lower 48 states by detonating an EMP weapon centered over the interior.

Using shorter-range missiles Iran could target selected cities easily from offshore, with lower-level EMP bursts. Ship-launch scenarios were one threat specifically identified by the 1998 Rumsfeld Commission report on growing ballistic missile threats. Not that this threat was new: in his 1949 memoirs Dr. Vannevar Bush, wartime science adviser to Presidents Roosevelt and Truman, warned of the threat posed by "atomic bombs smuggled in by innocent-appearing ships, to be detonated at the

---

54. Some countries claim a 200-mile limit to territorial waters, but such claims are not currently recognized under international law.

chosen moment." The U.S. successfully launched a Polaris ballistic missile off a commercial ship in 1962.

Infrastructure Vulnerabilities

AMONG THE warnings issued by the congressional EMP panel in 2008, perhaps the strongest concerned the risks of infrastructure interdependency, specifically its tendency to increase the time needed to recover after an EMP attack:

> Safeguards against single point failures generally depend on the proper functioning of the rest of the national infrastructure, a plausible assumption for high reliability infrastructure systems when they experience random, uncorrelated single point failures.... Planning for multiple failures, particularly when they are closely correlated in time, is much less common....
>
> No currently available modeling and simulation tools exist that can adequately address the consequences of disruptions and failures occurring simultaneously in different critical infrastructures that are dynamically interdependent.

In other words, if neighboring communities cannot help, recovery time is much longer. "Edge" communities can bring in supplies, give shelter, and send in needed funds, but we cannot predict how much help they will be able to offer. Recovery from Hurricane Katrina included large-scale resettling of displaced residents, with some even choosing to become residents in edge communities that hosted them. A wider circle of destruction would have hindered recovery everywhere.

The second report issued by the EMP panel examined 10 specific infrastructures and detailed their potentially greatest vulnerabilities. It should be noted that one major change in the past half century has increased societal vulnerability: the shift from vacuum tubes to silicon chips inside America's electrical infrastructures. The latter are less resistant to EMP damage.

Electric power drives virtually all infrastructures in the United States. Backup is provided by generators whose life typically is 72 hours or less, along with batteries with a life of a few hours at most. Even a short blackout can cause losses of between 18 and 60 percent of production in the affected area.

Note that in the past 20 years the margin of redundant capacity for emergency needs has halved, from 20 to 10 percent. Increasing use of wind power, a mode that relies on the vagaries of fickle weather, can place unpredictable demands upon the system, increasing reliability problems. Overseas factories often produce (and customize) high-power transformers that step up and down voltage levels as electric current travels between power generation and customer distribution. But these transformers are not an immediate-term solution; the lead-time to order one is about a year, and there are 2,000 transformers in the U.S. electric grid.

As with computers, digitally controlled power systems can suffer extensive damage if shut down without the proper procedures. Thus the electric grid transmission system that links generators and consumers is, the panel said, "highly vulnerable" to EMP.

Telecommunications networks are another major potential weak spot. Backup power typically lasts 4 to 72 hours. (One significant exception: EMP can't hurt fiber optics, which lie outside the frequency range EMP effects occupy; but computers, telephones, etc. are electrical, and thus the end points of fiber networks are susceptible.)

Banking and finance networks are highly automated electronic digital systems. These networks are impossible to operate without communications connectivity. In the past three decades, the transaction volumes that these networks carry have jumped by several orders of magnitude. A generation ago, a *10 million*–share trading day on the New York Stock Exchange was huge, whereas today trading volume averages *several billion* shares per day. The public securities markets trade trillions of dollars of securities annually; other specialized financial networks also trade trillions of dollars in value. In all, financial communications networks daily carry several times the amount of data held in the entire print collection of the Library of Congress.

The financial industry is well protected against localized outages, with significant backup redundancy. But the industry's assets are not hardened against EMP, and likely are highly vulnerable. The industry is so automated that reversion to a cash economy may not be feasible in event of a protracted outage; the United States might have to revert to a barter economy. A major disruption for even one day, let alone weeks or months, could be devastating. The Treasury Department and the Securities and Exchange Commission agree that even a single day without power could cause wide-scale disruption and risk to critical markets. In a situation where an EMP crippled electronic systems needed to recover lost data, the panel warned that an "irrecoverable loss of critical operating data and essential records on a large scale would likely result in catastrophic and irreversible damage to U.S. society."

Petroleum and natural gas flow through an extensive physical infrastructure in America. Backup systems can run this energy infrastructure for a few days, but energy transport systems, run by easily fried specialized digital control systems known as SCADA (Supervisory Control and Data Acquisition), are vulnerable. (It is SCADA systems that were damaged by the Stuxnet cyberwar software. When the SCADA systems went haywire, they caused Iran's delicate centrifuge equipment to operate erratically, ultimately rendering nearly 1,000 inoperable.)

Transportation is another source of vulnerability. Coal supplies currently on site at some power plants could last up to a month; other plants have only days' worth of coal on site. Repair and recovery of railroads would take days to weeks, with manual control able to operate at only 10 to 20 percent of normal capacity.

Modern vehicles have up to 100 microprocessors controlling operations, so an EMP attack could disable most of the nation's over 200 million vehicles, including the ones that carry about 80 percent of manufactured goods between manufacturer and consumer.

Some 100 deep-draft ports (capable of handling large ships) move 95 percent of overseas trade (75 percent by monetary value); typically, ports have 10 to 20 days' fuel on the premises.

Aircraft have lots of redundancy. Modern airliners and regional jets carry hydraulic backup, driven by pressurized fluid power and unaffected by EMP or other electrical interference. EMP would zap electrical systems and radar, but planes could fly on hydraulic power and land under visual flight rules, weather permitting. Spacing of landing aircraft would be a problem; air traffic control radars have limited redundancy. Once on the ground, though, planes would stay there until power is restored, save for emergency missions. As food and water ran low and communications closed down, a major EMP strike could bring most air travel to a standstill.

Agriculture requires immense water table and electric grid support. The grid is also essential for food processing, primarily for refrigeration.

Supermarkets are the weakest link—the current reliance on just-in-time delivery (using electronic databases) means that supermarkets have one to three days' supply of food. In 1900, almost a third of Americans were farmers. Today the figure is 2 percent, meaning that there is a shortage of skilled farm personnel to help in a crisis. (Farm productivity, meanwhile, is up fiftyfold.) There are not enough workers to process food in the low-tech ways of earlier times. Gas ranges would work, but most gas-powered ovens built since the mid-1980s would not, as they are made with components more vulnerable to EMP disruption. And these newer models cannot be ignited with a match.

Starvation, in the event that the food infrastructure collapses, would impair mobility and strength within a few days. After four or five days judgment would be impaired. After a fortnight people would be incapacitated. Death would result in one to two months.

The water infrastructure includes over 75,000 dams and reservoirs; thousands of miles of pipes, aqueducts, and distribution and sewer lines connect buildings with many thousands of water treatment facilities. Filtration and disinfectant systems require electric power. So do the pumps that raise water against the pull of gravity (as in skyscrapers). Irrigation and cooling are 80 percent of water consumption. As for drinking water, stores typically carry one to three days' supply. Overall, because it relies heavily on electricity and digital control systems, the water infrastructure is highly EMP vulnerable.

Emergency services are provided in the United States by some 2 million firefighters, police, and emergency medical personnel. Emergency communications have enhanced backup, but they depend upon other infrastructures functioning. (A minor east coast earthquake in 2011 generated such a huge surge in cellphone traffic that congestion prevented most callers from getting through. An EMP strike would be far worse.)

Space systems orbiting at low altitudes are vulnerable to EMP (as well as to other radioactive elements dispersed by a nuclear explosion, should their orbit take them through an affected zone). However, many vital satellites—such as communications and broadcasting satellites in their geosynchronous orbits, 22,300 miles above earth in deep space—are EMP safe.

Government depends upon all the above services, and is thus vulnerable. It would need to handle public dissemination of information following an attack. People may panic in the face of remote but unexplained dangers: after the 2001 anthrax attacks people took precautions against the disease, despite the astronomical odds of their becoming victims. After an attack, people would want to know about their family, understand what had transpired, and be assured that the authorities were managing the situation. Otherwise panic, or even posttraumatic stress, could result. After Japan's 2011 earthquake and tsunami megadisaster caused several partial nuclear plant meltdowns and released locally lethal radiation, Americans on the West coast bought iodine tablets, fearing that they otherwise would get thyroid cancer. Many people ignored statements from public health authorities that such precautions were unnecessary (because by the time the iodine crossed the Pacific its toxicity would have been drastically reduced).

Reducing EMP Risk

THE COMMISSION concludes that while an EMP attack on civilian infrastructure is "a serious problem," it can be managed by public and private cooperation. This may prove optimistic. America may well need other countries to serve as "edge communities" and come to our aid.

A modest investment along the lines indicated in the commission's report—hardening of key facilities and stockpiling of critical infrastructure components—would surely represent a small fraction of potential exposure and could add a lot to America's security. The panel listed a set of remedial measures that appear to cost in aggregate perhaps $5 billion. At many times that amount the investment is a bargain.

Hardening vital infrastructures would also protect our lives and trillions in economic value from one phenomenon against which a deal with Moscow will not help: geomagnetic storms from the sun, which interact with the Earth's magnetic field as does EMP. In 1859 a powerful geomagnetic storm inflicted major damage worldwide. With today's vast infrastructures global catastrophe could result if another such storm occurred.

Missile defense—intercepting missiles before they reach detonation altitude—could amplify this protection. The threat is hardly theoretical; as indicated above, Iran has successfully tested a missile in EMP mode. A big and unanswered question is when Iran will have an ICBM ready, to cover the 6,350-mile distance between Tehran and Washington, D.C. One report has Iran already having purchased a pair of Chinese DF-31 ICBMs, whose range is 5,000 miles. These have sufficient range to cover all of Europe.

Iran has already launched small satellites into space. Doing so requires accelerating a rocket to an orbital velocity of five miles per second, faster than the four-mile-per-second velocity achieved by ICBMs that traverse space en route to their targets. Iran's ICBM quest awaits two milestones: when it miniaturizes nuclear warheads, so they are small and light enough to be carried by Iran's ballistic missiles; and when it achieves sufficient accuracy to put those missiles close to intended targets. Because Iran's likely targets will be cities, the ICBMs they deploy need not have the pinpoint accuracy, within the radius of several football fields, achieved by U.S. ICBMs.

Currently Iran has the intermediate-range Shahab-3, with a 1,200-mile reach. To reach the continental United States, a Shahab-3 would have to be launched from a base inside the Western Hemisphere. And as it happens, Iran has found just such a base in Venezuela, courtesy of Venezuela's anti-American president Hugo Chavez. From Caracas to Miami is 1,000 miles, well within the range of the Shahab-3. But being smaller than an ICBM, Shahab missiles will require warheads of greater miniaturization than those for an ICBM. Chavez may succumb to cancer before 2012 ends, but if his followers seize power, then Iran's basing option will remain open. Meanwhile, six Persian Gulf states have indicated interest in deploying a missile defense shield backed by the U.S., to counter the growing Iranian threat.

Currently deployed missile defense systems can shoot down intermediate-range ballistic missiles (IRBMs), which travel at about two miles per second. At twice that speed ICBMs are far too fast for existing defense systems to reliably track and destroy. America's current deployment is minimal, and not effective against an EMP launch.

Such launches pose an additional as yet unmet challenge: they follow a steep trajectory that today's missile defense systems are not designed to intercept. Existing systems intercept warheads as they descend. But an EMP warhead is detonated at maximum altitude, and will have done its work before today's systems can perform their defensive mission.

What is ultimately needed is a system like the recently cancelled Airborne Laser, which was carried on a Boeing 747 aircraft and aimed at missiles as they rose off the launch pad or in early stages of flight. The

ABL was ended because its technology was considered not good enough. We must put American ingenuity to work anew on this vital task. New directed energy systems—especially those based on ships, which would draw from the vast electric power produced aboard ships (far greater than that generated in any aircraft)—offer promise for improved missile defense in the medium and longer term.

Missile defense needs were examined in the Rumsfeld Commission report, which presented four unanimous broad conclusions:

1. Nuclear missile threats posed by hostile nations to America and its allies are growing.

2. Emerging offensive missile capabilities are "broader, more mature and evolving more rapidly" than realized in the intelligence community.

3. The ability of our intelligence to provide "timely and accurate" estimates of these threats is eroding.

4. Warning times are shrinking and may in some cases be minimal.

Given emerging perils, it is essential that missile defense technology be unleashed, not retarded, by existing arms accords, including New START, and that development on multiple types rapidly proceed. The need for this technology is urgent.

Which makes all the more worrisome President Obama's identification of missile defense as of "particular" interest in accommodating Moscow's desires after the November election.

The danger of EMP may seem remote. But failure to protect against it—by hardening essential infrastructure and strengthening missile defense—greatly increases the payoff for surprise attacks, and thus the chance they will be carried out and succeed. The potentially catastrophic consequences of EMP underscore the importance of nuclear-age history's Eleventh Lesson: NEVER ALLOW SINGLE OR LOW-NUMBER POINTS OF CATASTROPHIC VULNERABILITY.

14.

THE PERILOUS PRESENT: BEYOND MYTHIC PASTS AND FANTASY FUTURES

*How the Great Democracies Triumphed, and so Were able to
Resume the Follies Which Had so Nearly Cost Them Their Life.*
STATED THEME OF VOLUME 6 OF WINSTON CHURCHILL'S THE SECOND WORLD WAR

LESSONS DRAWN FROM THE NUCLEAR AGE DURING ITS FIRST TWO-thirds of a century cannot predict every crisis to come. History does not always repeat itself, but if we are to disregard what history teaches we should have good reason to do so—reason grounded in facts, and logical inferences drawn from those facts. We also should hold a keen appreciation of the intractability of human nature and how that nature affects global politics.

The civilized person recoils at the utter moral insanity and ultimate strategic futility of nuclear war. But defending and preserving civilization from its worst enemies, some of highly dubious stability, necessitates considering how to prevent the very real prospect that nuclear weapons will be used for the first time since 1945. The prospect of such a hideous, civilization-altering event seems to be growing as time passes. There is no time to waste in remedying unfortunate turns in nuclear policy and restoring more prudent policies so as to confront emerging nuclear dangers.

The select community of serious nuclear strategists, often satirized as enamored of matters at once esoteric and macabre, diligently and creatively pondered ways to avoid nuclear Armageddon. They got things right enough to help guide the civilized world through the era of super-power contest. Their collected wisdom coupled with history's nuclear-age lessons offers the civilized world the best—and the last—chance to

226 / Sleepwalking with the Bomb /

defeat the emerging, malignant nuclear actors of the twenty-first century before nuclear demons seize the world stage.

The bombs of 1945 generated a powerful current of opinion among leaders and the citizenry—the belief that those blinding atomic flashes had rendered traditional principles of geopolitics and war obsolete. The advent of the nuclear age coincided with the creation of the United Nations, which was to accomplish after World War II's global carnage what the League of Nations had failed to do after the slaughter of World War I's trenches. It is understandable that with tens of millions of lives already lost in what was to prove history's bloodiest century, the prospect of destruction on a vastly greater scale—made possible by the potentially unlimited thermonuclear power of the hydrogen bomb—would drive pacifist passions and utopian yearnings.

Events since 1945 have proven the dolorous refutation of such beliefs and hopes. The nuclear genie is not only still out of the bottle, it has multiplied. Malignant actors are now in possession of nuclear technology and could well have it within their power to fatally wound modern civilization in the not-too-distant future. The five members of the original nuclear club have been joined by four more, with only one of these, Israel, a truly stable democratic state that would not use nuclear weapons save if its literal survival required it. India is a democracy, fairly stable, but going through an economic and social transformation that will test that stability. Pakistan is rife with Islamist fervor and anti-American passions. A mysterious clique of xenophobic tyrants runs North Korea. Iran is approaching nuclear membership but is neither stable nor pacific in its strategic aspirations. Its revolutionary leaders desire to attain regional hegemony in the Mideast, driving American influence to the periphery, and then ultimately to destroy Western civilization.

Despite the clear lessons offered by this history, many have embraced mythic pasts. According to these myths, the threat of extinction posed by an all-out nuclear arms race is sufficient to create a fundamental commonality of interest in mutual survival. Thus patient diplomacy can bring about a nuclear-zero world in which we "end the nuclear nightmare" once and for all. The genie can, in this view, be put back into the bottle after all. There is no serious evidence to support this view. A companion myth is one of benevolent world government, though even a cursory look at the United Nations shows how chimerical such a vision is in real life.

For those who harbor such beliefs, arms control has become a doctrine that transcends geopolitics. Like all utopian beliefs, it is based upon revelatory rather than empirical truth and is thus beyond refutation by concrete evidence in the form of actual events. Arms treaties are inviolate, leading supporters to deny or minimize violations, lest they lead to abandonment of the treaty. Each treaty stands as a step towards nuclear zero. There can be no steps backward on this path. There are, in this view, no undetectable clandestine caches, nor implacable enemies.

Arms-control doctrine further holds that nuclear war is unthinkable because "a nuclear war cannot be won," and that if somehow a nuclear war starts, the use of even one weapon will inevitably lead to all-out nuclear exchanges. Thus only a truly insane leader could even seriously contemplate starting a nuclear war. And thus the concept of "nuclear superiority" is meaningless, because there can be no winner in a nuclear confrontation. Nuclear weapons are unusable, except to support "mutual assured destruction" as a deterrent to their ever being used. International institutions acting in accord with "world opinion" can mediate seemingly intractable differences between nations. And in saving the human race from mass self-destruction, geopolitics can be redeemed.

But such beliefs presume that our adversaries share our core civilizational values. They do not. These values are scorned by the likes of North Korea's blinkered Stalinist dictatorship, attempting to use its nuclear bombs for blackmail and to expand international commerce with aspiring rogue nuclear powers. They are scorned by atavist Islamists seeking to seize power in Pakistan so as to gain control over its growing arsenal of nuclear weapons, already about 100 bombs. And they are scorned by the fanatical revolutionary clerics ruling Iran, who might well use nuclear blackmail to undermine the existing world order, starting in the oil-rich and turbulent Mideast. We continually imagine moderates in governments where they are a scarce commodity at best and an extinct species at worst.

During the Cold War doves imagined that each new Soviet leader might prove to be one who would liberalize the system and reach peaceful coexistence. When former KGB chief Yuri Andropov ascended to power upon the death of Leonid Brezhnev, for example, rumors promptly surfaced that Andropov, architect of the bloody suppression of the Hungarian revolt, was a closet liberal who liked scotch and jazz. In fact he liked neither, nor anything else Western and liberal.

Stir into this poisonous nuclear geopolitical brew a Russia that is a stagnant petrostate, consuming its natural resources as its population dies off at a younger average age by the year. Add a China that is determined to vault to preeminence on the world stage, restoring its long-lost greatness via economic primacy and cyber-dominance coupled with regional military intimidation. While neither Russia nor China is a plausible candidate to initiate nuclear war, any shift in the nuclear balance in their favor could alter their behavior during a major crisis, as happened with the former Soviet Union during the 1973 Yom Kippur War.

We would do well under the circumstances to recall the words of Senator Daniel Patrick Moynihan, speaking on the Senate floor about the Reagan administration's response to the December 1981 Soviet crackdown in Poland: "We court great danger when we invite the contempt of totalitarians."

If a powerful America is often the object of anger and resentment, it is also feared. But a weak America, far from engendering sympathy, will earn the contempt of allies and adversaries alike. Allies will seek alternative arrangements—including their own nuclear weapons—to secure their position. Enemies will plot potentially lethal trouble. Further, "setting an example" by our own steep arms reductions will not reassure smaller powers like India and Pakistan, who feel threatened and lack a superpower guarantor they trust.

A weak England and France invited Hitler's contempt, and got World War II. A weak Depression-era America invited Japan's contempt, and got Pearl Harbor. A weak JFK invited Nikita Khrushchev's contempt at the Vienna Summit, and got the Berlin Wall and the Cuban Missile Crisis. A weak Jimmy Carter invited the Ayatollah Khomeini's contempt, and got the 1979 hostage seizure. Ronald Reagan's failure to respond to the 1983 Marine barracks bombing, and his efforts to negotiate the release of hostages, invited contempt, and got an upsurge in hostage taking and terrorism across the Mideast (while his bombing of Qaddafi in 1986 restored a measure of respect). George H. W. Bush's failure to answer the Pan Am 103 bombing, and his failure to cap Desert Storm by finishing off Saddam Hussein, invited al-Qaeda's contempt. So did Bill Clinton's hasty departure from Somalia, and his serial failures to respond to escalating terror attacks by al-Qaeda. Osama bin Laden saw himself as the strong horse and his adversaries as weak horses. The upshot was a series of attacks, culminating in the atrocities of September 11, 2001.

George W. Bush's failure to respond forcefully to Syrian and Iranian roles in killing U.S. troops in Iraq and Afghanistan invited Iran's contempt, as had earlier failures of his predecessors to respond. Iran paid us back in the cruel coinage of American soldiers slain and maimed in Iraq and Afghanistan, by Iranian munitions (some Russian made) supplied to Islamist terrorists.

The threat from fanatics is only partially distinct from that posed by the clinically insane. Fanaticism is often considered a synonym for insanity in Western societies, whose people feel that no "rational person" would contemplate nuclear use. Thus anyone who does contemplate it is deemed insane. True, Hitler was both a fanatic and insane, but not all fanatics are like him. And "rational" people can commit supremely irrational—even insane—acts.

Because we are limited in our ability to see inside the human mind and precisely pinpoint who is crazy and who is a fanatic, we should instead focus on the more prosaic task of inferring intent from action. Where, as with Iran and North Korea, a pattern of activity indicates a penchant for risk taking and gambling, we should expect more of the same. Nor can we reasonably expect anything from negotiations with fanatics whom we cannot coerce at gunpoint. Such adversaries will repudiate voluntary commitments as long as they remain in power.

In 1962 one leader—Fidel Castro, a fanatical Marxist revolutionary—apparently did indeed contemplate an all-out nuclear war, even knowing it would obliterate his own island and captive subjects. His masters in Moscow thought better of the plan, and Nikita Khrushchev instead labored with President Kennedy to pull the superpowers back from the nuclear precipice. Many people do not regard Castro as insane; to the contrary, he remains widely lionized, despite ruling a country he has utterly impoverished. Thus can fanaticism and widely perceived rationality be joined in a leader who desires to use nuclear weapons.

Despite mutual desire to avoid all-out war, large powers can find themselves involved in a nonnuclear crisis that evolves into a nuclear one. Thus the 1973 Yom Kippur War—unlike the Cuban confrontation 11 years earlier—began not as a superpower nuclear power play but rather as a regional war over lost territory. The superpowers involved themselves when the United States sought a primary diplomatic role, and the Soviet Union—eager to reestablish influence in the region that had been lost when its prime client, Egypt, sundered their alliance relationship a year earlier—sought a military role as well as a diplomatic one.

The Soviet Union, smarting from having to back down in the face of overwhelming nuclear strategic superiority in the Cuban Missile Crisis, had vowed never to be caught in a similarly weak military position again. It accelerated over a quarter century of nuclear and conventional force buildup, as America, at least, partially pulled back. As its arsenal swelled, the Soviet Union became more aggressive in moving across the global geostrategic chessboard.

The second nuclear confrontation between the superpowers—in the Mediterranean in 1973 rather than the Atlantic in 1962—ended differently than did the first, in no small measure because in the interim the strategic superpower nuclear balance had changed. The eventual diplomatic compromise reached did not restore the Soviets to their former strong position, but spared them a replay of their humiliation of 1962.

The 1973 Yom Kippur War crisis confirmed a hard truth about a power's perception of the strategic nuclear balance: the balance matters if *any power* in a major confrontation acts as if it does. For such action will have consequences that affect how a crisis unfolds and how it ends. The United States responded sharply to Soviet escalation and prevailed, because the Soviets had not attained the position Brezhnev foresaw he would attain in 1985. Yet thus fortified, albeit ultimately his prediction for the USSR proved the polar opposite of what transpired, Brezhnev acted more boldly than did Khrushchev over Cuba, at least in part because of the vast increase in the Soviet nuclear arsenal.

And superpowers' actions can have long-lasting consequences beyond those envisioned at the outset, as was the case with the Suez Crisis of 1956. The failure of the U.S. to back its allies (Britain, France, and Israel) against a Soviet client (Egypt) triggered a series of disastrous events that unleashed both secular and religious hyper-aggressive tyrannies, waves of terrorism that spread globally, demoralization and thus weakening of key American allies, and independent nuclear proliferation by allies. The reverberations of Suez continue today, to the detriment of American ability to influence events in the Mideast.

Deterrence did eventually prevail during the Cold War. The massive uncertainties unavoidably attendant on launching a large-scale nuclear attack provided real-world deterrence far more credible than a deterrent threat to commit reciprocal suicide if attacked. Deterrence cannot reliably work against the truly insane, even those with small nuclear arsenals. What will be tested, should Iran go nuclear or Pakistan's arsenal fall into jihadist hands, is whether fundamentalists can transcend their ideology and accept deterrence. It is a proposition imprudent to test if we can avoid it. Preventing fanatics from obtaining nuclear weapons beats relying on a calculus of deterrence.

There is a further danger in relying upon retaliatory deterrence alone: the potential for a terror state to engage in nuclear blackmail by proxy. A common fear among those who assess potential nuclear threats is that a terror state transfers several bombs to a terrorist group. The group sets off one bomb in a major American city. It then announces that there are bombs already placed in several other cities, and that if America retaliates against any suspect group or state, or if any nuclear search team approaches the hidden weapons, more bombs will instantly be detonated. It is far from clear that any American president would order nuclear retaliation under such circumstances.

Securing the existing global nuclear arsenal, and thus preventing sale, gift, or theft of nuclear weapons, necessarily entails nuclear-capable states cooperating and nuclear-aspirant states being denied access to nuclear status.

A constant companion to mythic pasts has been the fantasy future of rapidly moving towards a nuclear-free world. Some Manhattan Project scientists joined disarmers in the aftermath of the bomb's use to end World War II. Ronald Reagan, to the consternation of Lady Thatcher, sought to strike such a bargain at the 1986 Reykjavik summit. His idea was checked only by Mikhail Gorbachev's insistence that Reagan limit missile defense to the laboratory. Reagan refused, and the moment was gone. And Reagan, at least, hedged his offer by insisting on retaining a robust missile defense program, as a national security insurance policy against clandestine nuclear cheating.

The latest movement pushing for nuclear zero includes former senior national security officials who served American presidents over the past 40 years. In an article published as this book went to press, Henry

Kissinger and Brent Scowcroft set eight criteria for moving to lower levels, in the process rejecting the idea leaked by the Obama administration for a rapid push to a U.S. nuclear arsenal of 300 weapons.

They argue for retaining sufficient, diversified forces; stronger verification; extending force reductions to the growing arsenals of proliferating powers; factoring in missile defense and conventional long-range strategic forces; sustaining alliance guarantees to discourage allies from proliferating; and avoiding the mirror-imaging trap of assuming our enemies share our values, and the perspective on nuclear weapons that our values encompass.

Their viewpoint is a more carefully framed position than that taken by those who wish to rapidly reduce America's arsenal to 300. But two large problems face those following this gradualist prescription. First, until we know the size of China's arsenal, and know more about sophisticated nuclear weapons that China and Russia are testing and deploying, we should not entertain further reductions. Second, the cause of rapid disarmament gains momentum from prestigious officials advocating it, and may lead to a stampede of popular opinion. Let a single nuclear weapon detonate anywhere, and the cause will pick up potentially irresistible momentum. Cautionary advocacy of gradual reductions could well fall by the wayside. What is needed is action to bring about positive regime change in hostile states and, if necessary, preventive action to delay nuclear club membership in aspirant hostile states in the interim.

Well-crafted arms agreements can contribute to strategic stability, if arms control is viewed as an essential foreign policy tool rather than an always-paramount goal—an inherently good end in itself. Establishment of hot-line channels of communication, arrangements guarding against accidental war, verifiable arms reductions, notification of maneuvers, and careful information sharing can all enhance security.

Yet we must "trust but verify." The closer we move to nuclear-free status, the higher confidence we must have in our means of verification. And as verification will never imaginably be ironclad, we will need to hedge against nuclear surprise. This will require newer technologies that can provide superior means of detection, defense against, and disarming of nuclear cheaters. Such technologies must also be fully able to deter conventional and unconventional nonnuclear threats, to provide a full spectrum of national and global security.

A strategy based on past failures will itself fail, and a sufficiently serious failure in nuclear arms policy can destroy Western civilization. Between mythic pasts and fantasy futures lies the perilous present. Fundamentally, nuclear policy must be defensive in orientation: nuclear policy makers should resist reaching for the nuclear-zero stars, and instead concentrate on avoiding the nuclear Armageddon abyss. Unless the West changes policy soon, a Doomsday scenario looks increasingly likely.

The Bulletin of the Atomic Scientists, a publication founded in the dawn of the nuclear age to promote the gospel of arms-control doctrine under the guise of empirical science, in 1947 set its "Doomsday Clock" at seven minutes to midnight. The clock metaphor was chosen by the editors to signal how close they thought the world then was to nuclear extinction.

Periodically the editors set a new time, when they decide that a significant event has altered the world's nuclear risk level. Twice the clock reached two minutes to midnight—in 1949, upon the first Russian A-bomb test, and in 1953, after the 1952 American H-bomb test. It stood at three minutes to midnight in 1984 when Ronald Reagan allowed the Soviets to walk away from the bargaining table. When the INF Treaty became reality four years later, on Ronald Reagan's terms, it was moved back to six before the witching hour. The end of the Cold War in 1991 pushed the clock back to 18 minutes to Doomsday—the furthest from Doomsday it has ever been. During President George W. Bush's second term it was pushed to five minutes to midnight, as the hydra-headed Islamist monster surfaced and struck. On January 14, 2010, following U.S.-Russian arms talks and President Obama's call for a nuclear-free world, it was moved back to six before. On January 10, 2012, the clock was moved back to five minutes to midnight, due to lack of progress in arms reduction over the past two years.

It is tempting to dismiss the clock as all for show, and indeed those positioning it have conceded that its original time setting was theater to grab public attention. It is certainly not scientific, in any real sense. Rather, it is ideological. Only arms agreements seem to move the clock back, while saber rattling or breakdowns in negotiations seem to nudge it forward. Yet, with proliferation attained by rogues, and Islamist fanatics in search of their jihadist nuclear genie, time is running out. After two-thirds of a century without a nuclear attack, even a single nuclear detonation would tragically alter the course of history, causing catastrophic loss of life and damaging the global economy to the tune of trillions of dollars—a reality even President Obama recognized in his 2009 Prague address. Depending upon what form such a nuclear attack takes, Western civilization would at minimum suffer a devastating blow to societal cohesion; in an absolute worst case it might be extinguished permanently.

It is not too late to act. But we must act decisively and soon, focusing on threats of today, understanding the past as it actually unfolded and the lessons it teaches, and deferring utopian projects for a nuclear-free future and benevolent world government. THE BEDROCK GOAL OF NUCLEAR STRATEGY FOR CIVILIZED NATIONS MUST BE TO AVOID WHAT MIGHT BE CALLED THE "APOCALYPTIC TRINITY" OF STRATEGIC NUCLEAR OPTIONS: MUTUAL SUICIDE, GENOCIDE, OR SURRENDER—in the words of strategist Raymond Aron—submission "to a detestable world order provided it dispels the agonies of individual insecurity and collective suicide." This goal makes up the Twelfth—and most fundamental—Lesson of nuclear-age history.

We must take preventive action to foster regime change in nations whose acquisition of nuclear weapons creates grave risk of nuclear catastrophe. As a last resort, if other means fail, a preventive military option must be preserved. Failure to take necessary active measures to defend against nuclear-armed missiles and passive measures to harden societal infrastructure essential to life and health greatly increases the payoff for surprise attacks. Such lapses simply increase chances that attacks will be carried out and succeed.

"I know not with what weapons World War III will be fought," Albert Einstein said, "but World War IV will be fought with sticks and stones." To have the best chance to avoid nuclear catastrophe, we should absorb the right lessons from the two-thirds of a century we call the nuclear age. We should keep in mind Dean Rusk's tart quip that "only one-third of the world is asleep at any given time and the other two-thirds is up to something."

President Obama's utopian rush towards nuclear abolition ignores the vital lessons nuclear-age history teaches. His abject failure to support the Iranian uprising of June 2009 by leading an allied coalition to impose strong sanctions then, instead of pursuing talks that had no plausible chance to succeed, exemplifies why we are sleepwalking towards an avoidable nuclear catastrophe. Equally risky is his desire to "set an example" for other nations to follow in reducing nuclear arms, when our adversaries are more likely to increase their arsenals instead, in pursuit of greater power and influence.

History's Twelve Vital Nuclear-Age Lessons

Two-THIRDS OF a century offer up twelve guidelines for leaders in public office.

1. Arms control cannot be viewed in isolation, but rather must be considered along with an adversary's conduct.

2. Arms agreements must be based upon genuine, not presumed, commonality of strategic interest.

3. Revolutionary powers cannot be contained; they must be defeated.

4. Nuclear weapons give nations a "dying sting" capability that virtually precludes preemptive action and confers near-total survival insurance.

5. The nuclear balance matters if any party to a conflict thinks it matters, and thus alters its behavior.

6. Civilian nuclear power inherently confers military nuclear capability.

7. Intelligence cannot reliably predict when closed societies go nuclear.

8. Ally proliferation can be prevented only by superpower constancy.

9. Popular pressure for unilateral disarmament can prevail unless Western governments explain its hidden, grave dangers.

10. Disarming hostile powers cannot be done by negotiations alone.

11. Never allow single or low-number points of catastrophic vulnerability.

12. Nuclear policy must be fundamentally defensive: its goal is to avoid the apocalyptic trinity of suicide, genocide, and surrender.

In applying these lessons it is supremely important to distinguish between three classes of adversary states: rivals, rogues, and revolutionaries. Rivals, like China and Russia, do not desire our outright destruction; their interests are too intertwined with our survival to allow for that. But they do desire to displace us in primacy of influence in world affairs. China desires to attain the supreme position it enjoyed for most of the past two millennia as the world's preeminent power; it is beginning this quest by seeking to become primary power in the western Pacific region. For its part, Russia desires to regain the territories it controlled before the end of the Cold War. Rivals, however, may aid rogue regimes by transferring military and nuclear technology.

Rogues, like North Korea, do not necessarily seek to dominate a region. Rather they seek to ensure their own survival. Towards this end, nuclear weapons are the best survival insurance policy their leaders can purchase.

Revolutionaries, like Iran, seek not merely to adjust their position in the existing global order, but to overturn that order and establish a new one. Iran's leaders are militant Islamists who ardently desire the destruction of Great Satan America and Little Satan Israel. These regimes are least likely to be peacefully persuaded to change their course.

Of the 12 lessons history offers as to nuclear policy, lessons 3, 6, and 11 are those that address the most immediate threats facing the civilized world: a revolutionary Iran in hot pursuit of nuclear weapon status (3); the danger of more rogue proliferation through careless diffusion of civilian nuclear technology (6); and the risk of nuclear blackmail if leaders leave their country open to potentially catastrophic single-point strikes from hostile powers willing to take extreme risks (11). Failure to fully meet these challenges would present civilized peoples with apocalyptic choices, with the least bad achievable outcome a Pyrrhic victory.

Over the medium term, the possibility of a nuclear crisis between major powers is also growing. Russia's immense modernization program, encompassing diverse advanced technologies, is not consistent with a desire to move towards nuclear zero. China's stunning half-century surge in strategic forces is hugely inconsistent with a focus on reductions. Its vast network of cavernous Underground Great Wall tunnels, clearly intended to house China's advanced nuclear arsenal and shelter its leadership cadre, is way out of proportion to direct war threats China faces. We must convene an outside "B-Team," one free of the intelligence community's bureaucratic tendencies, to reliably ascertain the size of China's nuclear arsenal before considering more disarmament. A "B" Team should also look at Russia's broad range of nuclear modernization programs, especially risks of breakout via hidden nuclear assets.

Our peril grows as America's pool of nuclear weapons experts drastically shrinks. Declining steadily over the past two decades, American expertise may be entirely gone from government labs in five years. The great nuclear scientists who retired take with them a matchless trove of expertise gleaned from decades conducting and assessing sophisticated nuclear tests. Unless their knowledge is captured and a sustainable growth path for nuclear weapon expertise is created, America in a decade or two may find itself with less overall nuclear weapon expertise than resides elsewhere. There is plenty of work for designers to build a replacement generation of safer, more reliable nuclear weapons. These would be more credible as deterrent weapons, and thus less likely to be used.

It is only in the long term—almost certainly decades, if not generations—that any decisive move towards nuclear zero might responsibly be countenanced. Premature disarmament can plunge the civilized world into a nightmare world order dominated by the most ruthless states and leaders on the planet.

If reelected President Obama must reverse his present course, or his successor must reverse course before it is too late. Else the nuclear Doomsday Clock likely will strike midnight once and for all, and the world will never be the same.

APPENDIX 1:
FICTION'S WAR AGAINST
NUCLEAR REALITIES

T HE COLD WAR SHAPED PUBLIC ATTITUDES FOR 55 YEARS. BUT THE focus on superpower nuclear war shifted dramatically after September 11, 2001, and attention turned to the possibility of terrorists using nuclear weapons. Nonetheless, attitudes implanted by fiction a half-century old persist in the public mind.

Nuclear tests above ground etched the mushroom cloud image indelibly on the public mind. Nuclear war became perceived in the public consciousness as inevitably an all-out exchange of the kind that ended Stanley Kubrick's black comedy *Dr. Strangelove, or How I Learned to Stop Worrying and Love the Bomb*. The 1964 film was loosely based upon Peter Bryant's 1958 novel, *Red Alert*, which had a happier, peaceful ending. Nuclear scientists and generals were portrayed in the film as lunatics, and the misleading image of one mistake triggering all-out superpower war became a staple. Nevil Shute's *On the Beach* (1957) posited a global war fought with "cobalt bombs"—nuclear devices laced with intensely radioactive cobalt-60—in which survivors in Australia live out mankind's last days. The war in that novel was started by Albania, and spread to larger powers until Russia and China exchanged massive cobalt-bomb salvoes, unleashing lethal radiation that atmospheric wind currents eventually spread worldwide. In *Alas Babylon* (1959) Pat Frank based all-out war on a single air-to-air missile with a conventional warhead fired by a U.S. Navy flier that missed its Russian target and slammed into a Russian military depot in Syria.

The novel *Fail-Safe* (published in 1962 and set in 1967) posed a scenario in which the American president avoids all-out destruction after the accidental obliteration of Moscow by consenting to a deliberate destruction of New York, equally without warning. And the thriller *Seven Days in May* (1962) featured a liberal president whose arms-control treaty induces a right-wing Caesar-general to attempt a coup; the general, readers and viewers were led to believe, would have unleashed a first strike against the Soviet Union.

A later, more credible take on nuclear peril was the 1980 thriller by Dominique Lapierre and Larry Collins, *The Fifth Horseman*, which has Libyan dictator Muammar Qaddafi, at the time instigator of numerous terrorist acts against the West, developing a three-megaton hydrogen bomb via stolen French technology. The device is smuggled into New York City, where its detonation could kill nearly 7 million people. The weapon is disarmed seconds before it is to detonate, thanks to intrepid detective work. In fact, since the mid-1970s Qaddafi had made a standing offer to purchase nuclear weapons from any seller.

Public perceptions were fueled by factual inaccuracies and outright absurdities in the fictional works. In *Strangelove* American bombers, once aloft, proceed to their targets when not recalled to base before they reach their designated standby stations aloft; in reality the opposite has been true for over 50 years, with bombers turning back unless given an affirmative order to proceed from authorized commanders.[55] In *Fail-Safe* the pilots fly bombers at speeds of 2,000 mph at impossibly low altitudes, skimming terrain in the dead of night; they also are instructed to disregard a recall order coming even from the president, as his voice might be faked. And Moscow refuses for hours to accept information on how to destroy the bombers headed its way out of national pride! None of this was or is true or plausible. *Alas Babylon's* escalation scenario has the Russians launch an all-out strike because a single base is damaged with one conventional warhead. *On the Beach* posits nuclear-armed states launching weapons in such massive numbers so as to destroy the human race. Only an entire collection of Armageddon-inspired fanatics might do this. As for *Seven Days in May*, its coup scenario is utterly implau-

---

55. Albert Wohlstetter was instrumental in conceiving the "fail-safe" protocol. Perhaps due to the film and its notoriety, it later was renamed "positive control."

sible, because America's military has a civilian command structure and a deeply entrenched culture of deference to civilian authority.

Later scenarios were based upon more realistic prospects. In *Blink of an Eye*, former secretary of defense William Cohen sketched out a scenario involving a possible terrorist nuclear bomb. His real-world senior-level crisis management experience lent gripping realism to his account of how government officials would act in extreme crisis.

Yet in the end, a nuclear crisis will arise in a context likely unforeseen in many aspects, and will impose stress upon leaders and world politics of a kind never seen in human history. Nuclear events might well prove stranger than nuclear fiction.

APPENDIX 2:
IMPROVING CONTROL OVER
NUCLEAR WEAPONS

In 1961 a B-52G crashed in Georgia with a pair of hydrogen bombs. By one account, recovery teams discovered that five of six safety switches had been flipped on one of the two hydrogen bombs it carried. That bomb was perhaps 1,000 times more powerful than the Nagasaki bomb. The plane crashed in a rural area. Still, had the bomb gone off, it would have caused massive loss of life in several states, *via dispersal of millions of tons of lethal fallout.*

This particular account, however, has been disputed. The alternate version holds that because the bombs were equipped with Permissive Action Links (PAL) trigger locks, a random series of stresses could not have flipped five of the six switches needed to detonate the weapon. This version appears more likely correct, as later-model bombs were equipped with PALs.

Either way, such a scary mishap showed how far the U.S. had to go in protecting its nuclear weapons from accidental detonation. Efforts to control use of bombs had begun not long before with behavior protocols, as L. Douglas Keeney details in *15 Minutes.* In 1956 the Atomic Energy Commission instituted a "two-man rule" for control of every nuclear weapon: "A minimum of two authorized persons, each capable of detecting incorrect procedures… will be present during any operations requiring access to the weapon." In 1957 aircrews of nuclear bombers began carrying envelopes printed with a code word. When the Strategic Air Command base station gave a two-word code, the pilot opened the envelope. If the word inside matched the SAC's second word, it meant to continue past the fail-safe point.

A second 1957 innovation was the "sealed-pit" bomb. Before, when a flight crew heard the authorization to proceed, its members had to insert the core of a bomb into its canister. In a sealed-pit bomb, the bomb canister already contained the core.

In all, the U.S. ultimately implemented 24-link, chained safeguards, each of which must be surmounted to detonate a weapon. There are weak and strong links, as Keeney explains. An electrical "capacitor" that can send an electric signal to detonate the bomb would be an example of a "weak link." The heat of a plane crashing and burning would melt the capacitor, disabling the bomb. A mechanical switch that has to be physically closed before detonation can proceed would be an example of a "strong link."

During the Cuban Missile Crisis, U.S. control was modest at best and Soviet control virtually nonexistent—local commanders could ignore Moscow's orders, and communication channels were minimal and slow. There was no technological control, only the human nuclear chain of command. Both superpowers saw that to reduce the risk of war by accident or by a field commander's impulsive act in a crisis, better arrangements for control over weapons of mass destruction were essential.

In the mid-1960s, the first major technical control steps followed the ideas of behavioral protocols. The installation of the Hot Line after the Cuban Missile Crisis created a channel of instantaneous long-distance direct Teletype and telephone communication between superpower leaders for the first time, enabling them to gauge risk of conflict and escalation more acutely and take steps to minimize it. With the new technology of built-in trigger locks (PALs), leaders were finally able to restrict final authorization to a small level of senior commanders acting upon direct instructions from the president. Within U.S. missile silos, two launch keys 12 feet apart had to be turned within a two-second period to fire a missile. The U.S. made security technologies and techniques available to the Soviets, to improve their secure storage and thus reduce the risk of accidental or unauthorized nuclear war.

But the Soviets, to the end of the Cold War, relied upon human controls—orders from superiors. Since then they have adopted technical controls as well. In August 1991, during the coup that toppled Mikhail Gorbachev, Soviet military officials made sure the rebels did not have control over nukes. When Boris Yeltsin emerged, control was given to him.

Nuclear safety locks use methods such as limiting the number of tries to a few (like password log-ins on computers), with astronomically large possible codes to defeat "brute force" crunching of every possible combination. Environmental sensors are implanted inside U.S. missile warheads—the warhead locks unless the sensors have detected stresses comparable to those in ballistic missile or air-dropped bomb flight.

A distant commander must authorize the launch—the President or such senior commanders as the Commander-in-Chief designates. With U.S. weapons based in NATO countries, independent authorization to launch must be received by the host government as well. This situation leads to some interesting results. In the case of Eastern European NATO countries, it undermines Russian assertions that defensive missiles based in Eastern Europe might be fired at Russia. The prospect that approval would be granted by any sane Eastern European leader, given the certitude of an apocalyptic Russian response, is virtually nil. No order thought insane by its recipients would be obeyed.

The case of Western European NATO countries during the Cold War was the mirror image of Eastern Europe today. Both British prime minister Thatcher and West German chancellor Helmut Schmidt turned down a U.S. offer of a "dual key"—a trigger lock allowing them to veto a launch from their soil. Both feared that the Soviets might conclude that the weapons would never be launched, because the host country would not fire U.S. missiles at Russia, thus weakening the credibility of U.S. "extended deterrence" of possible Soviet attacks against its allies. The allies wanted U.S. consultation before launch, but not a power embedded in technology to veto a launch outright.

In the 1950s, the Strategic Air Command introduced the Special Weapons Emergency Separation System (SWESS). If an aircrew were disabled during an attack while over enemy territory, SWESS would automatically release bombs on board, once the plane fell below a specified altitude. This became known as the "dead-man's switch."

For 30 years the Strategic Air Command kept an airborne command post aloft, originally named National Emergency Airborne Command Post, or NEACP (pronounced "kneecap"), and ultimately called Looking Glass. This ever-flying patrol enabled the U.S. to retaliate, even after a surprise attack. When the Cold War ended, so did the 24-hour airborne command post patrols.

APPENDIX 3:

INTELLIGENCE BIASES AND THE NUCLEAR BALANCE

MUCH HAS BEEN MADE OF THE "ACTION-REACTION" INTERPLAY OF the superpower arms race and of imaginary missile gaps allegedly invented to spur the U.S. arms buildup. The truth is more complex: what many observers (and even some senior-level policy makers in various administrations) thought was conspiracy was in fact, as is usual in human affairs, a case of blunder.

In 1976 Albert Wohlstetter proved that American intelligence estimates consistently underestimated Soviet deployments, with even high-end estimates often below the actual Soviet numbers. *Far from improving with experience, these estimating errors grew worse with time.* Convenient assumptions guided intelligence policy, rather than logical inferences from incoming evidence.

Intelligence underestimates beginning in the mid-1960s are best understood against the earlier overestimates of the late 1950s and early 1960s. Then, the focus was on a "missile gap"—the idea that the United States, with some 200 ICBMs, had fewer than the Soviets. Because these early overestimations of the Soviet arsenal have been a huge marker in nuclear policy debates for half a century, they merit closer examination.

In *The Wizards of Armageddon*, Fred Kaplan discusses "the gap that never was." In 1960, President Eisenhower's last year, intelligence analysts projected that the Russians would field 50 to 200 ICBMs in the early 1960s. But U-2 reconnaissance flights—flying up to 70,000 feet above land—revealed no ICBMs. On August 10, 1960, the air force launched the first Discoverer satellite (circling in highly elliptical polar orbits, these satellites swoop low—a few hundred miles[56]—over the target area). Only then did the U.S. acquire the ability to cover all of Soviet Russia's vast territory, which spans 12 time zones. The new satellite found only four ICBMs, sited at Plesetsk in northeast Russia. In February of 1961, Kennedy's secretary of defense, Robert McNamara, concluded that there was and had been no ICBM missile gap (or rather, the gap went the other way—America had more ICBMs than Russia). The issue that the new president had flogged so successfully in his campaign was mooted. In June, the CIA issued an intelligence estimate for 1961 that said the Soviets might have up to 50 to 100 ICBMs—and potentially up to 200 by next year (the high end of their earlier 1960 estimate, which they only repudiated that September).

In his landmark book, *One Minute to Midnight: Kennedy, Khrushchev and Castro on the Brink of Nuclear War*, author Michael Dobbs writes that in 1962 the Pentagon estimated the Soviets had 86 to 110 ICBMs (versus our own 240), but that the actual Soviet total was 42. Surely a contributing factor was Khrushchev's public bluffing as to how the Soviets were growing ICBMs like sausages, while privately telling his son Sergei that the USSR had little of either product.

However, Paul Nitze explained that there was a second gap: Russia led in medium- and intermediate-range ballistic missiles. These were the main spearhead of Russian missile deployments in Cuba. The threat posed by these missiles guided U.S. policy during the 1962 crisis. Nitze also cited a Soviet budget expert's assessment that the beginning of a 25-year Soviet strategic force buildup began at least a year before the Cuban Missile Crisis. The early intelligence overestimates of Soviet ICBM deployments surely were a large factor in later intelligence underestimates, via the classic pendulum swing that often follows major organizational failures.

---

56. Anything less than a thousand miles above Earth is "low" for a satellite, whereas a hundredth of that is high for a plane. Spy planes like the U-2 (and its faster-flying successor, the SR-71 Blackbird, which could cruise at 85,000 feet, or 16 miles above earth) are among the highest-flying manned non-rocket aircraft. The SR-71 was retired in the 1990s.

Nitze points out that the theory of National Intelligence Estimates (NIEs) is that they look to non-U.S. capabilities only, and do not attempt "net assessments"—those based upon comparing forces. Yet forward net assessments became what most NIEs did, due to bureaucratic biases in favor of trying to look ahead. It was a task rarely done well, due to biases built into assumptions.

APPENDIX 4:
MISSILE DEFENSE VERSUS
MULTIPLE WARHEADS

THE FUNDAMENTAL CONCEPTS OF NUCLEAR ARMS CONTROL WERE developed in the West long before small powers of questionable stability came into possession of nuclear weapons. Calibrated to the threat from a hostile superpower, decisions taken 40 years ago created a mindset that persisted past the demise of that superpower 20 years ago.

Failure of the U.S. to deploy an effective missile defense against a small-power attack is a product of superpower arms control. Binding arms-control constraints began with SALT I in 1972. The Anti-Ballistic Missile (ABM) Treaty severely limited missile-defense design and deployment in the United States. Defensive system design since then has aimed not for the best products that technology and innovation can produce. Rather, system design has been governed by the maximum technological result deemed permissible under strategic arms-control principles as they were understood forty years ago. The result has been systems of perilously stunted capability, making a successful strike by a small power achievable.

Just how this came to pass teaches a crucial lesson in arms-control efforts: how limitations that to many appeared reasonable in one strategic context—the Cold War face-off against a massively armed superpower—proved obsolete and even dangerous decades later, when emerging powers in possession of or seeking small arsenals of far less sophistication menace the free world. Missile defense against 1,000 ICBMs might never work within the limits of existing technologies; defense against 10 or 20 ICBMs might work.

Missile defense became inextricably intertwined with MIRV—multiple independently targeted vehicles (warheads). Put simply, the more warheads could be directed at targets, the harder it would be for defensive systems to intercept them. During the late 1950s and early 1960s, missile defense systems increasingly faced offensive systems whose growing size and hence payload capacity enabled carrying initially lightweight decoys and then, as warhead sizes drastically shrunk, multiple warheads. As attacking warheads increased, the burden on missile defense increased commensurately. As decoys confused sensors, the task of shooting down warheads became far more daunting.

These large offensive systems with multiple warheads were first deployed in 1964 on the U.S. Navy's Polaris A-3 submarine-launched ballistic missile. Soon after, it became possible to design a missile that dispensed a series of independently targeted warheads. The navy was first to deploy these MIRV systems in 1971. MIRV developments in America and Russia went along roughly in parallel—most American officials were convinced that American restraint on MIRV would not be reciprocated by the Soviets.

Missile defense capabilities deployed to date cannot intercept ICBMs, which travel at four miles per second (nearly equal to the five-mile per second orbital velocity of satellites), twice the speed of intermediate-range missiles and about four times the speed of a short-range missile (like the Scud). Such superfast warheads cannot be tracked and intercepted by existing defensive systems.

But the Russians feared that America would be able to surmount missile defense limitations. When U.S. Secretary of Defense McNamara lectured Soviet Premier Alexei Kosygin on the dangers of missile defense at the 1967 Glassboro (New Jersey) Summit, Kosygin countered him with Occam's Razor (a rule of preference for the simplest explanation): "When I have trouble sleeping, it's because of your offensive missiles, not your defensive missiles." McNamara was focused on defensive missiles because he accepted MAD. There is no credible evidence that the Soviets accepted MAD, except, perhaps, as Mainly America's Destruction. The Soviet Union's extensive civil defense program indicated a desire to save its population, which is utterly inconsistent with MAD. Even if the shelters would have proven useless, the government's intention in building them was to protect the very people MAD was supposed to hold at risk. (Nor did America fully accept MAD, as noted in the text.)

As arms talks progressed in the Nixon administration, domestic opposition to ABM—an acronym of Cold War origin that denotes anti-ballistic missiles, still used by many—began to build. Such systems were far more widely known than MIRV, and thus became the primary focus of arms-control attention.

The ABM/MIRV case was a classic example of strategic systems whose development was so closely linked that the "action-reaction" cliché often used by arms controllers—that each side's programs were primarily driven by similar moves by the other side—held an initial measure of validity. That theory, however, suggested that American restraint would have been reciprocated. By the mid-1970s it became clear that far from emulating American decisions, the Soviets were continuing their massive military buildup despite considerable American restraint, including freezing offensive forces at 1967 numbers. This should not have come as a surprise, in that American and British restraint during the 1920s and 1930s pursuant to the interwar naval treaties did not dissuade Nazi Germany and militarist Japan from rushing pell-mell to build far beyond the limits they had nominally agreed to accept. Nor have the post-1967 proliferators—India, Pakistan, South Africa, North Korea, and nuclear-club wannabe Iran—followed U.S. nuclear restraint.

The 1972 ABM Treaty did not halt development of MIRV. The price of gaining broad support for the first arms-control treaty between the U.S. and USSR included deployment of several modern strategic systems, including those incorporating MIRV. The rationale driving deployment was that as Soviet missiles became more accurate a smaller number of missiles would survive a surprise attack, and these would need enough warheads to be able to fully retaliate and thus preserve deterrence.

While MIRV development continued, ABM development was brought to a virtual standstill. The ABM Treaty permitted each side to deploy 100 missiles to defend a chosen land-based missile-silo basing site and another 100 to defend the national capital city. America deployed its Safeguard ABM in 1974 at the missile base in Grand Forks, North Dakota. Safeguard consisted of a two-layer defense: the Spartan missile designed to intercept ballistic missiles above the atmosphere, and the Sprint missile designed to intercept at low altitude missiles that Spartan missed. The system was never deployed around Washington, D.C., due to very understandable popular resistance to deploying five-megaton warheads close to heavily populated areas. The system at Grand Forks was dismantled in 1976. A 1974 protocol (add-on) to the ABM Treaty limited Russia to 100 ballistic missile interceptors.[57]

The systems ultimately deployed by the United States were "dumbed down"—deliberately made less capable of intercepting incoming warheads—in order to conform to arms-control agreements as interpreted by arms controllers. Specifically, radar capabilities and access to satellite tracking data were restricted. Thus when a Scud missile (a short-range, primitive Soviet ballistic missile system sold to several Mideast countries) destroyed a barracks and killed American servicemen in Dhahran, Saudi Arabia, near the end of the Gulf War, the dumbed-down Patriot-3 system failed. It is reasonable to believe, though not definitively provable as it is the road not taken, that unfettered development of missile defense technology would have produced a system able to destroy the Scuds launched during the Gulf War (most landed in Israel). *Thus arms agreements already have plausibly prevented deployment of lifesaving defensive systems.*

Much of the opposition to missile defense was based upon the sheer infeasibility of defeating a massive missile salvo of the kind the Sovi-

---

57. The Russians had first deployed 64 "Galosh" ABMs around Moscow in 1972.

et Union could have launched, using the kinds of systems deployable within arms-control constraints. The uncertainties were similar to those faced by prospective attackers using a large fleet of missiles. Put simply, systems were tested in small numbers, with many tests solo. There is no way for technologists to gauge from such tests how the same systems will perform when used on a large scale. Test trajectories and war trajectories differ, with aim "bias" introduced by asymmetries in the Earth's magnetic fields. System performance, in a nutshell, may not scale in uniform, linear fashion. Thus offensive system behavior in situations other than those specifically tested cannot confidently be predicted by attacker or defender.

Systems currently deployed intercept missiles either in their final (terminal) phase of flight or in midcourse. Terminal-phase intercept involves separating heavier warheads from lighter decoys in the closing seconds, made possible when warheads encounter friction in the atmosphere, which then separates the two based upon weight and density differentials. But with time so short, taking out a large salvo—even if defense radars were not destroyed, a highly shaky assumption—is a complex task. Midcourse intercept targets ballistic missiles coasting in space on unalterable trajectories (like artillery shells), but where the zero gravity of space makes separating warheads and decoys extremely difficult.

The result is a set of complex trade-offs, well illustrated by Paul Nitze in his memoirs. The early U.S. systems relied on nuclear warheads to destroy warheads with near misses. The altitude at which decoys begin to slow down sufficiently to be separated from actual warheads is about 250,000 feet, just under 50 miles up. Under 100,000 feet—19 miles up—marks a line below which detonating nuclear devices is out of the question when defending cities. This offers some 30 miles in which to engage decoys; below 19 miles, nonnuclear or kinetic-impact missile defense warheads must be used. Silo defense is less demanding, as incoming warheads can be engaged well below 100,000 feet, where lighter decoys are out of the way, and thus genuine warheads will be easier to identify.

Ultimately perhaps more promising, but strongly opposed by the Russians, are boost-phase intercept systems that target missiles shortly after launch. The missile is traveling far more slowly than in space; decoys cannot be released and thus intercept could well work, even on a large scale. But such systems, which employ lasers, have had to compete for funding with other defensive ideas. Because such intercepts would likely take place over the attacker's territory, potential attackers, including Russia, vigorously oppose their deployment.

In the 1970s the Russians conducted extensive laser beam defense experimentation at their Sary Shagan site in central Asia. Their technology was simply not up to the exacting task then, nor does it appear to be even today. American efforts have shown promise, but to date no system has proved itself against ICBMs. President Reagan was much taken by H-bomb father Edward Teller's X-ray laser concept: when an atomic device detonated, a laser based in space would emit intense X-rays that could destroy large numbers of attacking warheads in flight. Teller's concept was highly original, but eventually was abandoned, partly due to arms-control considerations about space weaponry and partly due to technical reservations. All large laser systems raise serious power problems. As noted in chapter 13 the Airborne Laser program was cancelled for this reason. (It used lasers mounted on a 747 aircraft to target missiles.).

The Russians even objected to a midcourse intercept system promised to the Czech Republic and Poland in 2006 by President Bush, claiming that it would also be capable of tracking missiles in boost phase and possibly intercepting them. This gave President Obama a rationale in 2009 to justify unilaterally abrogating the 2006 deal. However, he negotiated not with our Eastern European partners but with Moscow, notifying the affected allied leaders a mere 25 minutes before announcing the swap of a land-based missile defense system for a sea-based one.

The Obama administration asserted that the new system is better than the one promised our allies in 2006, but if this were true, why didn't the United States approach these allies and tell them what a great deal it is? Thus did Cold War arms-control doctrine govern President Obama's signature arms treaty, and trump concerns of two of our closest allies.

David Hoffman's *The Dead Hand* offers a prime example of how hard violations issues are to definitively resolve. The Russians built a massive radar tracking facility at Krasnoyarsk, 1,869 miles inside the Soviet Union, with radar oriented inward. The ABM Treaty limited each side to a single radar protecting the capital, plus perimeter radars at the coastline. This was intended to prevent radars being used for "battle management": directing large salvos of missiles to thwart a large-scale attack. At the perimeter, radars could take out individual missiles or small salvos but not represent a comprehensive shield. The U.S. maintained that the Krasnoyarsk facility was illegal because it was centrally located and also designed for battle management. On location the U.S. was clearly right. As to the system's purpose, Hoffman contends it was to plug a hole in Russian defenses, not manage a large-scale defense, and thus a minor violation. In 1989 the Soviets openly admitted that the Krasnoyarsk facility indeed was a violation of the ABM Treaty.

That it took a confession by the Russians to establish a violation showed the infirmity of Cold War arms treaty enforcement. Russia could violate the ABM Treaty with impunity, without fear of being condemned for it. Absent a supervening legal authority capable of rendering judgment, let alone enforcing same, protesting Soviet violations amounted to shouting into the wind.

Thus has missile defense, for 40 years, been held hostage to arms control limits—even *after* the U.S. exited the ABM Treaty a decade ago.

BIBLIOGRAPHY

Technology

Arnold, Lorna. *Britain and the H-Bomb* (2001).

Bernstein, Jeremy. *Nuclear Weapons: What You Need to Know* (2008).

Bernstein, Jeremy. *Plutonium: A History of the World's Most Dangerous Element* (2007).

Bodanis, David. *E=mc2: A Biography of the World's Most Famous Equation* (2000).

Bryan, Jeff C. *Introduction to Nuclear Science* (2009).

Bush, Vannevar. *Modern Arms and Free Men* (1949).

Cohen, Sam. *Shame: Confessions of the Father of the Neutron Bomb* (2000).

Garwin, Richard L., and Charpak, Georges. *Megawatts + Megatons: The Future of Nuclear Power and Nuclear Weapons* (2001).

Harford, James. *Korolev* (1997).

Hoddeson, Lillian, et al. *Critical Assembly: A Technical History of Los Alamos During the Oppenheimer Years, 1943–1945* (1993).

Macrae, Norman. *John von Neumann: The Scientific Genius Who Pioneered the Modern Computer, Game Theory, Nuclear Deterrence and Much More* (1992).

McPhee, John. *The Curve of Binding Energy* (1974).

Miller, Richard L. *Under the Cloud: The Decades of Nuclear Testing* (1991).

Muller, Richard. *Physics for Future Presidents: The Science behind the Headlines* (2008).

Sakharov, Andrei. *Memoirs* (1990).

Serber, Robert. *The Los Alamos Primer* (1992).

Stine, G. Harry. *ICBM: The Making of the Weapon that Changed the World* (1991).

Tsipis, Kosta. *Arsenal: Understanding Weapons in the Nuclear Age* (1983).

Van Doren, William G. *Ivy-Mike: The First Hydrogen Bomb* (2008)

Willrich, Mason, and Taylor, Theodore B. *Nuclear Theft: Risks and Safeguards* (1974).

Wohlstetter, Albert, et al. *Nuclear Policies: Fuel without the Bomb* (1978).

Wohlstetter, Albert, et al. *Swords from Plowshares: The Military Potential of Civilian Nuclear Energy* (1979).

Strategy
Aligica, Paul Dragos, and Weinstein, Kenneth R., eds. *The Essential Herman Kahn: In Defense of Thinking* (2009).

Brodie, Bernard, ed. *The Absolute Weapon: Atomic Power and World Order* (1946).

Bruce-Biggs, B. *Shield of Faith: Strategic Defense from Zeppelins to Star Wars* (1988).

Bruce-Briggs, B. *Supergenius: The Mega-Worlds of Herman Kahn* (2000).

Freedman, Lawrence. *The Evolution of Nuclear Strategy* (3rd ed., 2003).

Friedman, George. *The Next 100 Years: A Forecast for the 21st Century* (2009).

Kahn, Herman. *On Escalation: Metaphors and Scenarios* (1965).

Kahn, Herman. *On Thermonuclear War* (1960).

Kahn, Herman. *Thinking about the Unthinkable in the 1980s* (1984).

Krepinevich, Andrew F. *7 Deadly Scenarios: A Military Futurist Explores War in the 21st Century* (2009).

Marshall, Andrew W., Martin, J. J., and Rowen, Henry S. *On Not Confusing Ourselves: Essays on National Security Strategy in Honor of Albert and Roberta Wohlstetter* (1991).

Zarate, Robert, and Sokolski, Henry D., eds. *Nuclear Heuristics: Selected Writings of Albert and Roberta Wohlstetter* (2009).

Arms Control
Albright, David. *Peddling Peril: How the Secret Nuclear Trade Arms America's Enemies* (2010).

Kaufman, Robert Gordon. *Arms Control during the Pre-Nuclear Era: The United States and Naval Limitation between the Two World Wars* (1990).

Newhouse, John. *Cold Dawn: The Story of SALT* (1989 ed.).

Nitze, Paul H., et al. *The Fateful Ends and Shades of SALT* (1979).

Reed, Thomas C. *At the Abyss: An Insider's History of the Cold War* (2004).

Reed, Thomas C., and Stillman, Danny B. *The Nuclear Express: A Political History of the Bomb and Its Proliferation* (2009).

Sokolski, Henry, et al. *Pakistan's Nuclear Future: Reining in the Risk* (December 2009).

Taubman, Philip. *The Partnership: Five Cold Warriors and Their Quest to Ban the Bomb* (2012).

Wohlstetter, Roberta. "*The Buddha Smiles*": Absent-Minded Peaceful Aid and the Indian Bomb, Monograph 3, Final Report to the Energy Research and Development Administration (May 1977, rev. November 1977).

History

Ambrose, Stephen E. *Eisenhower: Soldier and President* (1990).

Anderson, Martin, and Anderson, Annelise. *Reagan's Secret War: The Untold Story of His Fight to Save the World from Nuclear Disaster* (2009).

Brown, Anthony Cave, ed. *Dropshot: The American Plan for World War III against Russia in 1957* (1978).

Bush, George W. *Decision Points* (2010).

Carlson, Peter. K *Blows Top: A Cold War Comic Interlude, Starring Nikita Khrushchev, America's Most Unlikely Tourist* (2009).

Cheney, Richard B. *In My Time* (2011).

Dobbs, Michael. *One Minute to Midnight: Kennedy, Khrushchev, and Castro on the Brink of Nuclear War* (2009).

Fischer, Benjamin B. *A Cold War Conundrum: The 1983 Soviet War Scare* (July 7, 2008 ed.)

Frank, Richard B. *Downfall: The End of the Imperial Japanese Empire* (1999).

Gordon, Michael, and Trainor, Lt. Gen. Bernard E. *The Generals' War: The Inside Story of the Conflict in the Gulf* (1995).

Gott, Richard. *The Evolution of the Independent British Deterrent* (1963).

Groves, Leslie M. *Now It Can be Told: The Story of the Manhattan Project* (1962).

Hoffman, David E. *The Dead Hand: The Untold Story of the Cold War Arms Race and Its Dangerous Legacy* (2009).

Karpin, Michael. *The Bomb in the Basement: How Israel Went Nuclear and What It Means for the World* (2006).

Kempe, Frederick. *Berlin 1961: Kennedy, Khrushchev, and the Most Dangerous Place on Earth* (2011).

Kissinger, Henry. *Crisis: The Anatomy of Two Major Foreign Policy Crises* (2003).

Kissinger, Henry. *Diplomacy* (1994).

Kissinger, Henry. *On China* (2009).

Kissinger, Henry. *White House Years* (1979).

Kissinger, Henry. *Years of Renewal* (1998).

Kissinger, Henry. *Years of Upheaval* (1982).

Kozak, Warren. *LeMay: The Life and Wars of General Curtis LeMay* (2009).

Lacouture, Jean. *DeGaulle: The Ruler, 1945–1970* (1991).

Miscamble, Wilson D., CSC. *The Most Controversial Decision: Truman, the Atomic Bombs, and the Defeat of Japan* (2011).

Nakdimon, Shlomo. *First Strike: The Exclusive Story of How Israel Foiled Iraq's Attempt to Get the Bomb* (1987).

Nitze, Paul H. *From Hiroshima to Glasnost: At the Center of Decision—A Memoir* (1989).

Polmar, Norman. *The Enola Gay: The B-29 That Dropped the Atomic Bomb on Hiroshima* (2004).

Polmar, Norman, and Allen, Thomas B. *Rickover: Father of the Nuclear Navy* (2007).

Rumsfeld, Donald. *Known and Unknown: A Memoir* (2011).

Rusk, Dean. *As I Saw It* (1990).

Thompson, Nicholas. *The Hawk and the Dove: Paul Nitze, George Kennan, and the History of the Cold War* (2009).

Timmerman, Kenneth. *Countdown to Crisis: The Coming Nuclear Showdown with Iran* (2005).

Trofimov, Yaroslav. *The Siege of Mecca: The Forgotten Episode in Islam's Holiest Shrine and the Birth of al-Qaeda* (2007).

Wittner, Lawrence S. *Confronting the Bomb: A Short History of the World Nuclear Disarmament Movement* (2009).

Reports

The Acheson-Lilienthal Report: Report on the International Control of Atomic Energy. Department of State Publication 2498 (March 16, 1946).

"All You Ever Wanted to Know About MIRV and ICBM Calculations but Were Afraid to Ask." *Journal of Conflict Resolution* 17, no. 2 (1973).

America's Strategic Posture: The Final Report of the Congressional Commission on the Strategic Posture of the United States. U.S. Institute of Peace (2009).

Damage Probabilities for a Small-CEP, Low-Yield, Airburst/Groundburst Attacks against Selected PVN and QVN Point Targets. RAND Corporation (August 1975).

The Effects of Nuclear War. U.S. Congress, Office of Technology Assessment (1979; reprinted 2005).

Meeting the Challenge: When Time Runs Out. Bipartisan Policy Center (June 2010).

National Capital Region: Key Response Planning Factors for the Aftermath of Nuclear Terrorism. Federal Emergency Management Agency (November 2011).

World at Risk: The Report of the Commission on the Prevention of Weapons of Mass Destruction, Proliferation and Terrorism. Vintage (December 2008).

Fiction

Bryant, Peter. *Red Alert* (1958).

Burdick, Eugene, and Wheeler, Harvey. *Fail-Safe* (1962).

Cohen, William S. *Blink of an Eye* (2011).

Collins, Larry, and Lapierre, Dominique. *The Fifth Horseman* (1980).

Forstchen, William D. *One Second After* (2009).

Frank, Pat. Alas, *Babylon* (1959).

Knebel, Fletcher, and Bailey, Charles W. II. *Seven Days in May* (1962).

Shute, Nevil. *On the Beach* (1957).

Wells, H.G. *The World Set Free: A Story of Mankind* (1914).

Winnick, Jack. East Wind (2010).

Film

The Atomic Cafe. Directed by Jayne Loader, Kevin Rafferty, and Pierce Rafferty (1982).

Atomic Jihad. Directed by Joel Gilbert (2010).

The Bedford Incident. Directed by James B. Harris (1965).

The Day After. Directed by Nicholas Meyer (1983).

The Day After Trinity: J. Robert Oppenheimer and the Atomic Bomb. Produced by Jon Else (1980).

Dr. Strangelove, or How I Learned to Stop Worrying and Love the Bomb. Directed by Stanley Kubrick (1964).

Enola Gay. The History Channel (1995).

Fail-Safe. Directed by Sidney Lumet (1964).

Iranium. Produced by Rafael Shore and Michael Pace (2011).

Kalifornistan. Directed by Jason Appuzzo (2009).

The Nuclear Tipping Point. Nuclear Security Project (2010).

On the Beach. Directed by Stanley Kramer (1959).

Red Dawn. Directed by John Milius (1984).

CPSIA information can be obtained at www.ICGtesting.com
Printed in the USA
LVOW131546010313

322320LV00004B/592/P